THE ENGLISH
CONVICT HULKS
1600s–1868

Dedicated to my wife, Lorraine, who has had to put up with far more than she should have and without whose understanding this work would never have been attempted.

THE ENGLISH CONVICT HULKS 1600s–1868

Transporting Criminals to Australia

Mick Davis

PEN & SWORD **HISTORY**

AN IMPRINT OF PEN & SWORD BOOKS LTD.
YORKSHIRE – PHILADELPHIA

First published in Great Britain in 2024 by
PEN AND SWORD HISTORY
An imprint of
Pen & Sword Books Ltd
Yorkshire – Philadelphia

ISBN 978 1 39905 449 2

Typeset in Times New Roman 11/13.5 by
SJmagic DESIGN SERVICES, India.
Printed and bound in the UK by CPI Group (UK) Ltd.

Pen & Sword Books Limited incorporates the imprints of Atlas, Archaeology,
Aviation, Discovery, Family History, Fiction, History, Maritime, Military,
Military Classics, Politics, Select, Transport, True Crime, Air World, Frontline
Publishing, Leo Cooper, Remember When, Seaforth Publishing, The Praetorian
Press, Wharncliffe Local History, Wharncliffe Transport, Wharncliffe True Crime
and White Owl.

For a complete list of Pen & Sword titles please contact
PEN & SWORD BOOKS LIMITED
George House, Units 12 & 13, Beevor Street, Off Pontefract Road,
Barnsley, South Yorkshire, S71 1HN, England
E-mail: enquiries@pen-and-sword.co.uk
Website: www.pen-and-sword.co.uk

or

PEN AND SWORD BOOKS
1950 Lawrence Rd, Havertown, PA 19083, USA
E-mail: uspen-and-sword@casematepublishers.com
Website: www.penandswordbooks.com

Contents

Introduction

On 4 December 1803 Captain Samuel Mottley, head of the Impress Service at Gravesend in Kent, was on duty along the Thames looking for men to impress into the navy. His luck was in and he caught two; one was my great x 4 grandfather, John Davis, apprentice waterman, aged 18 and a native of Dartford. John was to spend the next eleven years aboard His Majesty's ships being shipwrecked, flogged, blown up, falling overboard and close to starvation. His story was part of my piecing together the family history, which took many years but was an absolute joy, thanks to the fact that the Admiralty records at the National Archives detail the day-to-day events onboard every ship.

My research sparked an interest in the period and its wars, which, coupled with an interest in criminal history, led me to the present project. After serving on the *Belleisle* at Trafalgar, a ship that was almost reduced to matchwood during the battle, he was sent aboard the 104-gun ship of the line HMS *London* in December 1805. On 13 March 1806 his ship, with others, encountered a squadron of French troop transports and frigates under Rear Admiral Linois raiding trade between St Helena and the Canaries. The French ships, *Belle Poule* and *Marengo*, with a combined crew of 116 men, were captured after some fierce fighting. Among the crew of the former was Ambroise Garneray, soon to become a brilliant artist and author who spent eight years as a prisoner on the hulks. It is unfortunate that space does not allow the stories of the prisoners of the French and American wars to be included here.

My personal connection did not end there, however. In June 1809 John Davis was sent aboard the *Euryalus*, a frigate, the most glamorous type of ship in the navy, a fast-cruising warship of 36 guns and a crew of 230. He took part in the disastrous expedition to Walcheren of that year and was lucky to escape the rampant malaria that afflicted the British forces. In 1825 *Euryalus* became one of the hulks at Chatham used to house boys who had been separated from their fellow convicts, in the hope that they would not be further corrupted by those more villainous than themselves. In November 1814, with the coming of peace, John was discharged and began the chosen career that he had been forced to abandon so many years before, a Thames Waterman. He acquired a wife and two sons and continued to work until 1832 when he entered Greenwich Hospital, before dying in 1839 aged 54. His wife, Jane, died in the workhouse in 1842.

The subject of the hulks and transportation has been glossed over and neglected by generations of historians and genealogists, particularly in what we might call the 'host countries', possibly due to embarrassment over what they might discover about their forebears or lack of reliable documentation. Pick up any book on transportation and if the index mentions the hulks at all there are, at most, two or three minor entries. Those who were transported were largely illiterate, without the ability or opportunity to record their experiences, and their masters, who had control over them from prison to hulk to ship to eventual landfall, would have had very little interest in their own activities being recorded – quite the opposite, in fact, wishing to keep their business out of the public eye. For many, transportation was looked upon as a great release from the horror of the hulks, and if they could survive the journey and get through their initial period of punishment, there was freedom in a new land of opportunity.

Over the past few years there has been increasing interest in the story of transportation to Australia. There are now numerous books, comprehensive websites and growing databases, but the fascinating story of where and how they were housed before they left for a variety of destinations has been almost completely neglected. A book by William Branch-Johnson, published in 1957, was the first to be dedicated to the subject, but is now long out of print, and was produced in an age when research was far more difficult with many sources yet to be uncovered. It is a huge and fascinating subject covering eighty years of British criminal history and is worthy of in-depth research. Another book, by Charles Campbell, was published in 1993 and devoted to the subject, but again it is out of print and hard to find. A great many documents have been lost or destroyed during the intervening years, but this small book is an attempt to highlight some of the period's most interesting characters whose stories have survived, and to give an overview of the history and what life was like for those in the floating hell of all those years ago. As with any history, we are reliant on newspaper articles, reminiscences long after the event, dusty account books and long lists of names from court and prison records. We have to take a lot of these at face value unless there is compelling evidence to the contrary.

Throughout the period of the hulks, government was given constant reassurance on all sides that everything was fine, which is exactly what they wanted to hear. The alternative would involve the huge expense of building land-based prisons, and who cared about the comfort of a few convicts suffering entirely through their own failings? Better to acknowledge politely what they were told and move on to more pleasant topics. The reality was that the rotting remains of what were once proud and glorious ships, enlarging, defending and supplying the British Empire as it expanded throughout the world, were now as reduced in status as their ragged inmates. It has been estimated that more than 160,000 people passed through the hulks during their eighty years of service: starving children, murderers, thieves, fraudsters and distressed aristocrats, each with their own harrowing story to tell and many of them fascinating in their own right. The aristocrats of crime, the flamboyant Barrington and Dignam, for example, who, had they applied themselves to tedious but honest industry, would have died rich and respected men. We can only guess at their motivations, if they had any; possibly they just drifted from one desperate situation to another without thinking of the consequences. There were political prisoners like the Scottish revolutionary Thomas Muir, the Tolpuddle Martyrs, and the Irish republican John Mitchel, sent off to Bermuda in 1848. There was Richard Loader, who betrayed the trust of fellow officers and spent time in his own hulk. All this against a background of backbreaking work, near starvation, floggings, mutiny and the ever-present threat of dying from jail fever.

The majority of convicts were working-class people sentenced by middle-class judges with a mutual distrust and contempt; the lower orders trying to make ends meet and the ruling class defending their property against what they saw as a tide of undeserving wretches. This is not to class all convicts as victims: for every young man imprisoned for stealing a handkerchief, there are many rapists, murderers and psychopaths who thoroughly deserved all that was coming to them. A large part of the book consists of the biographies of Duncan Campbell and Aaron Graham, two remarkable men who controlled the operation throughout its formative and middle years and who ruled over thousands of unfortunates. Their stories are told here in detail for the first time.

The book is arranged chronologically as far as possible. In the first two chapters I have tried to set the scene and provide some background to the situation at home and the events abroad that made the hulks necessary. There are three chapters of personal stories from the various periods, which give some insight into their crimes as well as some of their experiences on the hulks. Much detail is given about the daily life of those on board, their work and their hardships. Tales of these alone could fill many volumes. Finally, I describe the sailing of the First Fleet to the new continent of Australia, and the final end to life on the hulks. It is unfortunate that lack of space discounts any account of the hulks in Ireland, which is surely worth a book of its own, as is the history of the prisoners of the French and American wars, which run parallel to our convict hulks. Again, size constraints mean that the book has a strong bias towards London and the Home Counties. It should also be borne in mind that many of the calculations regarding numbers of convicts on board the various hulks, and the amounts of money spent on the various activities, should be approached with caution as they differ, sometimes wildly, between accounts.

The complete wording of the Acts of 1717 and 1776 are included as Appendices at the back, along with a list of hulks compiled for Wikipedia.

Mick Davis
2023

Chapter 1

Vagabonds, Vagrants &
The Bloody Code

'Men are not hanged for stealing horses, but that horses may
not be stolen.'

George Saville 1st Marquess of Halifax,
1633–1695

The Criminal Law: Brutal and Bloodthirsty

It has been estimated that between 1509 and 1547, during the reign of
Henry VIII, an astonishing 72,000 people were executed. In the fifteenth
and sixteenth centuries Portugal, Spain and France had all used criminals,
undesirables and vagrants to help populate their colonies, but the Elizabethan
explorer and geographer Richard Hakluyt was probably the first Englishman
to suggest that English criminals be transported to America and put to work
on extracting resources from the land. In *A Discourse Concerning Western
Planting* written in 1584, Hakluyt observes:

> many thousandes of idle persons are within this realme, which,
> havinge no way to be sett on worke, be either mutinous and
> seeke alteration in the state, or at leaste very burdensome to the
> common-wealthe, and often fall to pilferinge and thevinge and
> other lewdnes, whereby all the prisons of the lande are daily
> pestred and stuffed full of them, where either they pitifully pyne
> awaye, or els at lengthe are miserably hanged. He proposes
> that: these pety theves mighte be condempned for certen yeres
> in the westerne partes, especially in Newefounde lande, in
> sawinge and fellinge of tymber for mastes of shippes, and deale
> boordes; in burninge of the firres and pine trees to make pitche,
> tarr, rosen, and sope ashes; in beatinge and workinge of hempe
> for cordage; and, in the more southerne partes, in settinge them

1

to worke in mynes of golde, silver, copper, leade, and yron; in draggine for perles and currall; in plantinge of suger canes, as the Portingales have done in Madera

Crime in England, and the number of prosecutions, reached unusually high levels in the 1590s, due in the main to a downturn in the economy, which increased the number of the nation's poor and unemployed. Most property crime during these times was committed by the young, the destitute or the homeless, and to address the problem, Parliament brought in new laws in an attempt to control the behaviour of these disadvantaged. One of the main social problems of the time was vagrancy, by which was meant any person not earning a respectable living by farming or practising a trade – living, it was assumed, by wandering the land begging and indulging in petty crime. After the peace with Spain in 1604, many of these rootless poor were ex-soldiers, brutalised by conflict, toughened by meagre rations and rough living, having returned to a land that had no use for them. Their desperate situation led them to commit numerous crimes against property, theft, burglary, highway robbery, acts of violence and begging. A law from 1572 had defined several categories of itinerants as vagrants, including unlicensed healers, palm readers and tinkers (travelling menders of cooking pots), and as such they risked being whipped, or subjected to some other physical punishment, unless they found a master or employer. Penalties for even the smallest of crimes met with vicious retribution, often accompanied by torture to extract a confession or the names of confederates.

While the fractured nature of society during this period caused the authorities to react viciously against anything they saw as a threat, many lesser crimes were also considered serious enough to warrant the death penalty. Simple murder would almost certainly be punished by hanging; women who murdered their husbands (petty treason) could be burned at the stake. Robbery, larceny (theft), rape and arson were also capital offences. Those accused of crimes had the right to a trial, but their legal protections were minimal with no automatic right of appeal.

The various 'poor laws' in support of the destitute had failed to provide for them adequately or deter crime, and the government began exploring other measures to control social groups that were considered dangerous or undesirable. Between 1546 and 1553, five 'houses of correction' opened in London. These institutions, otherwise known as 'bridewells' after the first one built at St Brides in London, were places where orphans, street children, the physically and mentally ill, vagrants, prostitutes, and others who engaged in what were considered to be disreputable ways of life, could be confined. Not all inmates of the bridewells had necessarily committed a crime, but they were restrained because of their marginal social status. As the name suggests, houses of correction aimed to reform their inmates, who were expected to work long hours under harsh conditions and were often preyed upon by the wardens for money or favours. They increased significantly in number throughout England during the sixteenth century, with perhaps 170 in the country by the early seventeenth, reflecting a growing interest in the idea that the state should aim to change a criminal's behaviour instead of merely imposing a punishment for offences.

Such prisons as did exist during these times were full, rife with disease and lacked the capacity to handle large numbers of prisoners. With the exception of debtors, unable to pay what they owed and confined until their obligations were satisfied, convicted criminals did not usually receive sentences that would have been an expensive option for the state. Jails were primarily places where suspects were kept while awaiting trial, or where convicts waited for their day of execution. Punishments for offences against the criminal law were fast, brutal and comparatively cheap. Sentencing criminals to long-term stays in prison to atone for their sins or to receive rehabilitation was a concept still many years away, and many thought that the idea of intentionally locking someone away in dreadful conditions was so inhumane as to be unimaginable. There was also a feeling that if children, petty thieves and debtors came into contact with professional criminals locked into the same institution they would be corrupted and guided towards even worse crimes. On the other hand, some thought that simple imprisonment in general was a soft option and not a harsh enough punishment, despite the fact that a convict was required to pay for his accommodation, keep his clothes in order and somehow get enough to eat and drink. Time in prison depended on what you could afford rather than the particular reason for confinement. Even those with money could not always pay for basic quarters for an extended period and were thrown back into the stinking cells with their poorer fellows once funds were exhausted. It is difficult to overestimate the sheer horror of finding yourself on the wrong side of the law in those early days.

The most trivial offences could bring the most horrific penalties, many inherited from the religious excesses of medieval times. Expanding urbanisation was partly responsible for the rise in property crime. Before the growth of cities, such crime was rare as personal possessions were few in number and most criminal offences could be dealt with by summary justice or informal sanctions. The growth and anonymity of towns also helped the rise of crime in general. No longer did everyone spend their lives in rural villages where families had lived for generations and people

3

knew each other. Being found guilty of antisocial behaviour was a public humiliation that would be remembered for many years, but the crowded streets of London and other cities provided many more temptations for theft and greater anonymity. The growing number of stalls and shops provided easy targets for thieves, the starving and the desperate, and the escaping criminal could easily disappear into the crowd. London's growth came, to a large extent, from people who were being forced out of the countryside and into the city to look for work, with overcrowding significantly adding to the increase in crime. Something had to be done.

The Vagabonds Act of 1597

In 1597 Parliament took the matter seriously, and in an attempt to address the problem of crime among the poorest sections of the community, they introduced new laws under 'An Act for the punyshment of Rogues, Vagabonds, and sturdie Beggers'. (39 Eliz. c. 4).

During that year, the harvest failed causing a shortage of corn, high prices, widespread suffering and hardship. Many thousands became unemployed, and the situation was made worse by the enclosure acts, which drove sheep onto the land and peasants off it and into the already overcrowded towns, or to wander the country roads. Things became so desperate that the government feared riots and even open rebellion. In London alone, there were an estimated 10,000 vagabonds. One MP called for them to be arrested, whipped and returned to their place of origin where they would be set to work in a house of correction until the overseers thought fit to release them. Vagrancy was becoming an increasingly national problem.

The government had not immediately taken up Hakluyt's idea of a decade previously, but this new act contained the first official sanction to allow the transportation of 'rogues and vagabonds' to the English colonies, which were experiencing a great shortage of labour. It was decided that a man condemned to death could be reprieved if he consented to be sent to an American colony and enrolled into a form of indentured service. The employer actually bought the servant and paid for their maintenance. At the end of the term of servitude, the master provided what was called 'freedom dues', which could be land, a commodity such as tobacco or sugar, cash, or some other form of exchange. Artisans and craftsmen among the convicts often received more favourable terms than common labourers, but not always better treatment during their time of service. Corruption and abuses of the system were commonplace at every level of English society, at home and abroad.

The act had the added advantage of not only expelling criminals from the country but also enabling them to be sold for use on the land in the labour-hungry colonies. In 1606 the tobacco plantations of Virginia were the first place to be recommended for 'idle vagrants', and from the time of the earliest settlements reprieved felons worked side-by-side with free planters. It was one way around the labour shortage as well as mitigating the heavy expense of poor relief at home.

Agents seeking to entice more upstanding citizens across the sea talked of land, houses, gardens and clothing, all provided at the company's expense. But the problem with attracting labour to a land so far away was that few people were prepared to risk making the journey via a hazardous sea voyage. This was a time when an excursion from the countryside to London was thought of as a great adventure. Perhaps as many as seven out of ten people still lived in the villages in which they had been born, or within a geographical radius of ten miles or so. Despite this, and aside from the criminal element, many destitute British subjects volunteered each year for terms of indenture in exchange for a passage to America. Thousands of the very poorest were finding that they were no longer needed on the land at home and had nowhere else to go.

Beginnings of Transportation 1600s

In 1611 the Marshall of Virginia, Sir Thomas Dale, imported 300 'disorderly persons' to labour on the plantations, the vast majority of whom proved to be unsuited to manual work or much else of use. Nonetheless, he persevered and appealed to James I to officially sanction the sending over of convicts held in prisons under sentence of death in order to furnish the settlement with able-bodied men. Far from being a soft option, those pardoned,

> may be constrained to toyle in such heavey and painefull workes
>
> as such a servitude shalbe a greater terror to them than death it selfe,
>
> and therefore of better example since execucions are so common
>
> as that wicked and irreligious sorts of people are no way thereby moved
>
> or deterred from offending

Judges did not have the power to sentence convicts to transportation directly, but under the new provision the king could pardon felons on condition that they leave the country. In 1615 the Privy Council decreed transportation be a lawful penalty in itself, and an act of 1619 issued a warrant creating a system for transporting felons by granting reprieves, on condition that they be moved to one of the plantations for a specified number of years, granting leniency to those who would otherwise have been executed.

> Whereas it hath pleased his Majestie out of his singular Clemencie and mercy to take into his princely Consideration the wretched estate of divers, of his Subjects who by the Lawes of the Realme are adjudged to dye for sondry offences though heynous in themselves, yet not of the highest nature, soe as his Majestie both out of his gracious Clemencye, as also for diverse weighty Considerations Could wishe they might be rather Corrected than destroyed, and that in theire punishmentes some of them might live, and yealde a profitable Service to the Common wealth in partes abroad, where it shall bee founde fit to employ them, for which purpose his Majestie having directed his Commission under the greate some of the prominent reformers of the day, was finally welcomed as a means of relieving the government from a most perplexing burden Seale of England, to vs and the rest of his privy Counsell, gyving full power warrant and Authoritye to us or and Sixe or more of vs whereof the Lord Chancellor or Lord Keeper of the Greate, Seale, to be two, to Reprieve and stay from execution suche persons as now stand Convicted of any Robbery or felony (Willfull murther, Rape, witchcraft or Burglary onely excepted) who for strength of bodye or other abilityes shall be thought fit to be imployed in forreine discoveryes or other Services beyond the seas.

Those who received a pardon were free from judicial supervision as long as they remained abroad during the required term, which could often amount to banishment for life as there were few means of returning under their own steam. Those sentenced to death for crimes excluding murder, rape, witchcraft or burglary could be deported and treated pretty much as slave labour, and if they refused to go, or returned before their allotted time, then their original death sentence could be enforced.

In 1620 there was an even bolder plan. The City of London provided £500 to clothe, feed and ship 100 children 'of the multitudes that swarm in this place' to be sent to Virginia as bound apprentices, thus 'redeeming so many poor souls from misery and ruin and putting them in a condition of use and service to the state'. Children were sometimes kidnapped from the streets and sold on so that the colony could grow its own labour force.

Other important changes during the period served to lessen the severity of punishments meted out to such groups as strolling players. These were imposed under a 1572 act wherein all 'masterless men', including 'all fencers, bearwards, common players of interludes, and minstrels not belonging to any baron of this realm, or to any other honourable person of greater degree, found wandering abroad without the license of two justices at the least', were subject to be 'grievously whipped and burned through the gristle of the right ear with a hot iron of the compass of an inch about'. Such groups were distrusted as gangs of thieves or troublemakers, particularly Irish vagrants who travelled in bands like a circus, and often assumed the title 'gypsies', a corruption of the word 'Egyptian', which is the supposed origin of the Romany race. Beggars were punished for what was termed the 'subtle crafts' of palmistry, fortune-telling, minstrelsy or unlicensed acting, activities most often associated with illiterate itinerant communities. Gaming was forbidden and innkeepers were expected to keep their houses in good order under the threat of prosecution and closure.

Further legislation allowed that 'Every vagabond or beggar [...] shall be stripped naked from the middle upwards and publicly whipped until his or her body be bloody, and forthwith sent to the parish where he was born [...] If any vagabond or beggar return again, he shall suffer death by hanging.' Rogues not in compliance could be arrested, branded and then returned to the house of correction nearest to their place of birth. They were viewed by Parliament as being migrants, and therefore should be returned from whence they came rather than becoming a burden on the State or upon the parish to which they had migrated. The act required every parish to keep a record of every resident, including potential vagrants who might go wandering across the realm. Typically, it was young men, either unemployed or engaged in petty crime, who 'deserved to be whipped or stocked' as a punishment for transgressions. Many, of course, were just desperate to find employment, something to eat, or a bed for the night.

Other, perhaps more enlightened, pieces of legislation during this period concerned measures for the relief of parish unfortunates, which remained in force until the twentieth century. These included measures to erect hospitals and 'working houses for the poor', which became the basis for the Victorian workhouse system. Unfortunately, most of the information regarding numbers and punishments have survived only from the larger cities, and the lack of record-keeping has meant that it is difficult to interpret how effective the act was during this period. The Vagabond Act remained in force until it was repealed by section 28 of the Vagrants Act 1713.

The Caribbean and The Bloody Code

In the early decades of the seventeenth century England had acquired a number of islands in the Caribbean and began to develop lucrative tobacco and sugar plantations. African slaves provided most of the field labour, but a demand also existed for indentured servants of European stock, who worked for a fixed period before obtaining their freedom. During the winter of 1636 a ship bearing a consignment of sixty-one Irish men and women set sail for Barbados, but by the time they arrived, in January 1637, eight of them had died. The remainder were sold, including ten to the governor for 450lb of sugar apiece. For the return trip the ship was loaded with sugar for London and then returned for another trip. It was a very lucrative business. An Irish slave fetched between £10 and £35, and more than 50,000 were transported to Barbados alone, many captured by Cromwell during the wars in Ireland and Scotland. In 1649 he ordered the few surviving members of the Drogheda massacre to be sent to Barbados.

The Irish did not always accept their fate. In 1655 some joined African slaves and began attacking militia forces on the island, killing plantation owners and destroying crops. It took the authorities almost two years to suppress the disorder and some who escaped joined the numerous pirate fleets that roamed throughout the Caribbean. The Irish became known as 'Redlegs', a reference to the sunburn on their pale skin caused by the tropical sun. By the mid-1700s most were nominally free, their places taken by Africans, but few rose to become farmers or artisans and formed a wretched and isolated community. The restoration of the Stuart monarchy in 1660 brought an end to such large-scale transportations.

The option of transportation was little used before the act of 1718, and most were sentenced at home 'upon manuall labors and to be kept in chaynes in the houses of correction [...] with food and raiment as shal be necessitie of life and no more'. Those fit and able were to be given the chance to live and work, even if under the most dreadful circumstances, but those old, infirm or unable to work were left to rot. In 1688 fifty crimes were punishable by death in England and Wales, but over the next century the list grew considerably. By 1815 there were more than 200 capital offences on the statute books mainly relating to property, including damage to gardens and cattle. It was assumed that the severity of the punishments would act as a deterrent to further criminal activity, protecting landowners and men of property. The thinking behind it was that as there was no certainty that criminals would be caught, potential criminals had to be too terrified to commit crime in the first place. The problem with this way of thinking, of course, is that there is no way of knowing how many crimes were not committed due to the fear of punishment and therefore impossible to know how effective it was.

The few alternatives to the hangman's rope included whipping, time in the stocks, fines, the pillory and the branding iron; incarceration was still not considered as a serious option. Public executions were held about every six weeks throughout the year in London. A labourer of the time received very few holidays apart from Christmas and Easter, but as many as twelve hanging days could occur each year, each one being declared a public holiday for the working class who were encouraged to witness the spectacle as a deterrent. On those days, convicted felons were paraded at a leisurely pace through the London streets to meet their final end at the Tyburn Tree. Author Henry Fielding doubted that public executions terrified potential criminals and turned them against crime. In *An Enquiry into the Causes of the Late Increase of Robbers* (1751), Fielding viewed executions as a 'Day of Glory' for those sentenced since the atmosphere was more celebratory than solemn. Execution was turned into a carnival with the sale of drinks, foodstuffs and broadsheets detailing the life of the condemned. He believed that the frequency of hangings actually taught felons to approach their executions as moments of triumph, and advocated making executions private, which he thought might inspire more fear. On such days, of course, pickpockets and thieves turned up in droves.

There was a huge development of commercial activity in London after 1660, with a rapid rise in river traffic requiring many more warehouses and docks to meet the demand for the amount of goods being transported in and out of the capital. Shops became more numerous and began to display their ever-increasing range of goods in a way that made them attractive and accessible to thieves as well as customers. The early 1700s ushered in wars, rebellion and a severe economic decline, all of which gave rise to an increase in lawlessness and the prison population. New measures were needed to neutralise and remove those felons who could not be disposed of by hanging or crippled by judicial mutilation. There was no effective police system to protect property, and the law still acted in the mistaken belief that 'severity would prove an effective deterrent'. The introduction of transportation was supposed to be a way out of such excesses, and a form of compassion, as were arbitrary local decisions where a reduction in the severity of the offence was allowed so that the offender was not subjected to the death penalty. The 'forty-shilling law' stipulated that theft of any article worth more than forty shillings was a hanging offence, but if during the trial its value could be quietly reassessed to a lower amount, it would save the defendant's life. Once condemned to death, there remained the royal prerogative of mercy, which George III dispensed quite freely. One consequence of not enforcing the very letter of the law was that the countryside was not decorated with rotting corpses, but the less the rope was used the more jails were needed and the country still had very few.

The fact that so many were sentenced for the crime of stealing a handkerchief is perhaps an indication that this was excepted as a token charge by both defence and prosecution. The judiciary itself was perhaps in some sense overawed by its power to execute men for the most trivial offences and sought a more humane solution. As Blackstone commentated later, 'the injured through compassion will often forbear to prosecute: Juries through compassion will sometimes forget their oaths, and either acquit the guilty or mitigate the nature of the offence, and judges through compassion, will respite one half of the convicts and recommend them to Royal Mercy.' In practice, the excessive severity of a sentence may have reduced the significance of gradations of punishment since offenders developed a 'might as well be hung for a sheep as a lamb' logic. It was also becoming increasingly obvious that the deterrent argument simply did not work.

During the Bloody Assizes following the Monmouth Rebellion of 1685 Judge Jefferies sentenced 856 rebels to death, but James II spared their lives and gave many to his friends to sell for use on the plantations. Technically, legally, and according to the plantocracy and authorities of the State, white 'servants' were not slaves, but, in reality, no labourers, indentured or enslaved, had any say in the conduct of their lives, regardless of contracts, and all were worked ruthlessly. Macaulay in his *History of England* describes their initial fate:

> more wretched than their associates who suffered death, were distributed into gangs, and bestowed on persons who enjoyed favour at court. The conditions of the gift were that the convicts should be carried beyond sea as slaves, that they should not be emancipated for ten years, and that the place of their banishment should be some West Indian island. This last

article was studiously framed for the purpose of aggravating the misery of the exiles. In New England or New Jersey they would have found a population kindly disposed to them and a climate not unfavourable to their health and vigour. It was therefore, determined that they should be sent to colonies where a Puritan could hope to inspire little sympathy, and where a labourer born in the temperate zone could hope to enjoy little health. Such was the state of the slave market that these bondmen, long as was the passage, and sickly as they were likely to prove, were still very valuable. It was estimated by Jeffreys that, on an average, each of them, after all charges were paid, would be worth from ten to fifteen pounds...The misery of the exiles fully equalled that of the negroes who are now carried from Congo to Brazil... more than one fifth of those who were shipped were flung to the sharks before the end of the voyage... Of ninety-nine convicts who were carried out in one vessel, twenty-two died before they reached Jamaica [...] They were, therefore, in such a state that the merchant to whom they had been consigned found it expedient to fatten them before selling them.

The 'Bloody Code' is a term sometimes used to describe the legal system in England between the late seventeenth and early nineteenth centuries, a name coined sometime later in acknowledgment of the system's increasingly gruesome nature. Legislation passed in 1706 permitted judges to sentence felons for up to two years in a house of correction, which could include enforced labour, a useful alternative to the usual catalogue of slaughter.

As the economic crisis deepened, the poor and unemployed became less able to feed and clothe themselves. They lived in dark and narrow streets running with sewage, with piles of rotting refuse upon which pigs browsed freely, and contagious diseases were rampant. Household rubbish was customarily thrown into the street, and swarms of beggars, thieves and prostitutes plied their trade unhindered after dark. Brutal laws reflected views on property held almost as sacred. By 1760 up to 160 felonies were deemed worthy of death, some the result of acts passed in the recent decades, and included sheep stealing, or petty larceny. A conviction for theft meant that the convict's possessions were liable to be forfeit to the Crown, and in order to buy time, some defendants refused to plead. In this event they were subject to *peine forte et dure*, which involved having heavy weights laid upon them increasing in severity until they were either crushed to death or appreciated the benefits of entering a plea. This form of torture was not abolished until 1714.

Average annual earnings for the end of the seventeenth century was estimated to have been £3,200 for a nobleman, £280 for a country gentleman, £200 to £400 for a merchant, £42 for a farmer, £30 for a tradesman or artisan, and £18 for a labourer. The poorest class had an annual income of about £5, which was well below subsistence level. After levelling off during the second half of the century, England's population nearly doubled over the following hundred years. Poverty always carries a potential for lawlessness, but permitting hunger to spread amid increasing wealth was certain to result in a rise in crime. One way out of confinement or transportation was to agree to serve in the army or navy, although those noble institutions were, at times, rather reluctant to accept such persons, fearing that they might not only bring disease but also discourage more upstanding citizens from joining.

Until the State took over the management of crime in the nineteenth century and a professional police force was created for the apprehension of suspects, instigating a prosecution was left to the private initiative of the victim, including the expense and preparation of any trial. Only rarely did the Crown or local constables actively prosecute offences. A simple case would begin with an examination before the justices of the peace, usually landowners with some knowledge of the law, who were appointed by the Crown and unpaid. These sat without a jury and tried petty offences put before them by the victim or parish constable. For a serious offence they would commit the prisoner to the assize courts, but the defendant was unable to call witnesses on their own behalf.

Mid-eighteenth-century England witnessed a dramatic transformation in society and the economy, due in part to the Industrial Revolution. From 1700 to 1740 the population of the country had remained almost constant at about six million; between 1750 and 1770 the population of London alone doubled, meaning that the median age kept dropping, saturating the labour market. By 1830 the population had reached nearly fourteen million. The fear of disorder and social unrest, real or imagined, was running high throughout this period. It was unprecedented and unprepared for, and people only needed to look to France to see what could happen.

Chapter 2

To the New World and Beyond

The Transportation Act of 1717

In 1717 a bill was introduced into the House of Commons by Sir William Thompson, the Solicitor General, a prominent lawyer who had long seen the flaws of Britain's sentencing system and had sought more flexible provisions for judges in handing down sentences. The result was 'An Act For the Further Preventing of Robbery, Burglary and Other Felonies, and For the More Effectual Transportation of Felons, and Unlawful Exporters of Wool; and For the Declaring the Law upon Some Points Relating to Pirates'. (4 George 1 c.11).

Thompson believed that transportation could be an effective means of dealing with persistent offenders who were unable or unwilling to support themselves and who would probably return to crime repeatedly. The act was partly inspired by the consequences of the Treaty of Utrecht between Britain and France in 1713, which ended twelve years of war. The outbreak of peace led once more to a sudden upsurge in serious crime as military demobilisation released thousands of young men back into the country with little prospect of employment. Two years before, the riot act had been passed allowing demonstrators to be charged with a capital offence if they failed to disperse when ordered to do so. As there was no full-time police force in London and other urban areas, keeping the peace depended on amateur guardians, inefficient constables and watchmen who laboured under a heavy workload and were easily bribed. It was hoped that the riot act would lend more powers to back up what little authority there was.

With the support of Privy Councillor Robert Walpole, Thompson became Recorder of London on 3 March 1715, and therefore the principal sentencing officer at the Old Bailey, with a responsibility to report to the Cabinet all those convicted of a capital offence. Thompson was elected to this position during a time when there was deep concern over theft and robbery in London, and he brought enthusiasm and new ideas for combating crime to the job. He believed that the rise in crime needed new approaches for policing the city and a new category of punishment. Thompson's achievements were extraordinary: within the same year he had devised the first registry to help identify repeat offenders. By some accounts, Thompson was not popular. Despite commentator Daniel Defoe characterising him as someone with a notable sense of humanity and justice, he was repeatedly accused of corruption during his time in office, and his early biographers accused him of greed in acquiring government positions and seeking power. Despite this, he served as Recorder for twenty-four years until his death in 1739.

Under the terms of the act a system was put in place that enabled convicted criminals to be sent to the colonies in North America and sold for a term of 'indentured servitude', a period of unpaid labour. Merchants and others could be awarded contracts to transport convicts, after giving a surety bond that the transport would take place and the term of service would be completed. 'The intent of the law,' remarked Thompson, 'being to prevent their doing further mischiefs which they generally doe, if in their power, by being at large.'

Thompson became the architect of the transportation policy under the Whig government, acknowledging the fact that previous punishments had failed to deter crimes such as robbery, burglary and larceny. So enthusiastic was he for his scheme that he oversaw almost every stage of its passage through the Commons, and then steered it through the Lords. After years of discussion and prevarication, a workable system of convict transportation finally became law. The Transportation Act now formally institutionalised convict transportation as a punishment and made the government responsible for transporting convicts out of the country. Under the old system of transportation, which had existed from the time of the first settlement in North America until 1718, around 5–6,000 convicts had been banished from the country. This number was about to grow at a rapid pace.

One of the most important businesses in the colonies of Maryland and Virginia was the growing of crops that England normally imported from other countries, and the most important of these was tobacco. The idea was that if England could grow these crops in the colonies for home use, it could improve the balance of trade and increase the country's overall wealth. The average trading ship was not large enough for the transportation business, and even though slave ships were sometimes used to transport felons, most were better suited to carrying tobacco and other commodities on the trip back than to transporting human cargo on the outward journey. The ships tended to wear out quickly from the frequent trips across the ocean, and their rotting timbers often required costly repairs that cut deeply into the profits of the convict contractors. Many were made in America, mainly Maryland or New England where abundant forests offered plenty of wood, with about a third constructed in Britain. An even smaller percentage were seized from the French as prizes during wartime.

Under the new act judges could remove criminals from the streets and lock-ups without having execution as their main option Previously, convicts had been sent out with a conditional pardon, providing that they did not return during the term of their sentence, and were thus free from legal restraint. The new law represented a radical shift: it introduced greater flexibility into the penal code, broadening the range of punishments and enabling previous good character and mitigating circumstances to be considered. Redemption was believed to be possible and convict labour viewed as a positive benefit to the State.

Between 1718 and 1775 around two-thirds of all convicted felons at the Old Bailey were sentenced to be transported for periods of between seven years – for lesser felonies – and fourteen years for more serious crimes in lieu of capital punishment. At the Old Bailey session on 23 April 1718 – the one directly following the act's passage – twenty-seven of the fifty-one people convicted of crimes were sentenced to serve their time abroad. Banishment proved to be so popular among judges that it quickly became their preferred sentence, mainly used in cases of petty theft, but even offences that normally called for the death penalty, such as the theft of anything valued over £2, could be commuted to transportation. Convicts in either category who returned to Britain before finishing their term were liable to the death sentence. The more heinous crimes would normally be settled at the end of a rope, but only one-sixth who received the death penalty during this period were executed. Not all of them saw this as progress. To many non-capital offenders transportation did not appear as an act of clemency; some preferred to be whipped or to join the armed forces.

Completion of the sentence had the effect of a pardon, and it has been estimated that around 36,000 felons sailed out of Britain before 1776, most to Maryland and Virginia. Once there, the conditions could be quite lax, depending upon individual circumstances – they were not, for instance, confined or shackled – the aim being to clear the malcontents out of the country rather than to punish them further. Britain became the only European country to transport convicts as part of a major governmental policy for many felonies. Mass executions and brandings were increasingly thought of as too barbaric and long-term imprisonment was too expensive; banishment was seen as a more effective deterrent to repeat offending than corporal punishment. Transportation not only consisted of removing a criminal offender from England's borders, it emptied the jails and systematically purged criminal elements from the ranks of the poor and destitute. And it was big business. The act simplified and hastened the process of criminal sentencing. Not only were undesirables to be removed from the streets, but 'in many of his Majesty's colonies and plantations in America, there is great want of servants, who by their hard labour and industry might be the means of improving and making the said colonies and plantations more useful to this nation.'

In 1720 the range of felonies for which transportation could be applied was extended further and county courts were given the authority to appoint two or more Justices of the Peace, empowered to 'contract with any person' for the removal of those felons sentenced to transportation. The county was to bear the cost of them being taken by land to the transporting ship. In effect, the authorities were distancing themselves from the problem and hoping that it would be taken up by entrepreneurs, which indeed it was.

As well as labourers, the tobacco plantations required domestic service of many kinds, from scullery maids to carpenters, and this could now be achieved to some extent through the emptying of English jails, workhouses, brothels and houses of correction. The problem was that the influx of so many criminals gave the southern colonies a reputation so dubious that it became difficult to attract new immigrants of standing or integrity. The new law caused much concern among established settlers who feared an increase in crime, to the extent that they tried to pass laws requiring purchasers of convict labour to give securities of £100 for the good behaviour of their workforce, though protests from the contractors meant that these were never implemented. They also passed laws against the importation of criminals on the grounds that the Habeas Corpus act made exile illegal. A clever way around this was to grant prisoners a pardon on condition that they agreed to be transported and become 'indentured servants', a system that worked until the situation was legitimised by the act of 1717.

There was ongoing confusion and debate about the nature of the punishment. Was exile itself the punishment? Was it being kept to servitude while exiled, or both? The question was debated long after the settlements were established in Australia.

Jonathan Wild (1683–1725)

Thompson's act was more than just a charter for transportation. The first part of its long title contained the words 'Preventing of Robbery, Burglary and Other Felonies', and with this wording he had a particular target in mind. Jonathan Wild was perhaps one of the most fascinating characters in English legal history. An apprentice to a buckle-maker in Wolverhampton, he was dismissed by his master and came to London in 1704 to work as a servant. He was imprisoned for debt, during which time he was initiated into the joys of criminality and joined a gang, working initially as a receiver of stolen goods. A man of great intelligence, he developed a system whereby he appeared as a defender of law and order while at the same time running a gang of thieves.

Wild would retain goods stolen by his team and wait for the crime to be reported in the newspapers, or become generally known, at which point he would claim that his 'thief taking agents' had recovered the stolen items, and offer them to their rightful owners for a reward. As well as recovering the goods, he would offer the authorities help in finding the thieves, who were often 'innocent' members of rival gangs or members of his own with whom he had fallen out. Wild ran a serious amount of crime in London, keeping records of all thieves in his employ, and when they had outlived their usefulness, he offered them up to the gallows. In public, Wild was a heroic figure, the man who recovered stolen property and caught criminals. In 1718 he called himself 'Thief Taker General of Great Britain and Ireland'. By his testimony, more than sixty thieves were sent to the gallows and his office in the Old Bailey became a hive of activity. By 1720 his fame was such that the Privy Council consulted him on methods of controlling crime in the city – much of it organised by Wild himself.

Wild's activities on the side of law and order made excellent press. He would write to the papers with accounts of his crime-fighting accomplishments, which were avidly read by a concerned and paranoid public. In July and August of 1724 the papers carried accounts of his brave efforts in rounding up twenty-one members of the Carrick Gang (with an £800 reward – approximately £25,000 in current value). To the public, this seemed like a relentless campaign against criminality, but in reality it was a gang warfare in disguise.

Some of those in authority were vaguely aware of his activities, and possibly not overly concerned, being hesitant to interfere with a system that brought so many criminals to justice. Thompson was not one of those. One of the provisions in his act was the first law to make receiving stolen goods a capital felony and was aimed specifically at curtailing Wild's criminal empire. This provision made it a crime for anyone to take a reward for returning stolen goods to their owner without capturing and giving evidence against the thief. Failure to do this could make the person taking the reward subject to the same penalty as the thief.

The clause was so clearly aimed at Wild that the Transportation Act was sometimes known as 'The Jonathan Wild Act'. Despite this obvious indication that the 'game was up', Wild continued his activities for many years. He knew that if he carefully covered his tracks, and received payment indirectly from his clients, it was virtually impossible to secure a conviction against him. Not only that, but the act had the effect of strengthening Wild's hold on members of his criminal empire. Under the new law, returning before a term of transportation had expired was punishable by death, and convicts who did so made ideal candidates for Wild's criminal network. Once he got news of a convict who had returned early to England, he could easily bring them into his gang by threatening to reveal their identity to the authorities. Returned convicts not only provided Wild with protection from the provision in the act aimed at him, but if they ever tried to betray him, he could turn them in for a large reward, and a possible death sentence.

Despite being a master at manipulating the law, it was his own arrogance that led to his downfall. He believed himself invincible and ignored all the signs that the glory days were over. In 1725 he was arrested for theft and receiving stolen goods. William Thompson drew up a warrant that included eleven articles providing details of his criminal empire. Wild met his end at Tyburn on 24 May 1725.

In 1728 King George himself became so concerned about crimes committed by convicts returning illegally that he wrote to the City of London justices, ordering that a reward of £40 be paid to anybody who could turn one of them in so that they be 'brought to justice'.

Jonathan Forward (1680–1760)

The new legislation and the system that developed in North America became a popular method of criminal punishment, helping to deal with society's more troublesome elements. One reason for its success was that it removed the cost of the voyage to the government. The Treasury agreed to pay merchants to transport convicts, and gave an exclusive contract to oversee transportation to Jonathan Forward, a 33-year-old London tobacco and slave trader who operated from a Cheapside house on Fenchurch Street. He had experience in the Atlantic slave trade, and was involved with the tobacco business in Virginia and Maryland, but, perhaps more importantly, he was strongly recommended by Sir William Thompson.

Forward was perfect for the job. He commanded a small fleet of ships, which made regular trips between London, Africa and the American colonies as part of his tobacco and slave business, and his experience in transporting human cargo had given him all the necessary connections with the plantation owners who would buy the convicts' labour. In 1717 he transported 131 prisoners to Maryland for the government while Parliament was still debating the Transportation Bill. One of the first ships known to have left these shores under the new act was the *Lewis*, which sailed for Jamaica transporting fifty-four felons at a cost of £108. This was followed in May 1718 by convicts being landed at Barbados and Antigua. However, exports to the West Indies were not very successful. The plantation owners were not at all happy with the quality of the new arrivals, who, they claimed, were a destructive influence on their existing workforce, encouraging desertion and indolence. America, on the other hand, was desperate for cheap labour and was to become the preferred destination.

Forward's first convict ship to America, the *Dolphin*, arrived along the Patuxent River, Maryland, in early 1718 with 134 convicts, seven having died during the voyage. The survivors were sold off to plantation owners, after which the ship was loaded with tobacco for its return journey to London. The total cost to outfit the vessel for the journey was £375, but his eventual profit is not known. Either Forward's keen business foresight or his connection to Thompson convinced him, even before the 1718 act, that convict transportation would become big business. Probably, in the hope that a more permanent contract would come his way, he decided not to charge the government for these first voyages and instead relied on the profits taken from the sale of the convicts and the tobacco crop on the return journey.

On 9 July 1718 Thompson appeared before Treasury officials and convinced them that Forward's proposed contract was a bargain. He claimed that no one else could transport convicts as cheaply and pointed out that Forward's flat rate included all fees to officials, the cost of leg irons, and the hiring of guards to accompany the convicts to the ship. Thompson also argued that an effective convict transportation system would actually save the government money, because one effect would be to lower the number of rewards the government would have to hand out for the recapture of escaped felons at home. The Treasury accepted Thompson's arguments, and one month later Jonathan Forward became the first Contractor for Transports to the government. Contracting out the punishment of convicts to private enterprise was a radical step for the government, which had never previously hired outside firms for this purpose. Eventually, the trade was run almost exclusively by two tightly knit groups of merchants: London, dominated by Forward, for the twenty-four years of his contract; and Bristol, by Samuel Sedgely & Co. Sedgely was a prosperous slave trader who had become Sheriff of Bristol in 1739. Between 1746 and 1775 Bristol shipped nearly 35% of almost 10,000 felons known to have been sent from Britain to Maryland.

Initially, Forward was paid £3 for each prisoner transported from London and nearby counties, with the right to dispose of them at the best price he could achieve. In 1727 he managed to get his fee raised to £5, a payment that had also to cover the jailer's fees for releasing the prisoners to be transported. One difference from the old system was that Forward was obliged to take every prisoner marked for transportation, regardless of age, physical condition or sex, rather than choosing those fit and healthy who would command the best price. There were other convict transporters outside of the Home Counties who were not in receipt of subsidies and were totally reliant upon sales. These retained the advantage of being able to pick the most financially rewarding of their convict cargo and leave behind any thought unable to work or fetch a reasonable price. For every prisoner who was discharged for transportation in London, the Keeper of Newgate prison charged 14s.10d., and their sentence did not begin until they were in the custody of the captain of the ship. Once the convicts were on board, shipmasters were required to obtain customs certificates confirming the safe delivery of their cargoes.

Forward's business was not without its difficulties, however. In 1725 two ships arriving at Maryland were refused entry under some hastily constructed local legislation that sought to impose expensive guarantees of the felons' continued good behaviour. There were further complaints that transportees were useless and unsuitable for the work. Other problems involved a number of court cases over the tobacco business, ships being lost at sea, convict mutinies and even ships being captured by pirates. Nonetheless, the expeditions continued to prosper: the contractors had relieved the government of convict maintenance and transportation costs, selling prisoners in labour-starved colonial markets such as the Chesapeake for a very good price.

It has been said that Jonathan Wild was one of his associates, and who would be better placed to know the names of those having fled from exile in America than Forward, who would pick up the gossip as soon as he delivered the next load of convicts. This does not necessarily mean that their relationship was criminal or corrupt. If Forward believed that Wild was genuinely in the business of apprehending escapees, as many did, he may well have handed over the names and details in good faith.

So popular was the scheme among those giving out sentences that a backlog built up. By November 1735 there were 139 convicts from five sessions at the Old Bailey lying in Newgate awaiting ships to transport them, costing the government to feed and maintain. Forward was summoned before the Lord Mayor to account for this situation and all he could do was to plead a lack of ships. In the end he was compelled to agree to clear Newgate three times a year, in March, August and December. Despite this, the problem continued, and in later years the authorities began to charge for additional expenses incurred in housing those who should have been transported. Forward's monopoly of the London convict trade continued until his twenty-four-year contract ended in 1742, when he was succeeded by Andrew Reid, his former tobacco agent in Maryland. Reid ruled the roost under the terms of a new twenty-one-year contract and seems to have been a thoroughly unpleasant and disreputable man who allowed the conditions on board ship to deteriorate into an even worse state than they were before. Having made his money, Reid retired to South Carolina and died in 1784.

Despite the loss of his prime position in London, Forward continued to transport felons from provincial jails until the late 1740s, setting precedents for the convict trade that would last for decades. He died in 1760 at the age of 80, a very wealthy man, leaving extensive estates in the West Country to his daughter, Elizabeth, who had, in 1734, married Robert Byng, son of Viscount Torrington, later becoming Governor of Barbados.

After Reid's retirement in 1763 he was succeeded by his partner, John Stewart, who became Contractor for Transport to the government. Little is known about him except that he had been in the convict service since at least 1755. Stuart also took on a partner, Duncan Campbell, and following his death in 1772 Campbell took charge of the entire business.

The Journey Begins

By the middle of the seventeenth century there were fourteen prisons in London, of which the oldest and the most notorious was Newgate. It has been estimated that some 20,000 offenders passed through this jail on their way to America, at least one third of all convicts transported to the colonies. It was a cesspit of filth and corruption, with fees demanded by the jailers for every common decency, from straw bedding to enough food to keep from starving and the weight of the irons that convicts wore on their legs. A prison warder was not a public servant but a franchise-holder, entitled to charge inmates a scale of fees of their own devising. Many prisons had taprooms, run for profit by the keeper, and John Howard discovered that in one London prison the beer franchise was let to one of the prisoners. In another, he was told that as many as 600 pots of beer had been brought into cells from the taproom during one Sunday. Richard Ackerman, the keeper of Newgate for thirty-eight years, a dining friend of James Boswell and associate of Dr Johnson, left a fortune of £20,000 when he died in 1792. All profits from the taproom, along with various other 'little earners' like private apartments in the jail rented out to convicts who could afford them, came to him.

Drinking, gambling and attempting to escape were the main occupations of those inside. If they had no money they were allowed to beg for food from charitable passers-by and many more prisoners died from hunger, disease and deprivation than ever went to the gallows. The fear of disease was such that doctors routinely refused to enter the prison, and it was not uncommon for 10% of the inmates to die in a single year. After sentencing, periods of waiting to be taken on board ship varied, but there was probably an average of two months in London while contracts were signed.

When they left Newgate, the convicts were chained together two by two, marched through the street and down to the docks. This procession occurred three or four times a year, and generated considerable interest among the local populace, who would follow, laughing, jeering or hurling abuse as the fancy took them while unfortunates hobbled their way for a mile down to Blackfriars at the edge of the Thames to board their transport ship.

Once they were on board, Parliament took no responsibility for their well-being. Private profit rather than penal policy was the guiding factor, and what happened during the voyage was entirely under the control of the contractors and the shipmasters. The captain, the jailer and other witnesses signed the transportation bond, which declared that the new felons were secured and safely stowed away. These documents were delivered to the Treasury to prove that the criminals had been safely transferred and that payment was due. This was normally paid to the contractor after a month or so and the documents were copied word for word into the Treasury money books. Once the paperwork was in order, the convicts were ready to embark on their voyage across the sea to their new home. Having money, of course, made life much easier, and even the most notorious felon could purchase a comfortable trip to their destination. They could even be set free upon arrival in some cases, having been taken by coach from prison to the awaiting ship. The less wealthy could pay a smaller sum and have their period of servitude reduced upon arrival.

Life was very different for the ordinary villain, of course, who was sent below deck to a prison hold where they spent most of the eight- to ten-week voyage until they reached port in America. As the contractor's profits depended upon the sale of their human cargo at the other end, it could be assumed that they would their do their best to keep the goods in as healthy a state as possible, but this does not always seem to have been the case.

And though the ship's captain would receive a percentage of the sale, many were more interested in the slave trade, which was much more lucrative. On board, conditions were so disgusting that many did not survive the journey, dying of many undiagnosed illnesses, or typhoid, known as jail fever, which, once imported from the prisons, continued to spread. Provisions were barely sufficient. The typical weekly ration consisted of 1.2lb of beef and pork, 13.3oz of cheese, 4.7oz of bread, half a quart of peas, 1.7 quarts of oatmeal, 1.3oz of molasses, half a gill of gin, 1.3 gallons of water – about 1,200 calories a day. Corruption was rife with many receiving a lot less than this, but those with money could buy what they liked. Mutinies were plotted and some attempted, but largely without success – the felons were nearly always stowed down below and heavily shackled, and most likely not in a physical and mental state to attempt such a thing.

The convicts shared space, but not quarters, with a number of indentured servants. Most were labouring men in their twenties who had signed themselves to the ship's captain having failed to find employment in their home country. Some, though, were just seeking adventure in the New World. The latter would normally be signed on for periods of five years or less, and came from a wealthier background than the convicts, with a more hopeful vision of what their destination held for them.

Arrival and Sale

Once the transport ships reached port it was time for the contractors to display their goods and auction off the cargo. Some of these sales took place on board ship, others at the port once the ship had been cleared. Payment was in cash, produce, or bills of exchange, but credit was also frequently given. The convicts had to be unloaded quickly as the ship had to be made ready for the return journey. At auction a slave could fetch between £30 and £60, whereas a convict would make only between around £10 and £15 and were often bought by poorer planters who could not afford slaves. A slave was sold for life, whereas convicts were only bound for a certain number of years. Also, most young slaves, depending upon their origin, would not have a criminal past and would be in much better shape physically. Potential masters examined the convicts in much the way as they would a horse by feeling their muscles and looking into their mouths to check their teeth. Conviction papers that contained details of their crime, length of sentence, and where they had been jailed in England were carefully examined. They were also asked various questions to see how intelligent or obedient they might be.

Felons with money were able to 'bid for themselves' and gain their freedom but had to remain in the colony for their allotted period. The less fortunate who were left over after the sale were sold in bulk at a cheap price to dealers known as 'soul-drivers'. They chained the convicts together and herded them off like oxen, to be sold singly or in groups as they passed each settlement inland, enabling the small planters and farmers who were unable to travel to the sale to pick up the cheap labour. In 1773 more than 300 convicts arrived in one place at the same time and American dealer Matthew Ridley reported to the merchant Duncan Campbell that he had sold all his cargo £10 a head as 'there were no country people among them nor seemingly a good tradesman or I might have got 10s a head more'. This ensured that the convicts were off the ship quickly and did not affect the long-term price. Once purchased, convicts worked alongside indentured servants and African slaves, their status falling somewhere between the two.

There was an important difference between slaves, classified as 'chattel' and held for life with the owner having complete legal control over them, and the indentured servants who were 'qualified property', owned temporarily and relinquished once they had served their term. The owner could rent out their labour to another planter or sell them to someone else, and corporal punishment was allowed as long as it was not deemed overly cruel. Several seventeenth- and eighteenth-century contemporaries expressed the view that servants had a slave-like status. In 1671 Governor Berkeley wrote, 'Not one in five of the English Chattel labourers survived indenture.' In 1769 a gentleman wrote to a friend in London that 'two thirds of the inhabitants, white or black, are now actually slaves'. Convicts could be prohibited from engaging in any trade outside of their normal duties on the plantation, and any money that they had managed to earn on the side could be confiscated. Because the time used for such activity was considered the property of their owner, it was a matter for the individual master what he chose to allow. If an owner died, convicts were passed along with the rest of the deceased's property.

The social rank of the new arrivals was also governed, to a large extent, on the skills they brought with them from England, coupled with the needs of the plantation where they ended up, and the temperament of their master. Buyers were especially on the lookout for joiners, carpenters, blacksmiths, weavers, tailors, and those with other important skills among the new arrivals. Those from the West Country were also sought after due to their assumed agricultural experience as the majority of the work was on the plantations. The lucky ones were treated more like servants and required to undertake a specific occupation. If they lacked any trade or aptitude they were likely to be sent out into the fields along with the slaves on the principle that 'as many of the poor who had been useless in England were inclined to be useless likewise in Georgia'. Between 1700 and 1775 a total of 585,800 immigrants arrived in the thirteen colonies from all over the world. Only about 52,200 of these were convicts and prisoners (9%). Slaves were by far the largest group (278,400; 47%), followed by those freely seeking a new life (151,600; 26%) and indentured servants (96,600; 18%). By around 1745 the Treasury was paying out about £1,400 per year to the contractors.

In extolling the benefits of transportation for the home nation, the British government gave little attention to any impact that it might have on the region that received the new recruits. One North American colonist was left to complain that 'America has been made the very common sewer and dung yard to Britain.' 'Very surprising, one would think,' wrote another American colonist in 1756, 'that thieves, burglars, pickpockets and cutpurses, and a herd of the most flagitious banditti upon earth, should be sent as agreeable companions to us!' Another concern of the local population was that convicts were bringing infectious diseases with them. In 1766 Maryland passed an act requiring that any ship arriving with sick passengers be quarantined to help prevent the spread of illness among the colony. The merchants fought the act, arguing that it seriously affected their trade, but lost the argument and the act stood, prompting merchants to provide their ships with ventilators and open portholes to air out the decks. These simple measures greatly cut the spread of disease and the mortality rate was much reduced within a short time. It has been estimated that between 1718 at 1736 the death rate during transportation was about 14%.

Women were not a popular commodity as their ability for hard manual labour was considered less than that of men, and they were liable to become pregnant. The children of slave women inherited their mother's status, as did the illegitimate children of servants. The removal of children from parents was as common in servitude as it was in slavery, but while the children of slaves belonged to the owner, the bastard children of servants were often sent out by the parish to a different master. Virginian masters were not legally obliged to maintain a servant's child. This responsibility was the father's, if he was known, or failing that they would become a charge upon the parish. Some masters took in the children of their servants, but it was always a possibility that these children were their own. Slaves were encouraged to procreate, whereas servants were not due to the temporary nature of their service. A pregnant female servant unable to work while pregnant deprived the master of profit from her labour, but a female slave was adding to the long-term labour the master could draw upon.

Masters were often keen to retain their servants after their time was over and in many cases the burden of proof that their time had expired rested upon the servant. Despite the legal position being that they were to be freed at the end of their service, time limits were often violated. Owners would often destroy indentures, many convicts arrived without documentation, and in some cases the shipping merchant neglected to provide any written records. If they went to court, servants had to provide proof of their indenture, with no recourse for those who arrived without one. The widespread evidence of servants being kept beyond their time shows that many masters would have preferred to keep their servants in the long term, just as they kept slaves.

Once free, many changed their names and moved to other parts of the country, keen to leave their disreputable past behind them. As they were mainly illiterate, there are few documents to tell their stories, and tracking the fates of individual transportees is almost impossible. Unlike the later settlements in Australia, convicts sent to America were not officially watched over or disciplined by any governmental authority, which is why it cannot be said that they had been sent to a penal colony. As a result, there was seldom any official documentation.

To the mother country, transportation was an ingenious idea that seemed to suit everyone and was considered very successful: the country was rid of its most undesirable elements, and the population of workhouses, 'houses of correction' and those entitled to poor relief were greatly reduced. But many Americans were disgusted by the practice, finding it contemptuous and insulting that the British should empty its criminals onto their shores. The country was new and inexperienced, a society held together by personal contact and trust, into which were thrown 'wretches, outcasts vermin and human serpents', the scum of the Earth that would destroy the customary networks that bound communities together, thus corrupting and endangering the foundations of a still-fragile society. Despite these fears, any attempt at restricting the trade or demanding bonds for good behaviour from the convicts was dismissed by Parliament, and various studies have shown that there were no great outbreaks of crime associated with the newcomers. This could be due to of lack of opportunity – there was less to steal – or close supervision, or perhaps many were just too exhausted by their physical labours to contemplate any wrongdoing.

Many refused to accept their fate and tried their escape for a variety of reasons – a change of ownership, bad treatment, or simply seizing an opportunity on the spur of the moment – often with some success, while others planned it well, managing to obtain forged discharge papers and identity documents. If they could survive the journey, the most favoured destinations were urban areas like Philadelphia or New York, which offered anonymity, employment or even opportunities for more crime, but the ultimate aim for many was to get aboard a ship and return home. This was easier than might be thought as many shipmasters would accept a bribe, sometimes from organised gangs in England wanting their labour force returned, even to the extent of having agents at the port to facilitate the process. On other occasions ships were grateful for the free labour in return for keeping quiet.

Despite returning convicts facing capital punishment, few were recaptured mainly due to a poor system of communications and lack of any organised crime-fighting force. Having said that, the main problem for the illegal returnee was where to go. Returning to their old haunts was fraught with danger as word would get around and there were plenty like Wild who would take money to turn them in. However, to go to somewhere completely new was to stick out like a sore thumb. The lack of positive identification and documents to prove previous crimes or transportation was a serious problem and it was often thought to be not worth the trouble of bringing a prosecution. Rather than the threatened execution, many who were caught, often in the commission of a new crime, seem to have been returned to exile.

The Colonies Revolt

A triangular trade existed for the convict transporters similar to that of slavers, but on a smaller scale. Once the convicts had been sold, the ship could be loaded with timber and sent to Jamaica to be loaded with sugar and rum for the home run. Not every trader followed this route, some sailed directly home with a hold full of tobacco, but a significant number did. Often a return load was ordered to be stored on the dock before the ship arrived, to ensure that the turnaround time was as quick as possible. American facilitators were crucial in these sales as they represented the London merchants on the ground. These were the men who organised return loads and the sale of the convicts.

Despite this cosy arrangement, other factors were at work that meant its days were numbered: the natives were restless. The colonialists were becoming increasingly angry at the way they were taxed without any representation in the British government. Whereas at one time they had a high level of independence, this was gradually being eroded by a number of acts intended to bring them under a more direct rule, presumably to extract yet more tax. Benjamin Franklin suggested that rattlesnakes might be exported to England in return for convicts, describing the practice as 'an insult and contempt, the cruellest perhaps ever one people offered another'. After a long period of mistrust, during which King George was described as a tyrant who disregarded the colonists' rights as Englishmen, the first military engagement between the two countries took place.

On 19 April 1775 British soldiers were sent to capture a cache of unauthorised military supplies and were confronted by the local Patriot Militia at Lexington and Concord in Massachusetts. In August of that year King George issued a Proclamation of Rebellion, which declared elements within the colonies to be in a state of 'open and avowed rebellion', marking the beginning of the end of any cooperation between the two parties. Ports were closed to British ships and the transportation system came to an end. The last convict ship reported as having been able to unload its cargo in America was the *Jenny* from Newcastle in April 1776. On 11 December 1776 a group of convicts who had boarded the *Tayloe* for transportation to America were pardoned on condition that they join the army. Ironically, rather than being sent to work for the colonists in America, they were impressed to fight against them. It was thought that this little difficulty with the colonials would soon be over and transportation could soon continue as normal. By the declaration of independence, England had shipped some 50,000 prison inmates to the colonies, about 19,000 of these from London, Middlesex and Home Counties, meaning that convicts represented as much as a quarter of all British immigrants to colonial America during the eighteenth century. During this time at least eighteen different colonies had received convicts at one time or another: eleven mainland colonies, Bermuda, and six islands in the Caribbean.

The glory days were over and, henceforth, government policy and the lives of thousands of convicted felons were to be in the hands of two remarkable men.

Chapter 3

Case Histories I

Having had a brief overview of the state of the criminal law and the beginnings of the system of transportation, it might be interesting to have a look at a few individual criminals who lived through this early period. Many of these tales are fascinating, many doubtless exaggerated, the stories often turned into broadsheets to be sold at the executions as the confessions or last words of the condemned felon. These 'biographies' were taken down in the cell of condemned by the chaplain as a few of the subjects were literate. Other accounts appeared in the press and scandal sheets of the time.

John Meff – 1721 (as told to The Ordinary of Newgate)

John Meff was arrested for a robbery that he had committed within the limits of a 'period of grace' granted by George I, a general amnesty for certain offences, and as such he could not be prosecuted. Unfortunately for him, he was recognised as having been transported for house breaking in 1717 and had thus returned before his sentence was completed. He was sentenced to death by hanging, as was mandatory at the time, but gave the following account of himself.

He was born in London of French parents driven from that country due to religious persecution and became apprenticed to a weaver. He served his time, but could not find work, and with a family to feed, he turned to house breaking. Meff was caught and sentenced to death.

Meff was returned to Newgate where his sentence was changed to that of transportation. Upon reaching Bermuda, on the way to America, his ship was captured by pirates who wanted the nine felons on board to join them. Those who refused were marooned on a desert island to die of hunger and thirst. After a number of days, during which they almost starved, a party of Indians arrived. The convicts managed to steal their canoe and eventually reached America where Meff could probably have settled quietly and had a good life. Instead, he joined a ship as a seaman carrying merchandise from Virginia to Barbados. Missing his wife and children, who he believed to be in the workhouse, he foolishly returned to England and fell back into his life of crime. That was one story, but it seems that he married a second time and lived with this new wife for nine months. He was recognised and arrested before long and returned once more to Newgate. He escaped and made his way to Hatfield, presumably the home of his second wife, where he was discovered and arrested once more. Despite these several opportunities to avoid his fate, Meff met his end at Tyburn on 11 September 1721, at the age of 39.

Mary Young – 1733

Contemporary accounts of female convicts assumed that most were either prostitutes or career criminals. *The Complete Newgate Chronicle*, which detailed the exploits of celebrated villains, commonly featured women like Mary Young, alias Jenny Diver. Young, originally from Ireland, who was both attractive and fashionably dressed, became a successful cutpurse in London and amassed a large following of accomplices, becoming both wealthy and famous. In fact, Young became the basis of the character 'Jenny Diver', who betrayed MacHeath in Gay's play *Beggar's Opera*. When eventually caught in 1733, she was sentenced to be transported to Virginia, but even then her relative fame and prosperity ensured her a comfortable passage. Remarkably, she managed to take onboard enough goods and possessions to load a wagon. She was afforded every possible convenience and accommodation during the voyage, and upon her arrival in Virginia she disposed of her goods and for some time lived in great splendour. Despite seeming to have fallen on her feet early in her sentence, she was determined to return to London and made a successful escape by bribing a ship's captain. She returned to her old trade and was caught again in 1738 under an alias and sentenced once more to transportation. Nothing if not determined, Young escaped again, and by using the same strategy she was back in London within the year.

By now, after a long and successful career, she had turned 38 and suffered from arthritis. The skills of her youth were deserting her. A hamfisted attempted robbery of a young woman led her to try her hand at highway robbery, which resulted in her capture in January 1741. This time she was recognised and her previous life caught up with her. This latest crime, and her illegal return from transportation, meant a death sentence. On 18 March 1741 Jenny and nineteen other condemned prisoners were taken from Newgate for the two-mile journey to the gallows at Tyburn. Jenny's wealth allowed her final trip to be taken in a black mourning coach pulled by black horses decked out in black cloth. At the fatal time, she and her fellow prisoners stood in carts while the executioner secured the hanging rope to a beam. Then, the horse-drawn cart was whipped from under them and they dropped a few inches. If lucky, she would have lost consciousness quickly, otherwise it was a case of slow strangulation.

Bampfylde Moore Carew – 1738

Of all the tellers of tall stories, imposters, larger-than-life characters and bare-faced liars who seem to have greatly enriched the eighteenth century, few could have been more outrageous than Bampfylde Moore Carew. Born in about 1693, the son of the vicar of Bickleigh in Devon, he was enrolled at the famed Blundell's School in Tiverton, where, by all accounts, he applied himself diligently to the study of Latin and Greek. At 15, Bampfylde and some of his schoolmates antagonised local landowners by damaging their crops while hunting. Fearing the severity of their impending punishment, the boys ran away from the school and went to a local pub where they met a gang of gypsies and spent the day carousing before joining their number.

One of his first capers was to convince a rich lady in Taunton that for twenty guineas he could use his special powers to find a large amount of money she thought was hidden on her land. He told her that she could only dig on a certain date – by which time, of course, he had long gone. Within this gypsy group it was regarded as decent and honourable to deceive for financial gain those who were not of their kind, provided no personal harm was done and the victims were not severely impoverished by such actions. This 'mumping', as they called it, was justified on the grounds that 'mendicants are in a constant state of hostility with all other people'. Carew became a master of disguise. A shipwrecked seaman was one favourite, picking up takes from those returning from voyages. Another was a vicar who had fallen on hard times.

After marriage to a respectable woman and further years as a vagabond, Carew claimed to have been elected King of the Gypsies. He was imprisoned by a judge with a grudge against him for living as a vagrant, and after two months in jail was told that he was to be transported for seven years to '*Merryland*' after cheekily correcting the chairman's pronunciation of Maryland. Carew feigned gratitude, saying it would save him five pounds for his passage to a country he had dearly wished to visit. After an eleven-week journey aboard the *Julian*, Carew was auctioned, along with the other convicts, and upon being asked his trade declared that he was a rat catcher, a mendicant and a dog merchant. Unsurprisingly, he wasn't chosen, but managed to slip away when nobody was looking. He was soon recaptured, subjected to the cat o' nine tails, and had an iron slave collar fixed around his neck.

Carew was set to loading ships, but upon hearing that some of the local Indians were quite friendly, he made his escape once more, and according to his own account, became a great friend of the Indian chief. Despite this, he felt the need to move on and travelled to Pennsylvania, where he adopted the guise of a Quaker and lived quite well off their money before convincing them to pay for his passage on a ship back to England. Having heard that the press gangs were on the way to imprison the crew, he devised a cunning ruse to avoid being drafted. He pricked his arms and chest with a needle, then rubbed in bay salt and gunpowder, which made it look as if he were suffering from smallpox. His concerns turned out to be well founded, and upon arrival at Lundy Island off the coast of Devon, the entire crew were impressed, apart, of course, from the one with smallpox who was dumped in Bristol.

He didn't stay long, and returned to his travels, visiting Sweden and Paris in various guises before returning to Exeter where he was recognised and, without trial, kidnapped and sent once more to Maryland where he escaped yet again, eventually making it to Boston and another covert passage back to England. By now it was 1745, and upon hearing of Bonnie Prince Charlie and the Jacobite rebels he inexplicably decided to join them. Not having the stomach for combat, he pretended to be very lame and sick and just hobbled along with them to Manchester where he had his first sight of the young Prince. From there they moved on to Derby where a rumour was spreading that the Duke of Cumberland was coming to engage them in battle, at which point Carew decided that it was time to go home. Reunited with his wife and daughter, he purchased a house in Bickleigh, his birthplace, and spent his remaining years in obscurity, outliving his wife. Before his death, in 1758, he saw his daughter marry. He was buried in the churchyard at St Mary's Church in Bickleigh. There is no doubt that he had a fascinating life, and his story was reprinted many times, and though greatly embellished, its essential parts appear to be true.

Eleanor Conner – 1748

In one notable case, a convict was rescued from the tedious journey to America even after sail had been set. On 4 April 1748 an Irish woman, Eleanor Conner, or possibly Tobin or Woods, was arrested for picking the pocket of a farmer named Hewitt. She was sentenced to death but agreed to be transported to America for fourteen years. It was said that Conner was

among the most noted pickpockets of her day. Covent Garden and the area
around the London theatres were her favourite haunts, but there were few
public places she didn't frequent as she seldom missed any opportunity
that presented itself. She was committed to Newgate jail in Bristol, and
remained there for almost two years before boarding a brig named the
Nightingale bound for the American plantations. The ship was owned by
Thomas Benson and captained by John Lancey.

So valuable were her skills that her gang did not want to lose her, and
while the ship was under sail, not far from port, Conner was on deck:

> whether by accident, or thro' design, the consequence seems to
> declare for itself; for, she was no sooner upon deck, than two
> boats were ready to receive her, one of which took her up, and
> carried her clear off to shore, where it was most convenient:
> there is scarce any doubt by whom the boats were manned,
> her old companions, who were then in that part of the country,
> procured attendance for that purpose. And it is reported, that
> when one of the ship's crew declared a woman was overboard,
> 'twas was replied with an oath, "She is not worth taking up;
> it blows a brisk gale, and I'll not run a risque of losing my
> voyage to save her life."

After this daring escape, she and her old companions continued to travel up
and down the country plying their trade with great success, until they decided
to try their luck in Dublin. It was here that they bumped into an old associate,
John Poulter, highwayman – or according to him, retired highwayman –
trying to run a pub and lead a quiet life. Once the secret was out, his house
was flooded with criminal colleagues old and new, causing much unwanted
attention. He fled back to England with Conner close behind him.

She settled in Liverpool for a while, running a chandler's shop as a
cover for the gang's activities, but inevitably she was caught once more
and committed to Liverpool jail to take her trial at the next assizes. She
had been there some time when her old gang managed to break her out
once more. Rushing the turnkey one evening, they created a fight, enabling
her to clamber over the struggling heap and get away. The rescuers also
managed to escape, and one of them went to London with her to carry on
their old trade, but it wasn't long before they were recognised, and – as
there were good rewards for capturing escaped criminals – they were seized
and committed to Newgate by Justice Fielding. Part of their undoing was
that highwayman Poulter had been arrested, and as part of a plea bargain,

he stated that Conner was still alive and active (it had been assumed that she had drowned attempting to leave the *Nightingale*.) It didn't do Poulter much good, though; they hanged him anyway.

The magistrates in Bristol soon got wind of her recapture and before long she was on trial for 'returning from transportation'. They sent the town clerk to London 'at their own expense' with a copy of the court record. Her only defence was to claim that she was not Eleanor Conner and that Conner had drowned, but, unfortunately, three witnesses from her previous case in Bristol gave evidence that she was indeed the fugitive. She claimed that the captain of the *Nightingale*, John Lancy, had declared that they were two different people. He hadn't, and as he was also under sentence of death in Newgate for scuttling the ship in an insurance scam organised by the ship's owner, his evidence would have carried very little weight. (Captain Lancey was hanged at Execution Dock in Wapping on 17 June 1754 for his part in the affair.) Finding that this defence was going nowhere, she claimed to be pregnant to gain time for further contrivances. A jury of matrons was called and agreed that this was indeed the case.

Her execution was respited, and she remained without further enquiry until the September sessions, when it was estimated that if the matron's verdict in February had been right, she must be at least close to giving birth by that time. She replied that she was not yet delivered and pretended that her time was not yet due. In October she pretended to be very weak after labour, and begged the court would take it into consideration and sentence her to deportation for life. But it was to no avail, and she was ordered to her former sentence. On Monday, 9 December her luck finally ran out and she was hanged with others at Tyburn. She was about 35 years old.

Alice Walker – 1772

On 9 September 1772 Alice Walker, a 19-year-old Londoner, was tried at the Old Bailey for stealing a canvas bag worth one penny, and approximately £12 in cash, from a wagoner named Thomas Atkins. He claimed that Walker stole the bag from him while the two were having a drink at a local pub. Walker contested that Atkins had given her the money to 'buy me some wearing apparel', and that he had asked her to go with him into the country the following day. The next morning, the constable of Newgate prison found Walker with a man named Michael Johnson, a tailor. The constable found Atkins' money in Johnson's possession and the canvas bag in his tailor's shop. Despite her protestations of innocence, the court found her guilty and sentenced her to be transported to Rappahannock, Virginia, where she would be sold as a convict servant for seven years, one of about 5,000 women transported to America in the eighteenth century.

On her arrival, in March 1772, Alice was purchased by the Mathews brothers, Sampson and George, established members of Virginia society. Between them they owned a large number of slaves and convict servants, but their treatment was suspect, as large numbers ran away from their estates. In 1769 three slaves fled from the brothers, and in 1773 ten convicts managed to escape, among them Alice Walker. Newspaper advertisements for runaways provide some of the most detailed accounts of convict life in the colonies. The descriptions of women who ran away reveal scars from beatings, tattoos, and attempts to create relationships with other convicts. Winifred Thomas, a convict runaway, sported a tattoo on the inside of her right arm with the initials 'W.T.' and 'the date of the year underneath'. Another runaway, Isabella Pierce, had scars on her right ankle, causing her to limp. While most of the escapees advertised in the *Virginia Gazette* travelled alone, some ran away with other convicts. Alice escaped with two fellow convicts: John Steel, a cabinetmaker, and John Eaton, a ship's carpenter. The newspaper reports that Walker was going by the name of Alice Eaton at the time of her departure:

> Runaway last night, three English convict servants, John Eaton, by trade a ships carpenter, about 23 years of age and about 5 feet 3 or 4 inches high [...] Alice Eaton, alias Walker (who goes for the said John Eaton's wife) a low, well set woman, about 20 years of age, and has sandy coloured hair; had on a brown stuffed gown, a red stuff petticoat, and four red silk handkerchiefs. John Steel, by trade a cabinetmaker, about 18 years of age, 5 feet 5 or 6 inches high.

Alice managed to return to England following her escape, but whether she was with John Eaton, the man who posed as her husband, is not recorded. She was recognised in London the following year and indicted for returning from transportation before her time. At another appearance at the Old Bailey, she was sentenced to death, but the jury recommended mercy, and she was given a conditional pardon if she would agree to be transported for a further fourteen years. She was returned to America but no further trace of her has been discovered.

Following the American Revolution, Sampson Matthews went on to become a senator for the district of East Augusta, and his brother, George, became a sheriff during the colonial period.

Chapter 4

Duncan Campbell
1726–1779

As we have seen, the loss of the American colonies was causing the government much concern over the future management and housing of convicted felons. One businessman who stood to lose the most from the collapse of the American trade was merchant and trader Duncan Campbell. He was born in Renfrewshire, Scotland, in 1726, one of ten children, the son of Reverand Dr Neil Campbell (1679–1761) and his wife, Henrietta (1678–1761). His father studied divinity at Glasgow University, becoming a Presbyterian minister and the university's principal from 1728 until his death in 1761. A very controversial figure due to his unbending religious views, he was Moderator of the General Assembly of the Church of Scotland in 1732 and again in 1737, being appointed Royal Chaplain in 1734. The Campbell family owned sugar plantations in southwestern Jamaica, the first one being Colonel John Campbell (1673–1740), of Black River, one of the oldest European towns on the island. Campbell had been a military employee of the Scottish Darien Company, a failed enterprise set up by investors to establish, and profit from, new colonies. His son, Colin Campbell, of Black River, was appointed to the Council of Jamaica shortly after his father's death in 1740.

Few details of Duncan Campbell's early life and education are known for certain, but after matriculating he is believed to have followed his father in attending Glasgow University, despite describing himself as 'having been brought up a seaman'. A fascinating letter from 1748, held in the Argyll and Bute archives in Scotland, gives some insight into his early adventures and ambitions (corrected slightly):

> Dear Uncle,
>
> I most earnestly beg your pardon for not writing to you sooner tho I delayed some time expecting ships from Jama[ica] with accts from my Uncle James. His last letters say that he intends to be home this year at all events so that we expect him by the first fleet.

No doubt but you have heard of my double misfortune before this time, of which I shall give you a short relation. I was coming home chief mate of a ship named the *Betty Galley,* but in ye Latt of 47 and about 15 Deg west from England we meet with a most severe gale of wind (on the 1st of February last) in which we unfortunately lost our rudder which had likes to have proved fatal to us all, for the rudder by going away tore the rudder irons from the ship's bottom, drawing all the large nails out with it. The ship then all of a sudden made an immense deal of water, insomuch that we could hardly keep her free with both pumps working constantly. In this condition we continued for six days (I having only nine hands with me to work at that rate a ship of 800 tons, the master being sick in his cabin and several of our people a dying, some we buried) having hove good part of our cargoes over board to lighten the ship.

On ye 7th of February we were lucky taken up by a French letter of Marque Ship bound to the West Indies. But our ship having at that time about 4 feet water in her hold they abandoned the ship. The day after they took us up they met with a small South Carolina ship bound to London which they took, but the commander ransomed the ship again. This was lucky for us because we all went aboard that ship to come to England. But when we had got within forty leagues of the Land's End, met with the *Dover*, Man of War, they being in want of a date and men pressed me & our people. I continued – months during which I acted as mate but General John (John Campbell later 4th Duke of Argyll) got me my discharge so then I left her. My being detained so long aboard a Man of War was a great disappointment to me, for had I got home at that time I might had the command of a ship to Jamaica I am now staying here with cous: McLachlan […]

Mr Currie and Lachlan are concerned with Mr McNeil in a ship now in Jamaica which we expect home on 2 Nov. They have given me their promise of the command of her when she comes home. By their desires & that view I stay, tho I might have gone out first mate of a very good ship to Jamaica.

The country air has been of great service to my health which was in great measure hurt, what with fatigue and what with vexation […] There are […] we expect in a month if we have any accts. from Uncle James I shall acquaint. I need not tell you how I was when I left Jamaica because I left in Novr last so that you have had letters from him since that. I can't say but I long much to see him for he has been like a father to me ever since I saw him.

Loves to you, & I am, dear Uncle, your most obed[ient] and affec[tionate] nephew

Duncan Campbell

Campbell served on the *Dove* between February 1747 and May 1748, and was a midshipman on merchant ships to Jamaica before becoming captain sometime after 1749. His early patrons are not known but they were probably his West Indian relatives. Between 1749 and 1750 he voyaged between London and Jamaica on the ship *Elizabeth*, and was on the ship *Mary* doing the same run from 1751 to 1752, continuing in the merchant service to Jamaica from 1752–1754 on *Mary*, then again from 1754 to 1757 on *Britannia*.

In 1753, on the west coast of Jamaica, Duncan married his cousin Rebecca Campbell (1730–1774) of Saltspring, Hanover, one of the ten children of Dugald Campbell, a wealthy planter and brother to John Campbell, who had inherited the estate from his father. They had a daughter, Rebecca, in 1756 when living in Hooper Square, Whitechapel, and in the same year he voyaged to Madeira, possibly in connection with a wine shipment. He soon became prominent in the West Indies trade, owning both plantations and ships. In 1758 he was elected as a Younger Brother of Trinity House, a prestigious body concerned with shipping and the maintenance of lighthouses. They also managed the raising of ballast on the Thames, an ancient guild right that was to become very useful to him in the future.

It is not known how he was first involved in the convict trade to America, but he had been junior partner to one of London's largest convict contractors, John Stewart, the former partner of Andrew Reid. In 1758 Campbell took his first known trip on a convict vessel, the *Thetis*, and saw the American colony first hand. The new partnership had 'JS&C' stamped on hogsheads and printed on its notepaper, they operated from Black Raven Court, Seething Lane, Blackfriars, and shipped convicts to Virginia and North America, bringing back tobacco and sometimes bar iron, which they sold to the Admiralty. Campbell eventually became one of the capital's top ten tobacco traders.

Following the death of Stewart, in December 1772, at the age of 46, Campbell moved to Mincing Lane near Tower Hill, the site of the present Custom House. This location was ideal for his line of work, close to the river and to Lloyd's, Cornhill, with other merchants' haunts in the vicinity including the banker Francis Baring. On 7 December 1774 Duncan's beloved wife, Rebecca, died, leaving him with seven children and a newborn son, Duncan Jnr. She might have died in childbirth, but there are hints in his letters that he may have shared an illness with her as there is some indication that his own life had been in danger. It is possible that he brought home some disease from the convicts as he remained in a grief-stricken state for some months, incapacitated physically and emotionally, apologising almost tearfully to business contacts for his inattention and ineffectiveness. Luckily, his younger brother, Neil, was on hand to help with the business affairs while he recovered. It might be relevant that in January 1778, while inspecting the hulks with Jeremy Bentham, Campbell avoided any risk of jail fever – or typhus as it's known today – by refusing to enter the hulk's hospital.

Until 1775 Campbell had been one of the leading London merchants dealing with the tobacco colonies, but since the beginning of the war the money owed to him by his former American trading partners had not been paid and was causing him great concern. By early 1777 he was beginning to consider the possibility that Britain might lose the war with America and a North American mercantile lobby was formed, which gradually came under his leadership. He was a signatory of the petition to Parliament in 1778 requesting that if negotiations for peace were begun the Americans should be required to pay their debts in full. Some of his country's enemies had once been his valued agents; the total amount owing was said to be between £2.5 and £5 million, depending on how the count was taken and if interest was to be included for the duration of the conflict. The loss of trade with America wasn't the only problem Campbell faced in 1776. The military forces manning the garrison at Hanover in Jamaica had been reassigned to fight in America and word spread through the plantations – apparently a prearranged signal for the parish's slaves to attempt a general uprising. The plot was discovered and put down before it got very far but for Campbell it must have been a very worrying time.

The Hulk Act of May 1776

The loss of the convict transportation business had a traumatic effect on the country's legal system. There was no backup plan and nowhere to send its seemingly never-ending stream of felons, and jails were soon filled beyond capacity. Parliament needed to act quickly before the crisis of overcrowding got completely out of hand. Justices throughout the country were still imposing sentences of seven years to life to be served overseas, despite their intended destination being no longer available. It brought Campbell close to ruin. He had lost the incredibly lucrative trade in tobacco and was still responsible for housing and maintaining convicts for the journey regardless of the international situation; he couldn't just walk away. In 1775 Parliament charged William Eden, the Undersecretary of State, with finding a solution to the problem. Eden estimated that they would have to find accommodation for about 1,000 convicts a year, and there was literally nowhere to put them. It was assumed that the American market for convicts would reopen once the rebels had been defeated, and Eden proposed that Campbell use his ships on the Thames to accommodate those condemned to transportation 'in the usual manner and as if in due course for transportation'.

In May 1776 'An Act to authorise, for a limited time, the punishment by hard labour of offenders who, for certain crimes, are or shall become liable to be transported to any of his Majesty's colonies and plantations' (16 Geo.3 c.43), otherwise known as the Criminal Law Act, the Hulks Act or the Hard Labour Act, was signed into law. The government put a brave face on its inability to dispose of its felons, claiming that the manpower that had been sent to America was:

> found to be attended with various inconveniences, particularly by depriving this kingdom of many subjects whose labour might be useful to the community [...] such convicts, being males, might be employed with benefit to the public in raising sand, soil, and gravel from, and cleansing the river Thames; or being males unfit for so severe a labour, or being females, might be kept to hard labour of another kind within England.

The act marked a profound change in the way that those convicted of crime were sentenced. Previously, prisoners were held under highly irregular conditions; there was no legislative precedent for transportable convicts being put to work on British soil and the whole unhappy enterprise was probably unconstitutional. Now hard labour at home had the force of law and was to replace the lucrative business of selling convict labour abroad, with the state assuming overall control of the private contractors. The act also required that regular returns should be submitted, initially to the Treasury but later to the Home Office.

Male convicts could now be sentenced to be 'kept to hard labour in the raising of sand soil and gravel from and cleansing the River Thames, or any other service for the benefit of the navigation of the said river'. The convicts were to be placed under the supervision of an overseer appointed by the Middlesex magistrates based at Hicks Hall in Clerkenwell, despite these gentlemen having a reputation for being totally corrupt. The magistrates gave no direction as to how affairs were to be organised, they were simply delighted to be able to pass the responsibility on to somebody else and have little more to do with it. Campbell's appointment as overseer was authorised by the Treasury and he was to enter into an agreement to take convicts off the government's hands at so much per head and hire men to manage them at his own expense. Noncapital offenders, who earlier would have been sentenced to seven years, were to be sentenced for a term of between three to ten years at the judge's order, and those pardoned from a death sentence were to be set to work on the Thames at His Majesty's discretion. Women and those unable to work were to be confined in houses of correction but still kept to hard labour. The act included a provision empowering every county in England to build a 'house of correction', although nothing was actually constructed during this time as the state was unwilling to build new prisons due to ongoing economic strain from the American and French wars.

The act did not concern itself with where this labour force was going to be housed, but for the time being they could remain locked up on the transport ships. Campbell began to reorganise immediately, and convicts were moved onto his two ships: the 160-ton *Tayloe*, named after a prominent Virginian family, and *Justitia*, a former 300-ton convict transport ship. These prison hulks – floating, unseaworthy vessels – were a cheap and workable solution, maintaining a much-needed workforce along the banks of the river. Prisoners began arriving from January 1776 in anticipation of the act passing, even though Campbell was not officially appointed until 13 July.

Specially created for the purpose, Campbell's office possessed powers over the convicted similar to those usually held by sheriffs and jailers and resembling the traditional powers of a ship's captain to maintain discipline. This gave him wider powers than a simple jailer – much to the surprise and consternation of those on board who would have been used to a more relaxed regime on shore. He was also responsible for ensuring adequate food and clothing for the inmates, quite a common situation in the jails of the time. Is unlikely that Campbell actively wanted this position. He had many business interests, including his trade with Jamaica. One of his major roles was to ship supplies to the plantations of his relatives in Jamaica, and in common with everyone else involved, he would have considered 'convict storage' as a temporary inconvenience that he had to organise until normality returned. Campbell's initial contract was for three years and worth around £3,560 a year. He was to provide a ship of at least 240 tons to house 120 prisoners – mainly from Newgate – at an average of

£32 per prisoner. This sum was also to provide guards with six lighters to work from, along with the necessary tools. The contract was to end or be renegotiated on 12 July 1779.

Not everyone saw the change in the law as progressive. A writer in *The London Magazine* commented, 'The sight of an Englishman transformed into a galley slave is humiliating [...] Englishmen, [even] in their most degenerate condition, are designed for a better fate.' A member of Parliament complained that 'the people have slavery daily before their eyes, it would at length become familiar to them'. Still another protested that the act was 'one of the many schemes of the crown for subverting the liberties of the people and destroying the essence of the constitution'. As overseer, Campbell was loathed by the London journalists, who also viewed the hulks as an affront to traditional views about English freedoms. His hulks were repeatedly referred sarcastically to as 'Campbell's Academy', by which was meant academies of crime.

Life on Board

After conviction and sentence at the Assize Court, the London felon would be taken off in chains to Newgate to languish in appalling conditions before being woken up one morning, chained to a few other unfortunates and marched down to Blackfriars Gate, where he would get his first view of the massive rotting hulks that were to be his future home. He would be rowed out in a longboat, stripped of the vermin-infested clothes that he had worn in jail, scrubbed down, and held for four days while being inspected by three surgeons for infection before being sent below to see if he were about to become ill or die. Once they had the all-clear, they would be issued with ill-fitting 'slops' and integrated into the stinking mass of their fellow criminals for a greater or lesser period, depending upon the time they had to serve and the availability of places on the convict ship. Keeping convicts on board the hulks was not the most satisfactory of arrangements. They would arrive from the prisons, diseased, starving and ill, which was normal, but instead of sailing away to the colonies they were trapped below decks indefinitely. The high death rate on Campbell's ships, and those moored in Portsmouth and Plymouth under the control of other administrators, was partially the result of diseases prisoners had contracted in the city and county jails. 'The ships at Woolwich are as sweet as any parlour in the kingdom,' Campbell asserted with some pride, perhaps being a little economical with the truth.

Campbell's ships were anchored initially between Gallions Reach and Barking Reach on the north bank of the Thames and came into use officially on 15 July 1776. Their conversion involved them being dismantled as ocean-going vessels by removing the sails, masts, guns and various other equipment that made the ship seaworthy and ready for battle. Sheds were constructed on the decks and used as stores and guard posts. The new hulks received as many prisoners as Campbell's contract would allow – and sometimes a few more. They came from all parts of the country and were stowed below decks in irons. Even Campbell found some of the sentencing inappropriate; in the initial stages of the scheme some inmates were more than 70 years old, some blind, crippled or mad, and there were boys under the age of 15. Conditions on board were poor, and mortality rates high. Inmates aboard the *Justitia* slept in tiered bunks with each having an average sleeping space of 5ft 10in long and 18in wide. These were soon removed and replaced with low, wooden platforms, 6ft long by 4ft wide, each accommodating two men with a straw pad and a blanket shared between them. The straw mattresses were nailed down to stop them being thrown about, which prevented them from being aired. Some decks were scarcely high enough to allow a man to stand straight and all were very overcrowded. When the *Censor* was fitted out in April 1777 hammocks were installed instead of the platforms, but the situation was reversed when it became apparent that climbing in and out of a hammock wearing heavy irons was not very practical.

Convicts were supposed to wash every morning, but Campbell commented that it was easier to get them to work than to wash. On one of his early visits, prison reformer John Howard observed that many men had no shirts, some no waistcoats, some no stockings, and some were without shoes – there seemed to be no consistent policy with regard to their clothing. Many depended upon friends to provide them with the barest of necessities and Campbell was quite willing to save his money while convicts received blankets from the outside. To the totally destitute he supplied a shirt, a brown jacket and a pair of breaches.

The sanitary arrangements were less than basic: the vessels had no adequate quarantine facilities and there was a continued health risk caused by the flow of excrement and filth from the sick bays. In October 1776 a prisoner from Maidstone jail brought typhus aboard, which spread rapidly. Over a seven-month period to March 1778, a total of 176 inmates died, or twenty-eight percent of the prison ship population of 632.

Many on board would have been familiar with prison conditions in London, where, despite the inhuman surroundings, visitors came and went pretty much as they wished, food sellers and hawkers plied their trade, business could be conducted via friends and family, and corrupt keepers and turnkeys were just part of daily life. By contrast, the hulks were austere, hard-to-visit, isolated and distant from the life of the city, and with ultra-tight security, there were few deals to be done. Hard labour as a form of punishment was to be dreaded, but what prisoners feared more than anything else was the isolation of the hulks. They were the end of the line, a living hell of jail fever, despair, filth and severe beatings for stepping out of line – the British concentration camp had arrived.

William Smith, who conducted a survey of London prisons during this early period, visited the *Justitia* and found that there was no medical help for eighty-nine transferred prisoners, of whom 'Twelve are now sick, and unable to move their heads from the boards on which they lie. Most of them complain of diarrhoea, few are free from scorbutic blotches, some with bad sores and venereal complaints, and all look thin and pale. The dozen confined to the boards are ill of a low nervous disease.'

When not out at work, they were crammed together like sardines, irrespective of age, level of criminality or physical condition, and without any supervision. The consequences of this are not hard to imagine. Below decks after evening lockdown, the strongest and most determined undoubtedly ruled. Any victims of robbery or assault were naturally reluctant to come forward, fearing retribution at a later date. Presumably, though, some form of equilibrium was reached – a consensus among those forced to live together – a sort of self-governing anarchy with its own pecking order. It would also have been realised that any large-scale disturbance would be brutally dealt with and would also interfere with their recreational activities like gambling, drinking, trading in government property between themselves, and carrying on traditional trades such as seeing how many counterfeit sixpences could be hammered out of a half crown.

Work

For the first few months of the new regime convicts were left pretty much to their own devices as no one was quite sure how things were to be organised. The silting up of the Thames was an ongoing problem and often commented upon in the newspapers, which claimed early in 1776 that the riverbed was in poor condition with the stairs on the docks at London and Westminster being made impassable by mud and gravel. At Woolwich major dredging was needed to correct a drift in the river, and convicts provided a cheap workforce. Campbell had ordered the building of lighters, or dredging boats, to be used in the raising of ballast and had them fitted with a machine for doing this – known as a 'David Machine' – which enabled each lighter to handle twenty-four tons of ballast at a time. Work began in August 1776, about two miles below Barking Reach, just downstream from Woolwich. The main area of activity was the foreshore of the Thames where the convicts cleared mud, sand and gravel to improve navigability and contributed to building works at the dockyard. Such was the novelty of their industry that they became something of a tourist attraction. A contributor to *The Scots Magazine* of July 1777 made the following observations:

> There are upwards of 200 of them who are employed as follows, some are sent about a mile below Woolwich in lighters to raise ballast, and to row it back to the embankment at Woolwich Warren, close to the end of the Target walk, others are there employed in throwing it from the lighters. Some wheel it to different parts to be sifted, others wheel it from the skreen and spread it for the embankment. A party is continually busied in turning around a machine for driving piles to secure the embankment from the rapidity of the tides.
>
> Carpenters etc are employed in repairing the *Justitia* and *Toyloe* hulks, that lie hard to buy for the nightly reception of those objects who have fetters on each leg with a chain between, that ties variously, some around their middle, others upright to the throat. Some are chained two and two, and others whose crimes have been enormous, with heavy fetters. Six or seven are continually walking about with them with drawn cutlasses, to prevent their escape and likewise prevent idleness. So far from being permitted to speak to anyone, they hardly dare speak to each other. But what is most surprising is the revolution in manners, not an oath is to be heard, and each criminal performs the task assigned to him with industry and without murmuring. It seems as if each convict was most desirous of showing his readiness and his obedience to discipline, being induced thereto but one only hope, viz., that of obtaining their liberty by good behaviour, which is the only means afforded to them to get their liberty before the legal expiration of their time. In the morning with breakfast upon a basin of soup from ox cheek or leg of beef. When the overseer pleases they are sent to the hulk to dinner, on one or other of those joints and when he pleases they return. Their drink is nothing but water.

All is discretionary with their keeper. They do not take it by turns to work, but turn out of the hulk into the long boat, and go on shore to work as he pleases, without distinction. If anyone appears to keep behind, he is certain of being employed the oftener. The greatest liberty allowed him is that of being permitted to go on to a neighbouring ditch within their boundaries to drink.

As well as dredging the river, inmates were engaged in the construction of the Royal Arsenal at Woolwich Warren, and many other menial tasks like shifting timber and scraping the rust from cannonballs, all directly or indirectly within a naval context. One of the reasons for intense activity around the Arsenal was that, as war became more of a long-term possibility, military building was being financed and encouraged. From 1776 both the Royal Brass Foundry and the Royal Laboratory were improved and enlarged. The convicts did the hardest, dirtiest work, and when Campbell set the convicts to work here and later on at other naval projects, he was simply playing his part in the military-industrial complex of the day. Not everyone was happy with the arrangement at first: Trinity House, a powerful institution, possessed an old guild right for raising ballast from the Thames by the labour of free men, which entailed also a right to the revenue obtained from distributing the ballast. Part of this sum went towards ensuring that the river could still be navigated, and some went to the upkeep of decrepit sailors – the activities on the hulks were in danger of interfering with these established traditions. Campbell was, or had been, a 'Younger Brother' of Trinity House and a financial agreement was soon agreed between them.

During the summer months the working convicts rose at 5am and were at work by 7am, labouring until noon and then from 1pm till 6pm. During the winter they began at 8.30am and worked without lunch until about three in the afternoon when they returned to the hulks, to be locked down on the lower decks by 7pm. The work was hard, dirty and dangerous, and often next to impossible in bad weather; many preferred to be locked down in the stinking hold than to risk their lives outside. It was hard to keep all the convicts employed all the time, so many sat about with nothing to do apart from plotting escapes and planning future crimes. Campbell's deputy, Stewart Erskine, Captain of the Hulks, who had been employed as his faithful subordinate since August of 1776, was in charge of day-to-day activities, and claimed that the work was harder than on the highways but not as hard as that performed by common labourers. Any convicts with particular trades, such as shoemakers, tailors or similar, were sent to work at other sites around the Arsenal or could be employed on the ship itself. They were unpaid during Campbell's time, but some could work on their own account, using any materials that came to hand, and were allowed to sell their products. Among those not sent out to work were those aged 15 or younger. They were confined on board with various light duties among the hardened villains; there was to be no separation between the various types or ages of convicts for many years.

Erskine had an eventual staff of forty officers between the two ships, *Justitia* and the *Censor*. The scope of the river work was decided in consultation with Trinity House and army ordnance officials. The value of convict labour was estimated at £6,053 – about one third of that of a free labourer who was able to work unencumbered by chains. He estimated that the ballast raisers had shifted 35,410 tons of ballast. If no double-handling was counted, as with the screening of gravel after ballast was raised, and if it was assumed that all ballast came from the riverbed, there were approximately 1,475 lighter loads at twenty-four tons per lighter, with great benefit to the navigation of the Thames. In the twenty months from August 1776 to April 1778, there were 85 lighter loads per month, which was deemed a reasonable working rate, given that the work could be interrupted by bad weather. These figures would, at a conservative estimate, provide a cost to government of £3 10s per lighter load of ballast. Any profit that Campbell made from ballast went to Trinity House or was deducted from his half-yearly payment from the Treasury. These arrangements demonstrated the ad hoc nature of the activities, as Campbell had not been officially directed to work the convicts at anything in particular. In practical terms, the idea worked. Campbell does seem to have had some genuine concern for the welfare of his charges, whom he termed 'poor creatures', reducing the hours of labour in winter, making sure that the lighters were not overcrowded and ordering more so that they would not have to stand in freezing water. He was also, on occasions, very sympathetic to those he considered worthy of being recommended for release and expressed genuine concern about rehabilitation.

Inevitably, the end of the punishment of transportation meant that Londoners were confronted first-hand with the sight of freeborn Englishmen put to work like slaves. They were able to observe in their own capital city what their fellow countryman had to face in the colonies, and for a time the prisoners were one of the more exotic London sights. Many came as simple thrill-seekers, but there was genuine concern among the local population about escapes by desperate felons and the risk of spreading disease. The longer the hulks remained on the Thames, the more they were regarded with fear, contempt and loathing, as was their overseer, who, in his first year, was seen to visit the hulks twice weekly. The newspapers found it all sensationally good copy and reported developments along the river as they unfolded. The sightseeing continued until Campbell built a wall to increase security, which also served to block the view, and the number of onlookers decreased significantly.

Expansion and Organisation

For some, incarceration was brief as the Home Office offered pardons for any who agreed to join the armed forces. By August 1777 nearly all those remaining on the *Tayloe* had been transferred to the *Censor*, a 731-ton captured French frigate that Campbell had purchased from the Admiralty. Since its tonnage exceeded the overall requirement, all the convicts contracted for were put aboard the *Censor*, the remainder having been pardoned, enlisted or died. Campbell kept the *Tayloe* and returned it to active service on the Jamaica runs. The Thames now had about 380 convicts, but pardons, deaths and escapes kept the situation in flux. By April 1778 Campbell, had secured pardons for about sixty offenders and wished to recommend the same for another thirty.

It does seem that Campbell was concerned for his charges. Correspondence exists between William Eden – now the newly appointed Lord of Trade – and Campbell, in which the latter makes various suggestions for the conduct of affairs: 'as our greatest Loss of People arises in great degree from a depression of the Spirits; from the dread of the term of confinement, whether the longest period might not be reduced to six and the sentence of the shortest confinement for smaller offences to one or two years; in which time with proper management great alterations may be made on the habits and minds of such persons.' But the tariff remained unchanged. Another of his ideas was that the operation be extended beyond the Thames to 'any other navigable river' in the kingdom. Britain would have had a system of mobile prisons for male prisoners, so that the convicts could be set to work repairing sea walls, dockyards or similar works. He proposed further that the overseers themselves should be allowed to remit part of the sentence for good behaviour rather than having to go through the courts. He suggested that the fine for assisting an offender should be increased from £20 to £50, or even £100, and that escaping from custody be made a capital offence to discourage the others rather than a doubling of the sentence, with execution only available for a second attempt.

Given the intensity of his religious upbringing, it is possible that Campbell had had enough of religion, his long experience with handling convicts does not seem to have been motivated by puritanical or Calvinistic views on punishment or redemption or any desire to impose religious views on those lacking remorse for the evils they had committed. In the first year the dead had been buried in unconsecrated ground along the foreshore of the Thames, but later Campbell obtained a piece of land near the Arsenal and had them buried there after a service performed by a ship's officer. When asked what the burial arrangements were, he replied that the dead were interned 'along the shore' and 'behind the butt' at Woolwich. Prison reformer John Howard complained that there was no chaplain and there were allegations of dead convicts being stowed away until a reasonable number was reached before asking the coroner to attend to save on fees. This was, of course, strongly denied.

In March 1777 Campbell was asked to provide for another 120 prisoners but at a reduced rate of £28 per person. He soon engaged his younger brother Neil, a clerk at the Board of Ordnance at Woolwich Warren, as his deputy, along with overseers to patrol the ships and the shores of the riverbank, but, despite this, escapes and outbursts of violence occurred regularly. Overseers were said to be afraid to descend the decks at night when lights were extinguished and portholes were shut. Campbell was a businessman, or merchant as he described himself, and organised the situation accordingly with maximum benefit to himself. As a private contractor, his management of the hulks was subject to little regulation, the quality of food was poor, jail fever, which became known as hulk fever, periodically ripped through the decks, and very few medicines were provided, unless you count vinegar – which was also used as the means to wash and fumigate the vessel – as a scurvy cure. Disease persisted as a threat to the community, and Campbell was constantly complaining that many convicts were dreadfully ill upon arrival.

Less than a year after the first use of the hulks, commutations of sentence were granted to several convicts who had impressed Campbell as good candidates for employment onboard. The undersecretary who forwarded the pardons made it clear to Campbell that if the released men were not retained as guards under his control on the hulks they would be sent into the navy. The county jails were still rammed beyond capacity and a system of pardons for the more trivial offences was seen as one solution, with the added advantage that many felons in the depths of despair could see the possibility of a way out if they behaved, though not all saw submission as the best option. Newspaper reports from October 1776 tell of thirty-two convicts who escaped from the *Tayloe* at Limehouse having 'lain six months on the river not knowing where they were to go'. They were soon recaptured, some in the commission of further robberies. The hulks were overflowing, despite the fact that magistrates had helpfully responded to the situation by ordering more whippings instead of confinement. Campbell was very soon overwhelmed and on 18 September 1777 he wrote to William Eden:

> When I had the honour of delivering to you my last Report of the Convicts ordered to Hard Labour on the River Thames, you would of course observe that our Number, notwithstanding those Pardoned & dead in the intermediate stage between that & the former Report, still exceeded the Compliment contracted for; since that time 11 have been pardoned & Discharged, and Twenty Six new Convicts Rec. as the Keepers of the County Goals are daily bringing up and applying to receive their several prisoners ordered to hard Labour I am much at a loss how to conduct myself, not having Received Orders to make a proper provision for the accommodation & employment of these additional people; I therefore request you will permit me through your means to submit this Circumstance to the Earl of Suffolk & that I may be favoured with a few lines in answer for my better Govt from the best calculation I can make there seems to be about 90 or 100 Convicts from the different goals & the Sessions at the old Bailey still to be provided for.
>
> With the greatest Respect, Duncan Campbell

Revolt and Discipline

It can be assumed that, in general, most prisoners were unaware of legislation governing their situation, but some in the hulks, possibly with access to newspapers or through visitors, watched the developments in legislation keenly, expressing their views via disruptive and mutinous activities. Prisoners on the transport ships on their way to America had always been prone to mutiny and the situation on the hulks was no different. The prisoners attempted a series of small but vicious revolts on their captors and the new terms of captivity; there were repeated attempts at escape, with very few succeeding and most being recaptured. Convicts were constantly finding ways to remove their irons but few of these attempts at defiance were reported in any detail, particularly those that had been successful; such stories would terrify those onshore and show the service in a bad light. Some, however, were much more serious, increasing government and public concern about the overcrowded state of the country's penal system.

In November 1776 five men seized the arms chest on the *Justitia*, locked up the warders and escaped in a small boat that their friends had drawn up alongside. In the resulting chase two were killed, two recaptured and one seriously injured. Not long after that, eight more made a similar attempt and got as far as Greenwich before being recaptured. Undeterred by the failure of previous attempts, within a short time twenty-two men forced their way into the captain's cabin, seized whatever armaments there were and rowed to the north bank. They made it as far as East Ham before they were overtaken by a party of sailors who engaged them in combat. Some managed to make good their escape into Epping Forest and were never seen again. Others were gradually rounded up and hanged. Lesser offences were dealt with by the cat-o'-nine tails, and threats to kill were dealt with by the culprit being heavily ironed for a week or a fortnight.

On 7 June 1778 there was another escape by thirty-six convicts who engaged their pursuers in a 'terrible battle'. Twenty escaped but were eventually recaptured, some after committing fresh crimes. September 1778 saw the most serious attempt to break out when about 150 convicts working on the shore armed themselves with whatever tools they thought most useful and advanced towards the gate. Stewart Erskine and twenty well-armed guards confronted them, attempting, in vain, to talk them down, and amid showers of stones they were forced to open fire, killing several and subduing the others. With outbreaks as frequent and as public as these, things could not go on as they were.

The Rise of Reform – John Howard

John Howard was the son of a well-to-do London upholsterer who began his attempts at penal reform in 1773 when he was appointed High Sheriff of Bedfordshire, giving him responsibility for the county jail. Unusually for a man in his position, he visited the local prison in person and was greatly distressed by what he found, being particularly appalled to discover that even prisoners who had been acquitted were still confined if they were unable to pay the jailer a discharge fee. Howard had been briefly imprisoned on board a French privateer in 1756, which may have given some impetus to his campaign. A driven man with strong religious beliefs, he visited just about every jail in the country and made numerous visits to the hulks in Woolwich, Plymouth and Portsmouth between 1776 and 1788. His criticisms were sometimes muted as he saw more merit in attempting to produce small improvements in food and conditions rather than an all-out assault on the system. He was able to improve sanitation and alter the basis of payments to jailers, but might have achieved more had he not announced his arrival before each visit and thus losing the element of surprise. When Howard first visited the hulks, in October 1776, he found the sick simply laid out on the floor of the forecastle with only a few boards nailed across to protect the healthy. A foul odour infested the vessels from end to end, emanating mainly from 'the necessary', as the toilet was known. Half of the portholes were blocked so that ventilation was almost impossible. The men lived in one big, unencumbered space below, where they slept and lived throughout the day when not at work, and many had barely enough clothing to cover themselves: 'a scarecrow collection of human refuse rowed ashore each day' to work at the Arsenal, as a contemporary account put it.

At meal times the men received rations modelled on that given to the navy. They were divided into messes of six and were allowed half an ox cheek undressed, or sometimes cheese, three pints of pease or oatmeal, and a quantity of bread or biscuit varying between 4½ and 6lb. Each man had a quart of small beer four days in the week and imperfectly filtered water drawn from the river. The ox cheek was sourced – cheaply – by Campbell from the slaughter yards on Tower Hill three miles from Woolwich. It was claimed that even if the cheeks were rotten they were still served up, but Dr James Irwin, Surgeon-General of the Artillery, who Campbell had used since the early days, discounted these reports as being without foundation. Friends and relatives of the convicts had been stopped from supplying extra food as it was found that they introduced saws, files and other instruments of escape into the packages. Howard remarked after his first visit that 'the biscuit was brought in two sacks one was all crumbs and the other broken, mouldy and green on both sides'.

In April 1777 Howard published his influential book *The State of the Prisons in England & Wales* to wide acclaim, bringing together the work and ideas of previous commentators as well as his own. Howard was keen on the idea of prison being a punishment in itself, but emphasised cleanliness, silence, hard work and, of course, religion. On a visit to the hulks during 1778 he asked Campbell why he didn't wash down the ships, to which the latter replied that he was afraid the convicts would catch cold. Howard replied that the healthiest jails were those washed down every day. He had little to say about the hulks in the first edition of his book, but by 1792 he was impressed by the increased cleanliness and food allowance. He had shone a light upon this hidden world about which the respectable and literate knew nothing and those who imposed the sentences were callously indifferent. His achievements lie mainly in the effect that his books and writings had upon those who came after him, like Elizabeth Fry and the soon-to-be-assembled Bunbury Committee. Campbell was stung by the mild criticisms in Howard's book and adjusted the convicts' diet enough to warrant mention by Howard on one of his later visits when he reported that the men looked a little healthier.

Two years after the passing of the Hulks Act, in early 1778, the problem of overcrowded jails had not gone away and was a continuing topic of conversation among establishment figures. Edmund Burke wanted transportation resumed to Nova Scotia or Canada; Sir William Meredith, who had originally been for the hulks, had changed his mind and now disapproved of them as being much more severe than transportation and 'totally repugnant to the general frame of our laws'. Another enemy of the hulks, Sir Charles Bunbury, quite unrealistically wanted transportation to America resumed, although most of his remarks seemed to be inspired more by resentment at the loss of the old system rather than anything useful. James Townshend and Sir Richard Sutton agreed that the act had not had the slightest effect on the number of robberies or crimes committed. Bamber Gascoyne, who had at least visited the hulks, thought the punishment on them very severe, and that too little value was got from the prisoners' labour. He was probably correct – closely supervised labour was expensive to deploy. Another way to dispose of the unwanted was to entice them into the armed services, and towards the end of 1778 a petition was presented to His Majesty:

> signed by upwards of 170 hearty young Fellows (many of whom are seafaring Men) sentenced to a hard Labour on the River for divers Felonies, praying His Majesty would be graciously pleased to extend his Mercy to them on Condition of their serving in the Royal Navy: In Consequence of which two Lieutenants on Monday last went on board the different Hulks at Woolwich, examined and took down the names of those they thought fit for the Service, which exceeded the Number the Petition is signed by. They were desired to behave well and every Endeavour would be exerted to obtain their Pardon as soon as possible. At going away the poor Fellows gave them three Cheers.

The following June two officers returned and took down the names of 200 'young fellows fit to serve His Majesty'. Despite this, on one of his visits to

Plymouth, Howard remarked upon 'many fine young fellows living in total idleness' aboard the *Chatham* and the *Dunkirk.*

On 2 February 1778 Campbell was awarded his third contract, which was due to expire on 12 July 1779. The 1776 Act itself came up for renewal in April 1778 and the terms of the 'temporary' measure were extended for another year. It was probably due to the influence of Howard and his friends that the Commons thought it necessary to enquire into the whole situation. A report was commissioned under the chairmanship of Sir Charles Bunbury MP, 6th baronet of Bunbury and Stanney, a former High Sherriff of Suffolk, more noted for his interest in horse racing than anything else.

The Bunbury Committee 1779

Bunbury had previously addressed the Commons on the subject of the treatment of prisoners when he told the House that the jails were overcrowded with prisoners sentenced to transportation, 'occasioning such scenes of cruel neglect and misery that are shocking to humanity and repugnant to sound policy'. He pointed out that more prisoners could not be sent to the hulks 'because there were too many there already', and put forward the idea that some of the male convicts could be sent as soldiers to the East India Company. Africa was another possibility, but others suggested that not one in 100 would survive their arrival.

In response to Bunbury's urging, the House appointed a select committee with the request that 'there be laid before this House an Account of Persons convicted of Felonies or Misdemeanours, and now under Sentence of Imprisonment in the Gaols and Houses of Correction in the City of London and the Counties of Middlesex, Essex, Kent, Herts, Surrey and Sussex specifying their respective Crimes, the Time when the Term for which, and by what Court each Person has been has been imprisoned; together with an Account of the Allowance made for the Maintenance of such Persons, and in what manner they are employed.'

The first meeting was held on Monday, 8 February 1778 in the Speaker's Chambers and the enquiry continued throughout February and March. The great majority of the evidence that they were to hear came from Campbell and his associates, in whose interest it was to present the hulks in a favourable light. Campbell was called to give evidence on the current situation and was at pains to explain to the committee the delights of the *Justitia* since improvements had been made in the previous year. As Campbell explained in his evidence:

It was now, 'a very roomy vessel with advantageous alterations in the barracks, the bed is upon a much more airy and roomy plan, a bed of six feet long and four feet wide was allowed to two persons, but he thought if there was quite a space between the beds it would be still more healthy to the convicts, there were portholes open during the night to admit fresh air.' Being asked whether the convicts did not make complaints of their want of provisions, he said he had 'never heard that they did except at the time of the insurrection since which he had enlarged their allowance of bread to 6lb a man per week, and half an Ox's head which weighed on average 5½lb was distributed daily to a mess of six men and that they had porridge for breakfast and supper. The bullocks heads, when not sweet, had been sent back to the contractor and two days a week were known as Burgoe [a sort of porridge made of coarse oatmeal and water] days on which each mess was allowed three pints of oatmeal made into porridge besides their bread and 2lb of cheese and that they had sometimes salt provisions on a Sunday, which were given to them as an indulgence upon their good behaviour.

Those who worked on shore were allowed by the Board of Ordnance a quart of small beer per day over and above their usual allowance of four quarts per week and in his opinion the provisions allowed to convicts were fully sufficient and better than labouring men usually had. A common allowance in workhouses was ten ounces of bread per day to each person and in the West India trading ships 5lb of biscuit per week to each man and 1½lb of meat per day. They had salt but no vinegar at their meals. He had never heard of the water being "brackish" till lately, nor did he think it so having tasted it himself and as the Navy filled there at low-water for sea voyages.

The behaviour of the convicts had been much better and they worked with more good will that last year and that they did as much as labourers employed on the highways in statute work but he thought they might do more if they were not chained.

The first period was taken up with reports on the state of county prisons before they came to Campbell's evidence. He began by saying that things had very much improved in the management of the hulks since last year when he was obliged to furnish 240 tons of shipping for 130 persons. He went on to say that now 250 convicts occupied a ship of 731 tons, the *Censor*, and 260 were on board the other hulk, the *Justitia*, a very roomy vessel. What disease there was had been brought in from the jails; but even he had to admit that in the first two years 176 prisoners out of a total of 632 had died and that when he was transporting them to the American plantations, 'upon an average of seven years the loss of conflicts in jail and on-board was one seventh.' Some 100 convicts had been pardoned since he began and he had only heard of six reoffending. He had sent twelve men on his own ships to Jamaica who had behaved very well during the whole time of the voyage, and he had recently applied to the Secretary of State for thirty or forty convicts under the age of 18 whom he thought deserved to be pardoned.

Campbell's deputy, Stewart Erskine, supported everything that Campbell had said, adding that the work given to the convicts was not excessively hard and that their diet was of a better quality than before. Dr Smith was called and stated that he had visited the hulks very recently and found everything greatly improved and very clean, but recommended some further changes in diet and suggested that there be a hospital on the shore. Sir Herbert Mackworth MP paid a visit and was impressed by the amount of work that had been done in moving soil and gravel at the Warren; he was given samples of brown bread and meat that he considered 'very good for a poor man to eat'. He stated further that he found all the convicts except a few invalids at work, mainly employed in moving soil in carts and wheelbarrows at the Warren to make a quay or wharf and others in constructing a large mound or butt, into which shells would be fired for testing along with a dock for barges, which he thought would be of great benefit.

John Howard told of his experience of men set to hard labour in various countries and suggested that the making of canvas bags and coarse clothes for soldiers might be added to their tasks in England. Thinking of plans for other types of work, and possibly influenced by John Howard's views, Bunbury suggested that the convicts be set to sawing stones while they were at hard labour as was done in Europe. It was also recommended that the prisoners make cordage or ropes for navy ships, which would render their work and maintenance less of a charge on the government and there would be few injuries as it was simple, healthy work and easily supervised. The materials would not be wasted or spoiled by the convicts, as happened from time to time in other areas. It was apparent that Bunbury knew very little about convicts, and would have seen them issued with saws, wedges, chisels and all manner of implements of destruction needed for stone-sawing work.

After these reports on the general situation on the hulks, the committee moved on to consider alternatives to America for the resumption of transportation and Campbell was recalled. He thought that although Virginia and Maryland were out of the running due to the political situation, Georgia and Florida were still a possibility, but could only take maybe 100 per year whereas on an average over seven years he had transported 473 convicts annually, 100 to 200 persons per ship.

Joseph Banks gave his opinion that Botany Bay on the coast of New Holland (Australia) could be ideal as the fertility of the soil might enable a colony to maintain itself after being supported for the first year. He had been there as a scientist and botanist with Captain Cook in 1770. His contemporary notes gave a rather different view, finding it, somewhat bizarrely, 'like the back of a lean cow [...] where scraggy hip bones have stuck out further than they ought, accidental rubs and knocks have entirely bared them of their share of covering.' Banks didn't think that there would be any opposition from the natives; when he visited there in 1770 he saw very few and those were 'naked treacherous and armed with lances but extremely cowardly'. The climate was as pleasant as the south of France and there seemed to be no wild animals. He observed the dung of 'what are called *Kangourous* which are about the size of a middling sheep but very swift and difficult to catch'. There was plenty of fish and a great abundance of water, timber and fuel. A colony could easily be established but would need to be furnished with a full year's allowance of food, tools, armaments, small boats, fishing tackle, etc. He recommended sending 200 or 300 felons at least, and escape would be very difficult as the country was distant from any part of the globe inhabited by Europeans. When asked if there would be any benefit to the mother country, he replied that once a colony was established and a civil government formed there would be great demand for European commodities. New Holland (Australia) was much larger than the whole of Europe, despite it being about seven months' voyage from England.

John Roberts, who had been governor of Cape Coast Castle, one of the commercial slaving forts on the Gold Coast, was asked if he thought a colony might be established in West Africa. He replied that he thought it was possible; it was named Yanimarew, about 400 miles from the mouth of the river Gambia. He believed that the local king would be very glad to have white people there, even though he knew they were felons, and would grant them a land at a moderate price. The land was very fertile with a great number of vegetables, fruits, water and timber. Roberts suggested experimenting with 150 men and sixty women, pricing the initial expedition at £7,049 7s 10d, and £2,816 for the second year, after which he would expect them to be self-supporting. There were further benefits to the country as the continent could be explored and exploited. Expeditions up the river had already returned with slaves, ivory and gold. He thought a fort would need to be built, 'in order to be safe from the Negroes', and he did not think that more than twenty out of 200 would die of the local fever. A settlement further inland in Senegal was another possibility.

A dissenting voice came from Richard Camplin, Secretary to the African Committee, who gave evidence that, from the beginning of 1775 to the end of 1776, out of 746 military personnel at Cape Coast Castle 334 had died and 271 were either discharged or deserted. The situation was so bad that they had been reduced to manning the garrisons with natives or the children of European soldiers born in the country. Colonel Charles O'Hara considered that the problem of defending any position against the native tribes was very difficult and that disease was rife. Sir John Irwin MP recommended Gibraltar, which he thought might be fairer to convicts wishing to return home after their time had been served. The committee noticed that their deponents had marked inclinations towards an Africa location.

The committee's report was presented to Parliament by Bunbury on 1 April 1779 and its observations were that:

1. The whole arrangement of the prisons is at present ill-suited either to the economy of the state or morality of the people and seems to be chiefly calculated for the safe custody of the persons confined without due attention to their health, employment or reformation.

2. That the Act, which was a temporary expedient intended only for the most daring and dangerous offenders who might otherwise have been crowded into dungeons or let loose again into society, has been extended to several criminals who, from their bodily infirmities, extreme youth or advanced age, might have been more properly subjected to some other mode of punishment. The mortality on board the vessels may be attributed to some degree to their very disordered constitutions [...] and appears in many instances to be occasioned by an extreme dejection of spirits observable in all prisons but more common and fatal in the hulks and most frequently affecting convicts from the country. The mortality has been increased by the number of convicts being too great for the space allowed, effluvia from the sick, by the contiguity of the beds, want of cleanliness which is extremely difficult to be enforced,

and perhaps too by some circumstances in the food, which might be better regulated.

It was agreed that the labour done was of solid advantage to the public and that continual improvements have been made since its first institution, but that 'further beneficial alterations may be made in it in case it shall be thought proper to be prolonged as a mode of punishment'. They thought that shortening the term of imprisonment by limiting it to a term not exceeding five years or less than one year rather than the current three to ten years might improve matters, as would somewhere apart from the vessels to receive the sick. They suggested that a piece of ground be set aside for growing vegetables and that a clergyman should attend on Sundays and assist at the burial of the dead.

Other suggestions were that regular inspections should be carried out by a magistrate, that convicts be employed in places other than the Thames in the repairs of seaports, embankments, etc., onshore houses should be set up within the home circuit as an alternative to the hulks as places of productive labour. Any boy under the age of 15 who consented to serve in the land forces or navy in the West or East Indies should be encouraged to do so having been vetted by two or more magistrates. In response to good behaviour, one sixth of the term of imprisonment should be remitted if a reputable tradesman would agree to employ the person and give security for his good behaviour for one year. It was noted that around half of English jails were privately owned, and often sublet to those who made their money by charging what they liked for the most basic of services.

3. As regards transportation to other countries, the plans suggested appear to be attended with many difficulties but "the sending of atrocious criminals to unhealthy places where their labour may be used and their lives hazarded in place of better citizens may in some cases be advisable; and in the instance of capital respites is indisputably just". However, as the laws respecting transportation are at present restricted, it is not in the power of executive government to adopt or pursue any new system of transportation.

The rather limp and limited conclusions of the committee were that:

1. Some alteration should be made in the laws respecting the maintenance and employment of convicted felons, confined by sentence of imprisonment, or by sentence or

imprisonment and hard labour in different places within England.

2. That it might be of public utility if the laws which now direct and authorise the transportation of certain convicts to His Majesty's colonies and plantations in North America were made to authorise the same to any other part of the globe that might be found expedient.

Banks was asked for his suggestions for a settlement, 'in case it should be thought expedient to establish a Colony of convicted felons in any distant Part of the Globe, from whence their escape might be difficult [...] and where, from the Fertility of the Soil, they might be able to maintain themselves, after the First Year?' Banks replied yet again that Botany Bay was a definite possibility.

On 5 May 1779, in summing up the findings of his committee, Bunbury recommended continuing the Act of 1776 until 1 June 1779, and that year saw the implementation of the Penitentiary Act, 'An act to authorise, for a limited time, the punishment by hard labour of offenders who, for certain crimes, are or shall become liable to be transported to any of his Majesty's colonies and plantations,' (19 Geo.3 c.74), drafted by the prison reformer John Howard and the jurist William Blackstone. It set out imprisonment as an alternative to a sentence of death or transportation and henceforth there were two modes of punishing those convicted: servitude on the hulks or transportation to anywhere outside Britain. There was also a strong recommendation that a network of state-operated prisons be created, but despite its passage through Parliament, no prisons were built at that time. However, the committee had made a considerable study of methods, alternatives and possible locations, but none of them seemed to be suitable. Despite all the discussions, the problem of where convicts could be sent remained unresolved. Blackstone's final comment was that he thought the act would establish 'a species of punishment in which Terror, Benevolence and Reformation are [...] happily blended together'.

Chapter 5

Duncan Campbell II
1780–1803

Attempting to keep an eye on what was happening with Campbell and his 'Convict Academy', Parliament asked that an annual set of accounts be prepared from April 1777 requiring that all monies paid to Campbell for 'maintaining the convicts who work on River Thames' must be laid before the House, and for the period 1775–1786 the total of all expenses came to £223,484.

Prison reformer John Howard asserted that the prison population of England rose by 73% in the decade after 1776, leading to an increased burden on local rates, which caused much discussion among those liable to pay them (and who objected to their money being wasted on criminals and the 'undeserving poor'.) Between 1783 and 1786 the number committed for trial at the Old Bailey was 40% more than for the previous three years. There was still a great and increasing concern over the number of escapes, desperate overcrowding, the likelihood of riots, spread of disease, corruption or immorality, causing fear in local communities and producing calls for the removal of convicts from town jails. The year 1780 had seen the Gordon riots, and with escalating unemployment those with property feared more of the same.

Hulk Fever

In Campbell's report to the Bunbury Committee he had stated that of the 132 convicts who had died since 26 March 1778 about 90 had died of a fever that he claimed was brought on board by convicts from the courts at Nottingham, Cambridge, Plymouth and Newgate, strongly denying claims that the cause was the water supplied to the prisoners, or that it was already on the hulks due to the filthy conditions. However, there were no reports of outbreaks in any of these jails at the relevant times. The argument really hinged upon the incubation period of the fever, which was a matter of debate as medical knowledge was very primitive, and the penal system was riddled with disease. Once the fever was on the hulks it would have been difficult to eradicate. Today, we know that the incubation period for typhoid fever can be between six and thirty days, which doesn't help much in tracing its origins or apportioning blame.

Jail fever was the most feared disease of the prison environment, a louse-borne form of typhus that began with a sudden headache, chills, stomach pains, and ended about three weeks later, usually in death. In the spring of 1750 disease had cast a long shadow over the convict population in London. The deadly diseases afflicting convicts could also kill their keepers, and at the Old Bailey infections killed more than fifty people including four of six judges, the lord mayor, four counsel, the under-sheriff, forty jurors and, presumably, a large quantity of prisoners. These were the first sensational cases of infection, which caused a fear of disease among any of London's middle and upper classes who might come in contact with offenders. The fact that convicts may have caught such diseases due to grossly inadequate accommodation, and medical ignorance about how such diseases were spread, went unrealised. In just over two months an epidemic of typhus swept through the decks and was there to stay in greater or lesser degrees. Dysentery from drinking dirty water was also rampant, along with venereal disease, which afflicted about half of those from Newgate, along with many other complaints associated with the unhealthy conditions. In later years pulmonary tuberculosis was recognised as the main cause of death.

Many of the medical professionals who visited the hulks and were asked to give opinions had spent most, if not all, of their careers among the poor, slum dwellers, convicts and seamen. Disease, cholera epidemics and a high death rate were nothing new to them, and after all, were these not just the dregs of society suffering through their own inadequacies and criminal behaviour? It was no real surprise that sympathy was in short supply.

Campbell seems to have had little interest in the medical condition of those on his ships, or the risk that colonials receiving sick felons might also become infected. He admitted that in the first two years, 176 out of a total of 632 in his charge had died, and in his view, the main cause was a 'universal depression of spirits'. Campbell visited the hulks twice a week, but he never entered the hospitals. Suicides and attempted suicides, along with deaths in custody, are entirely absent from reports on the hulks, as are injuries from fights among prisoners, though it's hard to believe that these weren't a fairly regular occurrence.

Campbell engaged the services of Dr James Irwin and his assistant, Dodo Ecken, from the nearby Woolwich Arsenal, both of whom seem to have been genuinely concerned about the convicts. Irwin recommended that they be given wine when sick, which Campbell paid for initially but was later reimbursed by the government. Ecken visited the hulks often and began to submit monthly reports suggesting that there be a properly established hospital ship set up to receive new arrivals, which would 'tend much more to the health of the convicts', although he thought that a house onshore would be more appropriate. He stated that he had known eight or ten convicts die merely of lowness of spirits without any signs of fever.

After Bunbury

The findings of the Bunbury Committee had certainly affected Campbell and caused him to pay more attention to how the hulks were organised. By 1780 he had accommodated 510 convicts and had purchased an old East Indiaman that he named, confusingly enough, *Justitia II*. He organised the *Reception* as a receiving ship and converted *Justitia I* into a hospital ship with three surgeons in attendance. The quantity of food was also increased, enabling him to claim that 'their rations were better than labouring men usually had'.

Despite these improvements at Woolwich, he was still lacking any clear instruction from the Home Office as to what the future held and was becoming increasingly frustrated. In letters to officials, he asked if more could be done for men after they had served their sentences to stop them reoffending, but little interest was shown. The *Northampton Mercury* stated that, according to the report of a Commons Select Committee, £21,500 was being paid annually to Campbell for maintaining the convicts, and that supporting Botany Bay cost £56,000, bringing, as they put it, a 'Charge of above £70,000 to support a Gang of Thieves!' Campbell was not, of course, involved with Botany Bay, and out of this seemingly huge sum he had to employ forty officers as well as many other obligations.

By 22 October 1782 Secretary of State Townshend had contacted London's Lord Mayor, Justices of the Peace and others demanding that 'strong measures' be taken against recent waves of robberies and other disorderliness. The following day, Townshend complained to the Duke of Newcastle about 'frequent Robberies and Disorders of late committed in the Streets of London and Westminster, and Parts adjacent'. He urged the judges and magistrates to take a firmer line, which resulted in an increased number of executions.

From 1781 the Campbell family lived at Blackheath, just behind Greenwich, and as an insight into his personal life, he was known to be a keen golfer and member of the Blackheath Golf Club, the second oldest established club in the country and the haunt of many like-minded businessmen with a strong connection to freemasonry. His premises in Mincing Lane had probably become his business headquarters. From the mid-1780s he invested in land around Blackheath and deeper into Kent, and in 1784 he bought a property of 2,000 acres in West Kingsdown for £21,458. His wife, Mary Mumford, inherited Shere Hall, Mount Pleasant, Wilmington, about twelve miles distant, in around 1789. The name Mumford is found in parish entries there from the 1680s and the family had considerable connections with the area around Dartford. John Mumford was High Sheriff of Kent in 1796, and is of Sutton-at-Hone, about three miles south-west of Dartford and about a mile south-west of Wilmington. By 1796 the Campbells had moved their London address to the hugely prestigious Adelphi Terrace, St Martin in the Fields.

In Jamaica his son, Dugald, was learning, reluctantly, to manage the Saltspring estate and had established a close friendship with Captain William Bligh, who was about six years his senior. Much later, Bligh (d. 1817) was to list Dugald as executor of his estate, although Dugald predeceased Bligh. The latter continued to sail for Campbell between London and Jamaica, still teaching Campbell's other son, John, the ropes.

The Penitentiary Act of 1779 (19 Geo. III, c.74) was due to expire on 1 June 1784 and at the end of 1783 the Commons initiated a series of inquiries into the state of current legislation. A bill was drafted and received royal assent on 24 March 1784 as statute 24 Geo III c.12, 'An Act to authorise the Removal of Prisoners in certain Cases, and to amend the Laws respecting the Transportation of Offenders'. The preamble went through the usual difficulties of transportation, fullness of jails, and accepted that time spent in them counted as part of the sentence of transportation. Apart from that, however, the rest of the act was a complete mess, seeming to empower the courts to transport convicts to anywhere they might think proper, which could, in theory, have pre-empted the king in his exercise of his prerogatives in the matter.

One problem with the act was the provision that 'nothing contained in this Act shall extend to authorise putting to Labour any Person, whilst he continues confined by virtue of this Act, who shall not consent thereto.' Charles James Fox, Secretary of State, viewed transportation as the *alternative* to hard labour, not an aspect of it, and the solicitor general, Richard Pepper-Arden, took a similar reformist view: 'Gentlemen did not think that persons under sentence of transportation ought to be compelled to hard labour in the places to which they should be removed from the gaols. In compliance to those gentlemen, he would consent to leave out the word "hard", but he could not conceive that it would be improper to make them work for their subsistence.'

How a system of voluntary labour was to be administered on a prison hulk posed immediate difficulties and Duncan Campbell sought the government's instructions as to how he should proceed. He, and doubtless, others, must have been listened to because in July, a redrafted bill was put before the Commons and received royal assent on the same day with the title: 'An Act for the effectual Transportation of Felons and other Offenders, and to authorize the Removal of prisoners in certain Cases; and for other Purposes therein mentioned', 24 Geo III c. 56. Hard labour was reinstated. Another problem was that the act allowed convicts to be paid 'half the profits arising from his labour for his own use', the intention being to encourage hard work and a sense of purpose. This clause was also removed and convicts were not paid for their labours. The act remained in force until 1 June 1787 and was to set things in motion for the First Fleet's voyage to Botany Bay two years later by authorising the sending of felons to any place appointed by the King in Council, or to any part beyond the seas appointed by His Majesty for the transportation of offenders.

The treaty with America was signed in September 1783, and with it hopes rose that transportation could resume. The topic was not covered in the text and the hope was that the market for cheap labour was still there and buyers still keen. In August the government hired London merchant George Moore, who gathered up 143 convicts and put them aboard the *Swift*, intent upon trying his luck. In case of a hostile reception from the Americans, the cover story was that they were indentured servants heading for Nova Scotia, though Maryland was the true destination. Soon after the *Swift* departed, the convicts rebelled, took over the ship and ran it aground on the Sussex coast. About a quarter of them managed to escape, although some were caught and consequently executed. After retreating to Portsmouth for a month, the *Swift* started out once again for Maryland, this time with only 104 convicts, and made it to Baltimore. As planned, the captain informed the authorities that the ship had run out of provisions and was forced to cut short its voyage to Nova Scotia. The convicts were landed but sales were slow and the operation lost money as they had to feed, clothe and maintain the prisoners. Despite these setbacks, Moore attempted another voyage with 179 convicts in April 1784 on board the *Mercury*. Once again, the convicts rebelled. The ship finally made it across the Atlantic, but unlike the first time, no American port would allow them to enter and they were finally unloaded in British Honduras, which was none too happy to receive them. Congress passed a law in 1788 that specifically prohibited the import

65

of convicts from Europe and all hopes of convict transportation to America were finally at an end.

On 20 November 1784 Campbell had his contract renewed as overseer and in February 1785 he attended the House of Commons at their request to present 'A list of the convicts on-board the *Justitia* hulk sentenced to hard labour on the River Thames', of which there were 261. To the annoyance of those living nearby, more hulks were being pressed into service and between 1784 and 1787 the whole enterprise had continued to expand. Since 1776 it had been intended that the hulks be mobile so that convicts could be placed near work sites, and the country would have a widespread and fully mobile prison system, which was an original and interesting idea. On 21 November, the day after Campbell's new warrant was signed, the Lord Mayor urged a strengthening of the guard on the hulks as he was fearful that demobilised sailors might set convicts free, causing devastation to the locality. The mayor also reminded the Secretary of State of the Gordon riots in 1780, when sailors were thought to have been prime movers in the devastation and setting fire to Newgate. Any legislation allowing the hulks to continue provoked the anger of Londoners who had always hated their existence, viewing them as holding bays for disease, sodomites, potential escapers and professors of crime and depredation.

Despite all the evidence presented to the Bunbury Committee, Africa was still being considered as a destination, at least by those instructing Duncan Campbell. In December 1784 he was preparing to send his 32-gun, fifth-rate ship *Ceres* to Africa and on 5 March 1785 the Attorney-General was asked to draft an Order-in-Council under the 1784 Act to send convicts there. The idea was to keep the convicts secure until the end of August when the rainy season would be over. The order was approved and a list of seventy-five convicts drawn up. Now that it was passed, all that would be required was for the judiciary to be instructed to sentence prisoners to Africa in particular rather than to transportation in general. Despite attempts to keep the destination quiet, rumours abounded, with reports in the press claiming that 'two frigates had been got ready with a number of marines to keep a constant watch to prevent any of them effecting escape'.

Edmund Burke attacked the proposed move as being 'beneath contempt, as the measure condemned prisoners to the hell of a tropical climate and a sure death'. Nonetheless, Campbell was prepared, as always, and had his deputy, Stewart Erskine, get the *Ceres* readied at Woolwich, ordering him to 'Man Your Ships well for fear of any Mutinous attempt, and be beware of any sort of violence or combination amongst them.' The prisoners who knew that they were destined for almost certain death in Africa remained in a very ugly mood and Campbell was fearing mutiny, but before anything could happen, another commons committee had been called to order.

Lord Beauchamp's Committee: 1785

The new enquiry, consisting of thirty-six members, was hastily assembled on 26 April 1785 under Lord Beauchamp, a Worcestershire MP, to consider options for convict transportation. In many cases it duplicated the work of Charles Bunbury, who remained disappointed that his 1779 recommendations for building prisons had not been implemented. Of the members, eleven had taken part in the Bunbury Committee. Notable members on this occasion were William Eden, Edmund Burke and William Wilberforce. Bunbury had been defeated in the general election of the previous year and did not attend.

Africa was soon top of the agenda. During their deliberations, Anthony Calvert, a London merchant whose business was mainly shipping slaves to Jamaica, offered his services as a convict contractor to ship 150 convicts at £8 per head to the island of Le Maine, 400 miles up the Gambia river. Evan Nepean supported the proposal, mentioning that 'the worst of both sexes' had been assembled ready to be transported to Le Maine, but when asked if the island was ready for their reception, he had to admit that it was not, 'but could be soon as it belonged to some native chief'. He explained that the convicts would be supplied with a framework for huts and tools, a medicine chest, and left to fend for themselves. The total cost, he assured the committee, would not be more than the amount spent on the hulks at home. The scheme was soon ruled out as unrealistic and a very inhospitable location for the dumping of convicts. The idea of a 'convict colony' of self-governing and isolated felons was seriously considered and rejected. Convicts would have to have strict government supervision wherever they were sent.

Reluctant to give up on Africa, it was decided that the mouth of the Orange River, at Das Voltas, in modern Namibia, should be investigated. Apart from other considerations, it might prove an excellent staging depot for naval supplies as it was sited right in the middle of the main sea route from Europe to the Far East, and a British Garrison there could offset the French base in Cape Town. Despite opinions to the contrary, it was decided that a sloop, the *Nautilus*, should be despatched in September to investigate the possibilities while the committee considered the West Indies, Canada,

Newfoundland and the west coast of Africa. Other locations mentioned were Florida, the former American colonies, any areas under the control of the East India Company, and an area of the Caffre Coast that Pitt had in mind. Botany Bay and Norfolk Island had also been suggested and New Zealand was referred to briefly. As discussion flowed back and forth it was becoming increasingly unlikely that the government was going to commit to building prisons.

Das Voltas was discounted when *Nautilus* returned and reported that it was unsuitable for landing convicts, or much else, as there was 'no bay, river or inlet but only a steep barren rocky shoreline [...] without [...] a drop of fresh water or a tree'. Various other African locations were considered, but one after another, experts confirmed that the continent was a place of disease and death with little strategic advantage in political terms. An army surgeon who had spent some years in Senegal said that two thirds of the army had died within a year of being sent there. Another who had lived on the west coast told the tale of 300 Frenchmen sent up the Gambia River to work the gold mines. Only three had returned. Convicts sent to the Gambia River would 'either die from disease or at the hands of the natives', he declared.

During the next six weeks of argument, and despite its logistical problems, Botany Bay was emerging as the favoured destination for the new settlement, as was Norfolk Island, 1,000 miles off the coast and believed to be rich in flax for making sailcloth and tall pine trees for making the masts of ships, neither of which proved practical. The pine turned out to be useless as it snapped like a carrot and the flax might have been okay if there was anyone there who knew how to process it. Joseph Banks was called and again recommended Botany Bay, as he had in his evidence before Bunbury. He declared that he found it in 'every respect adequate to the purpose'. His notes from 1770 gave a rather different view, as we have seen, but doubtless he had his reasons.

The government based its right to the occupation of Australia under the doctrine of *terra nullius* – 'no man's land' – under international law. Australia was, for the purposes of imperialistic or colonial activity, uninhabited and the right of 'first discovery' prevailed .The indigenous aborigines were considered just part of the exotic wildlife. Campbell estimated that the cost of transportation to New South Wales would be about £30 per felon, exclusive of crew costs, if 700 to 800 were shipped. If only 200 were transported then the cost would rise to £40 per man, including surgeon's fees and a profit for the contractor but excluding shipbuilding or hiring costs. Transportation to America had been around £12 without any return trade. Campbell was first and foremost a businessman and his proposed expenses would include a profit for himself should any future contract be awarded.

Beauchamp began to consider areas where a settlement could be founded with or without convicts but which would grow to be of some benefit to Britain. There were thought to be various strategic advantages in establishing colonies in various parts of the world as part of the ongoing conflict with the French. Equally, they were encouraged by the thought that a colony would be expected to become self-sufficient within three years, negating the need to send further supplies. Their attention was beginning to focus more and more on New South Wales, and despite the realisation that Australia was a vast distance away and would differ from America in that there would be no return cargo and no settlers to buy the convict labour, they were pretty much running out of options. Another drawback was that, to start with, every item would be a direct charge on the government and costs played an important part in their deliberations, hence the importance of the evidence given by Campbell. They had now been made aware that sending convicts to Botany Bay would be more expensive than sending them to Le Maine but less than keeping them on the hulks.

Apart from geographical locations, the committee had considered the growing feeling in Britain that convicts should be reformed to enable their rehabilitation into society – whether this was at home or abroad was irrelevant. It was not just a question of ridding the country of felons but putting them to use where they could feel valued, and be reformed, and though they might never return to their native land, still play some useful role in their new environment. It also rejected the idea that convicts could be 'settled' without strict government supervision. The opportunity for some commercial gain that would benefit the country as a whole never left the committee's mind, as was shown not only in the persons called to give evidence but also in the questions that they were asked. Add to this the individual interests of the committee members and it is evident that there were many commercial and political motives behind much of the thinking, as well as an attempt to solve the growing prison problem at home. Pressure was being brought on the government by the merchants in the Commons who dominated the committee.

Beauchamp produced his final report on 28 July 1785, but, in reality, he had got no further than Bunbury seven years before. The towns and cities in England and Wales still refused to build the expensive prisons required under legislation passed in 1778–9 and attention was still focused on a resumption of transportation.

Family and Finance

Aside from his convict interests, Duncan Campbell became chairman of a group known as the British Creditors, a body of more than 200 merchants set up in 1783 to lobby for the repayment of debts amounting to £2.5 million owed to them by various American merchants with whom they had been trading before the revolt. Campbell was owed around £38,000 personally from various contracts in Maryland and Virginia. Thomas Jefferson, then America's representative in Paris, met Campbell on 23 April 1786 while on a visit to London to discuss the matter. Contemporary descriptions portray Jefferson as 6ft 2in tall, large-boned, slim, erect and sinewy, with a ruddy complexion, sandy hair and hazel-flecked grey eyes. His carriage was relaxed but awkward, with a 'pleasant face' but not handsome. He was described as even-tempered and perhaps needed to be as they soon disagreed about the 40% interest on the £3 million that the Britons thought they were owed. Jefferson later observed of Campbell that the interest from 1775 to 1786 'was his only topic'. Campbell said he found the denial of interest 'a bitter pill he and his friends could never swallow'. Negotiations came to nothing on this occasion, and it is uncertain whether Campbell ever received money personally, but by 1811 various parties, including Campbell's descendants, received reimbursements of forty-four per cent following a British–American intergovernmental agreement made after the 1794 Jay Treaty.

Meanwhile, the problems associated with overcrowding continued. There were many people complaining about lack of suitable accommodation for prisoners as part of a general disaffection with government inaction on convict transportation. Parliament listened to a petition from the JPs of Chester complaining that the castle jail had become ruinous and unsafe for the custody of prisoners and needed to be rebuilt, but where were they to house the inmates? Their problem was common in the many counties and government still had no answer, except perhaps to increase the number of hulks. More political pressure was applied when two independent Devon MPs opposed the Duke of Richmond's plans for the fortification of the dockyards at Portsmouth and Plymouth. Both men had hulks in their constituencies and wanted transportation resumed, so much so that they were prepared to forgo all the benefits from the proposed new building. Pitt's government was drawing up contingency plans to shift 600–1,000 convicts during the following summer, destination unknown as there was still no strategy in place.

The end of the American war caused the crime rate to soar, real wages fell, prices began to rise, and the country had to cope with around 130,000 demobilised men from the army and navy. Newspapers contained reports, real and imagined, of gangs of ex-sailors or soldiers engaged in crime throughout the capital. Even *The Times* acknowledged the situation, commenting upon the large numbers of ex-servicemen 'who went abroad to fight for their country and came home to be starved or be hanged'. In 1786 the hulk establishment expanded to include the *Dunkirk* at Plymouth, the *Lion* at Gosport, and the *La Fortunee* and *Ceres* at Langstone Harbour, Portsmouth, and by July the total number of prisoners confined at these outlying ports came to 1,196. At Woolwich the *Stanislaus* joined the *Justitia* and the *Censor*, with 741 convicts. In 1783 eighty-nine inmates died out of 486 brought aboard; and by the first three quarters of 1786 forty-six died out of 638 inmates on the ships.

Around June 1786 Campbell moved from Mincing Lane, on the north side of the Thames, to 3 Robert Street, The Adelphi, by the Strand, a prestigious address designed by the Adams brothers, close to the north bank, with stairs down into the river. Importantly for a merchant, there were cavernous storerooms under the new address that Campbell could use to store his convict records. From December 1786 Robert Street was one of the points in London where the names of transportable convicts were check listed before they were delivered to the holds of the First Fleet. After all the arguments, committees, false hopes and disappointments, the first batch of convicts set sail for New South Wales on 13 May 1787. More than 1,400 people in eleven ships got under way from Portsmouth Harbour. Campbell's only part in this mass exodus was to perform his duty as hulks overseer and deliver the prisoners to the ship's captains. When the First Fleet sailed he was 61 years old, which may have been one reason for him taking a lesser role in proceedings. Another was the change in the law concerning the profit a private person could make from such opportunities. Legislation in 1776 had placed the convict, a commercially valuable legal entity, wholly at the service of the Crown. No longer could he profit from selling their labour to colonials in need of it. Nor could a convict servant buy out their own servitude, a transaction that he had sometimes countenanced as the government contractor. He could no longer contract with individual county officials or shipowners for the transfer of a convict. Reform had effectively nationalised the transportation market in servile labour.

Perhaps with retirement in mind, Campbell set about acquiring more land in and around Blackheath and Kent. While *Nautilus* was away and Beauchamp pontificated, he had some respite from delivering convicts and spent more time in the country. He had purchased land in Kingsdown,

Kent, from the estate of William Coke of Norfolk, later Lord Leicester, a man who happily spent his life discovering ways to improve agricultural science. One site was Brands Hatch, the site of the present racetrack. He enjoyed Blackheath and the surrounding countryside immensely, and now had more time to enjoy it. With his property at Wilmington, and ownership of the encumbered Jamaican plantation, Saltspring, Campbell was hoping to provide for his younger sons and was investing in land. Some of his final acquisitions included freeholds, farms and tenements; variously, Brands Hatch, Maplescombe, Little Maplescombe, Easthill, Knotts farm and Brands tenement. There were also quit rents, the manse or lordship of Kingsdown, and manorial rights. In 1784 he was living mainly at Blackheath. In August 1789 he moved to Wilmington and from 1797 to his wife's property, Shere Hall.

In May 1787 Campbell sold the 215-ton ship *Bethia* to the Royal Navy for £1,950. They renamed it the *Bounty* and equipped it for an expedition to collect breadfruit under Captain William Bligh. Campbell's niece, Elizabeth Betham, the pretty 27-year-old daughter of Richard Betham and Campbell's sister, Mary, had been married to Bligh since 1781. Betham was the collector of customs on the Isle of Man whose mission was to subdue smuggling on an island widely regarded as a haven for smugglers. An extremely intelligent man, he was a friend of economist Adam Smith and philosopher David Hume.

Campbell frequently employed Bligh to run his ships, and for four years he was plying the rum and sugar trade from the West Indies to England. Bligh was commanding Campbell's merchant ship *Lynx* at Green Island, Jamaica, in April 1786 and in May 1787 Campbell promoted him to captain of the *Bounty*, which was to be the ship for his trip to Tahiti and the famous mutiny of 1789. The original plan for the *Bounty* was to transport the first convicts to Botany Bay and then carry on to Tahiti to load up with breadfruit plants and botanical samples, but it soon became apparent that the ship was so well adapted for plant gathering that it would not be suitable for any other purpose and the transportation part of the mission was abandoned. The main aim of the voyage was to collect as many breadfruit seedlings as possible. These would then be taken to the West Indies to be grown as a crop for feeding the slaves on the plantations, as it was, allegedly, 'very nutritious and cheaper than other alternatives'. It is highly likely that Campbell suggested Bligh to Joseph Banks as the best man for the job. (After Bligh's second breadfruit voyage the slaves decided that breadfruit would form no part of their diet and resolutely refused to eat it except during emergencies, though nothing was wasted as it was fed to pigs and poultry.) Bligh arrived back at the Isle of Wight on 14 March 1790, having already written heartbroken letters to his wife, Betsy, and to Campbell, about losing the *Bounty*. Campbell does not seem to have been particularly upset about the outcome of the voyage or overly concerned about the mutiny.

In 1787 Campbell became a Jamaican plantation owner himself. His late brother-in-law, John Campbell, who had owned the Saltspring plantation and shipped his produce to Campbell in London, owed trading debts totalling £11,700 to Duncan as well as an outstanding mortgage on the estate. The Court of Chancery in Jamaica ordered the sale of Saltspring to allow Campbell to recover his debts, but he decided to take the plantation in lieu and had it managed by his eldest son, Dugald, who was reluctant to take on the job but eventually agreed. Political disturbances wracked Jamaica during 1787 and a hurricane caused damage of £50,000. This does not seem to have been a very astute move. Despite being a very clever businessman, Campbell had no experience of running a plantation and had to leave the day-to-day work to others. Letters between he and Dugald reveal that the plantation struggled to make money, and after Duncan Campbell's death, Dugald had to raise more cash by mortgaging the plantation to his late father's clerk.

The *Morning Star* of 10 June 1789 reported that £48,417 of the government's annual budget had been paid to Duncan Campbell 'for convicts'. He bought a plot of land in Woolwich near the Arsenal and employed some of his crippled prisoners as gardeners, growing fruit and vegetables. The plot continued in use until about 1850, although it is alleged that more produce went to the officers than the convicts.

Jeremy Bentham Visits the Hulks

The First Fleet began clearing out the hulks in May 1787, during which time it was estimated that the labour of the convicts had produced no more than two-fifths of the cost of their maintenance but were much cheaper in the short term than the erection of new prisons on shore. In late 1787, as the fleet was approaching New South Wales, Jeremy Bentham, penal reformer, legal theorist, polymath and one of those men of genius who seemed to thrive during this period, was developing design ideas for his model prison the 'Panopticon'. Bentham was no believer in the hulk system, missing the point that convict labour could be helpful to the State. At the heart of his Panopticon was a scheme for prisoners to make the jail self-sufficient by their labour. Bentham had been in Russia visiting his brother, Samuel, a brilliant mechanical engineer and naval architect employed on various projects there. He arrived back in London in early 1788, already well-informed of the trip to Botany Bay, and visited the Thames hulks, where he spoke to Campbell, took notes, and observed the methods that he and Erskine used to manage those under their control. He even gave prisoners small amounts of grog for the privilege of studying them.

Bentham examined the costs of the colony at New South Wales and estimated that it cost £48 per convict per year, four times the estimated costs for his Panopticon plan, with forty per cent of the sum being shipping costs. During 1791 he discussed with Sir Charles Bunbury his belief that the obstacles placed in the way of a convict with an expired sentence wishing to return to Britain was 'a very tyrannical and dishonourable if not illegal conversion of transportation for a limited term into transportation for life', as return was almost physically impossible. He thought that, perhaps, land owned by the Lord Privy Seal at Battersea Rise might be one site for his dream, otherwise Woolwich, or the Millbank site near Tothill Fields. However, Campbell had won the long battle of ideas; the hulks and transportation to Australia were already established and required no massive capital outlay. Despite repeated lobbying, the government failed to adopt the Panopticon and Bentham's efforts to see a rational prison system established came to nothing.

Campbell had suffered with rheumatism from a relatively early age and during January 1788 he experienced a severe attack of gout that kept him indoors. Later the same year, he had something different to engage his attention. Convicts on the new *Lion* hulk, moored off Gosport, near Portsmouth, and working on building part of the western defences of Portsmouth Harbour, were audacious enough to question the legal process under which they were confined, claiming that the relevant legislation had expired. They refused to go to work ashore and went on strike. The fact that the prisoners had shown some political understanding was disturbing and Campbell wanted them quickly disabused of their opinions on the legal questions. He was prepared to be relatively lenient with them when they expressed such views, but would have been just as willing to meet violence with violence should things escalate, which, on this occasion, they did not.

As the decade ended and the 1790s dawned no workable solution to the convict problem had emerged, and despite large numbers now being shipped to the other side of the world, the same old problems reoccurred. During 1789, complaints about overcrowded jails continued. Stafford Castle was another ancient and decaying jail urgently in need of renovation, necessitating the rehousing of a large number of convicts to prevent disorder and escapes. On 4 October 1789 Exeter jail officials reported an attempted mass breakout by twenty-six prisoners who had sawn through their irons, locked the turnkey in the cells and attempted to seize arms. Their plans had been sworn to secrecy, but one told his wife, who warned the jailer, causing the men to be rounded up by a waiting party of dragoons. London aldermen were still very concerned about the urgent need to remove convicts from Newgate, and government officials, including Campbell, were contemplating lists of up to 1,000 convicts for the Second Fleet.

In October 1789, with parts of the second major convict embarkation already underway, the Duke of Richmond, who was in charge of constructing fortifications at Portsmouth, became concerned about losing part of his skilled prisoner workforce. He sent the Home Office a list of 280 convict names from Portsmouth, Gosport and Langston Harbour, 'hoping that these men who have got into the track of our works and whose loss would be very inconvenient to us may be allowed to continue where they are most usefully employed'. In a sense, Richmond's request was against the law; if a prisoner had been sentenced to transportation, he should have been transported, not held back to hard labour at home simply because he possessed a skill. Nonetheless, the duke's political influence was sufficient to ensure that all but fifty-two of the 280 on his list remained on the hulks and at his service.

On 7 January 1790 four convicts, two from *Neptune*, were sent back to the hulks while their petitions for pardons were considered. An old convict, Gray, aged between 60 and 70, had sworn after his trial he would not see Botany Bay. *The Bristol Gazette* reported that after being sent back to the Portsmouth hulk, 'the hardened wretch thrust a lancet into each of his eyes, whereby he totally deprived himself of sight', and in Lancaster jail a prisoner was found hanged after declaring he would rather die than go to Botany Bay.

For a number of years Campbell's attention had been divided between his estates in Jamaica, bringing in returns of sugar and rum, and the convict business in London. Research in the National Archives indicates that his ships were not involved in the slave trade, although he was not in favour of abolition as it would hurt his sugar importation business, such as it was. For a slave owner, abolition was an alarming prospect. Campbell, who championed transportation and like measures, dreaded it; the Saltspring plantation would have had about 300 slaves and been totally dependent upon them. Campbell advised Dugald on Saltspring: 'WORK without overworking your Negroes, which is at all times to be avoided, as well from motives of humanity, as real benefit to our Interests. The folks who are for promoting the abolition of the Slave Trade, have now taken it up with as much Zeal as in the last Sessions: yet I cannot say I have such great fears as many of my friends here seem to have.'

In 1792 a Jamaica House of Assembly committee reported that since 1772, 177 plantations had been sold to pay debts, fifty-five had been abandoned, ninety-two were in the hands of creditors, and current legal action involved assets of about £22 million. Absentee landlordism was becoming more irresponsible. His son, Dugald, was still wavering as manager of Saltspring, putting the plantation at the risk of being managed by outsiders, and in danger of rendering Dugald a useless drain on family finances. To make matters worse, Dugald was apparently 'gallivanting on the continent' with his brother, Jack, instead of paying attention to the business. He was admonished by his father for playing 'a man of fortune' in Europe, allowing the estate to suffer while he was away. Dugald wanted to give up the responsibility, but grudgingly carried on as his father became more indulgent about allowing improvements, and gave him more power over the estate's affairs.

In London, representatives of slaving interests in Parliament were defending their industry, claiming that the mortality of slaves at sea was not as large as the loss in the transportation of British convicts. Campbell avoided that discussion as it would have drawn attention to himself as the major convict contractor since 1775, and it was his policy to avoid publicity at all costs. The death rate on convict ships to North America had been about one-in-seven.

It seems that Campbell's health had never been good and towards the end of 1791, now aged 65 and hoping to lessen his load, he wrote to the Foreign Secretary, Lord Grenville:

> Understanding that some plans are now in contemplation of Government for the future Management & Employment of Convicts, and the permanent establishment of a certain number of hulks for that purpose, I take this opportunity of requesting that you will have the goodness to inform my Lords of the Treasury, that from my advanced period of life and the effect of that anxiety of Mind I have experienced during the Number of years I have exercised the arduous Office of a Superintendent or Overseer, I have reason to fear the fatigue of Mind as well as Body in conducting so important a Charge, will be more than I can go through, and more especially in the

Charge and Direction of the Convicts employed at Portsmouth & Langston Harbour; I therefore most humbly request their Lordships will permit me to relinquish the Management of the Vessels so Stationed, and that the Contract made with their Lordships for the *Fortune,* and Agreement with the Secretary of State for the *Lion,* may cease and determine at the end of Three Months, or as soon as their Lordships shall be pleased to make the Necessary Arrangements for the Care & Employment of the Convicts these Vessels contain.

Should My Lords be so indulgent as to grant my request, my Superintendence will be confined to such Convicts as shall be employed in the *Censor & Stanislaus* on the River Thames or such other Hulks as it may be necessary to employ there, and I shall cheerfully continue to execute that trust I hope to their Lordships satisfaction. From the Arrangements which I have lately made as well in my Ships & Lighters as with the people employed under me, I find that by experience and mode of management which that experience has taught, I am enabled to make some reduction on the terms formerly agreed upon for the Care & Maintenance of these Convicts, and I beg the favour of you to acquaint their Lordships that from the 12th January when the quarter terminates I shall charge no more than 13 1/2 per diem for the whole expense, Chaplain & Bounties excepted, of such Convicts as may then be confined in the two Ships above mentioned or such other as it may be found necessary to engage.

I entreat you to inform their Lordships that I retain a most grateful Sense of the Continuance & Protection received during the executing of the duties of my Office; without their Aid, it would have been difficult if not impractical to have established any degree of good order among such a Number and description of Men as I had to Manage, with that benefit to the Public which I flatter myself has been acquired from their labour in the different Works on which they have been employed.

Dun: Campbell.

Meanwhile, Bunbury was back on his feet in the House. As chairman of the committee on the Offenders Bill, he was seeking information on conditions in New South Wales, and on 17 February 1792 he raised the question of transported felons and mentioned the dreadful events on board the *Neptune* during the sailing of the Second Fleet. He called upon the House to determine whether this was due to a deficiency of space in which the convicts were housed, a deficiency of provisions from their defective quality, or other causes. He asked for 'an account of the number of convicts embarked on board the *Neptune*, the *Scarborough* and the *Surprise*; of the number landed at the place of destination, and state of health in which they were so landed'. Events on board the *Neptune* and the Second Fleet are considered in chapter ten.

In May 1793 Bunbury moved six resolutions critical of the treatment of prisoners, including those awaiting transportation, their condition during the trip and their treatment once they arrived. He admitted that he had become a convert to Jeremy Bentham's penitentiary scheme and thought that it might at least be applied in the case of those awaiting transportation in place of the hulks. He and Bentham tried to convince the Home Secretary of the advantage of this kind of model prison, but without success. Bunbury was also in favour of the Felons Transportation Bill of December 1802, which advocated the separation of debtors from felons in prisons.

Between 1797 and 1801 evidence of Campbell's involvement with the hulks fades from the official records and his letter books as his health continued to fail. He appears as a signature on a document here, or a bill to be honoured there. His previous initiatives and innovations had now been largely adopted and there were fewer signs of his presence as the administration of the hulks became more bureaucratic and routine. His contract was not renewed in 1802 and he retired from his 'capital, double-fronted corner house at the West End of the Royal Terrace, Adelphi' to his house at Wilmington. He died on 24 February 1803, aged 77, giving instructions that he was to be buried 'in my own vault where my late wife is interred' at St John's Church, Hackney. His will, sixteen pages long and dated 21 February 1794, was proved on 9 March 1803, with probate being granted on 11 March. He was estimated to have been worth at least £200,000 when it was drafted.

He left a small annuity of £300 per annum to his wife, Mary, which was secured on the Saltspring Estate. This took into consideration the 'very ample provision made for her by her father's settling the whole of his fortune upon her and her children'. The estate itself he left, subject to this annuity, to his son Dugald Campbell, failing whom, half the estate was left to each of his sons John and Duncan, with contingent remainder to his sons Mumford and William Newell Campbell. His will refers to pieces of this estate, including Brands Hatch, which he left to his son John Campbell, and Maplescomb, in Kingsdown, which went to Duncan. He included significant financial legacies totalling £49,000 to eight daughters. No ships were mentioned in the will, and neither was his long-term deputy, hulks superintendent Erskine.

On 27 January 1801 Erskine informed the government that he was willing to take on the contract for the convicts in the Woolwich hulks. It is doubtful that he would have done so without knowledge of Campbell's impending retirement, and a week later it was announced that the whole situation was going to be examined. The transport commissioners recommended that the contract be renewed in Erskine's favour, but in May a London magistrate, Aaron Graham, was making proposals regarding the hulks and suggestions for improvements to the system. Erskine had been put in charge initially, but in June 1803 he was prosecuted at the Summer Assizes for assisting the escape of convict William Smith from the *Prudentia* hulk. The court's decision is not recorded and further details have not been uncovered, but it is hard to believe that after twenty-seven years of loyal service on the hulks, Erskine would have assisted an escape, and it seems likely that it was an attempt to ruin his reputation by those wanting him out of the way. He survived, and in 1813 Messrs Bradley and Erskine were still furnishing the convict establishment with provisions, clothing, etc.

Campbell's obituary in *The Gentleman's Magazine* read:

> Died at Wilmington, in Kent, Duncan Campbell Esq. He is succeeded as governor and overseer of the hulks at Woolwich by his deputy, Mr. Stewart Erskine, a gentleman possessed of great humanity, and of the strictest honesty and integrity and who has had the sole management of that concern for him ever since its first establishment in 1775. Mr. C. died possessed of much property, yet, to the surprise of their best friends, has not left any legacy to Mr E for his long and faithful services; though he seemed always to be considered himself much indebted to that gentleman for his great accumulation of fortune.

It is not known what Dugald did after his father died. His heirs and assigns inherited Saltspring in Jamaica. Dugald was to be an executor of the will of William Bligh, but he predeceased him. None of Campbell's direct descendants came to particular notice in history, although one grandson, Captain Charles Dugald Campbell (born 1814), was one of the first British to sail up the Euphrates River.

CAMPBELL'S TWO MARRIAGES PRODUCED A TOTAL OF 16 CHILDREN

1. **Rebecca Campbell**, 1730–1774, daughter of Dugald Campbell (1697–1744), married Duncan Campbell on 11 March 1753 at Saltspring, Jamaica. Duncan had the following children with Rebecca:

   Henrietta Campbell, 1754–1795, born St Mary, Whitechapel
   Rebecca Campbell, 1756–1781, born St Mary, Whitechapel
   Dugald Campbell, 1760–1817, born Walthamstow, Essex
   Mary Campbell, 1762–1846, baptised Barking by the Tower
   John Campbell, 1765–1848, born Black Haven Court Faethingame
   Ann Campbell, 1769–1801, London
   John Campbell, 1770–1841
   Launce Campbell, 1772–1856
   Duncan Campbell, 1774–1856

   Rebecca died on 7 December 1774, a few days after giving birth to Duncan.

2. **Mary Mumford**, 1756–1827, daughter of John Mumford (1723–1787) of Sutton Place, Sutton-at-Hone, Kent, and sister of John Mumford, High Sheriff of Kent, married Dunvan Campbell on 25 January 1776. They had the following children:

   Elizabeth Campbell, 1776–1847, married barrister Alexander Pitcairn (of the family that gave the name Pitcairn to the island which became the refuge of *Bounty* mutineer Fletcher Christian)
   Mumford Campbell, JP, 1778–1855
   William Campbell, 1779–1780
   William Newall Campbell, 1780–1856
   Colin Campbell, 1756–1784
   Louisa Campbell, 1784–1804
   Mary Ann Campbell, 1785–1844
   Neal Campbell, 1787–1793
   Augustus Campbell (dates unknown)

EXPENSES 1775–1786

1777: £1,879
1778: £14,348
1781: £15,487
1782: £14,719
1783: £14,452
1784: £12,212
1785: £13,578

In March of 1786 the Commons released the total amount of money issued to Campbell since he began in 1775 as follows:

To Duncan Campbell Esq.	£126,922/4/2d
To sheriffs for convictions	£92,840/0/0d
To George Moore for transporting felons	£1,512/17/6d
To John Kirby Wood Street Compter for taking care of convicts	£1,119/9/5d
To Anthony Calvert for transporting felons	£286/14/0d
To Thomas Cotton Esq clothing convicts and expenses at Plymouth	£803/2/7

Total of all expenses 1775–1786: £223,484

Chapter 6

Case Histories II
Aristocrats of Crime in the
Eighteenth Century

The convicts considered here were thought by those judging them to be part of their own class capable of reform, and often given the benefit of the doubt. Whereas the lower orders could be hanged for the most trifling offence, those with breeding and education stood a good chance of escaping the hangman's rope.

George Barrington

An Author! – Why, you have forgot that an author is the only *pickpocket* that *starves* by his *profession.*

    George Barrington,1787, Gentleman thief, pickpocket, convict transportee and governor of convicts in Australia

It is remarkable that a convict who earned his living by picking pockets should have his story told in six full pages of the *Newgate Calendar* and more than two pages in the *Dictionary of National Biography*, but then George Barrington was no ordinary thief.

He was born in County Kildare, Ireland, in 1755, the son of a silversmith. At about the age of 7 he was sent to school in Dublin and, along with a more conventional education, he started to train as a surgeon, but was expelled after an altercation with another boy. After relieving the school of twelve guineas and a gold watch, he took up with a troop of strolling players. He fitted in well and was described as having 'a speaking eye and expressive countenance, a tolerable theatrical figure, a very pompous enunciation and a most retentive memory'. The company was losing money and Barrington was 'persuaded' by a fellow actor to try his hand at picking pockets during a local fair, and a natural talent emerged.

By 1772 the pair were at it full time. Picking the pockets of the gentry was still a bit of a novelty and Barrington was able to pass himself off as one of them, assuming all the airs of a man of fashion, choosing his targets at fairs, drinking dens and gambling houses. Inevitably, his partner in crime was arrested, and having a narrow escape himself, he sold all he owned and moved to London in 1773 at the age of 18. Once there, his natural good nature and acting ability enabled him to mix easily with fashionable society. He spent some time, and the rest of his money, ingratiating himself with that set, but once the money had gone he had to get back to work.

Picking pockets at this level had its risks, but was very profitable, and his background raised him far above most of his rivals. He just needed a few successful coups to keep up appearances and make a decent living, but this could not be achieved in isolation. To be successful, he needed an accomplice. Once the initial 'dip' had been made, the prize needed to be passed on to an associate very quickly, who would then disappear with it into the crowd, leaving the original thief remaining where they were, a picture of innocence. The robbery was often carried out with the use of a knife or similar implement to cut the purse or open the pocket. If he was searched and his tools discovered Barrington had an explanation – he was a surgeon and these were the tools of his trade. He was especially skilful in the most delicate part of the operation, the removal of the booty without the victim noticing. In the days before an organised police force, it was very hard to prove a case against someone as slippery as Barrington, and any arrest was very much up to the victim and his friends to execute and prove in court. Once he had sufficient money, he would take time off, reading books, socialising and cultivating fashionable society, none of whom had any idea of the source of his wealth. An arrest or accusation would have been devastating.

Pickpocketing was considered a very serious offence in the eyes of the law. Grand larceny, defined as 'taking and carrying away the personal property or goods of another above the value of twelve pence', could carry the death penalty. Petty larceny, below twelve pence, was punishable by imprisonment, whipping or transportation, along with confiscation of goods. These incredibly harsh punishments had their drawbacks, as witnesses, jurors and sometimes even judges were very reluctant to convict unless the evidence was indisputable. In a typical year at the Old Bailey (1790-91), out of 1,533 prosecutions, 642 for grand larceny, there were only 551 convictions.

One of his first outings in London was to the celebrated pleasure gardens of Ranelagh in the grounds of Chelsea Hospital, and among the assembled company was the Duke of Leinster, a casual acquaintance of some of Barrington's friends. The duke was relieved of more than £80, a companion of his thirty-five guineas, and a lady of a gold watch. He must have been rather careless on this occasion as his activities were seen by a man named James. The outcome could have been disastrous but for a stroke of good fortune: James was a blackmailer and demanded a cut of the profits to ensure his silence. The two became partners and their success grew, but it could not last forever. During 1775 he found himself twice in the Bow Street police courts, though managed to talk his way out due to lack of evidence and the cases went unreported. He retired to Brighton and laid low for a while.

Back at work in the autumn, he attended the Covent Garden theatre and sat next to an Elizabeth West who, by a strange coincidence, was one of the most skilful pickpockets in London. She managed to empty his pockets, only to discover the tools of his trade, a knife, a key with a hook, and other implements that made his occupation obvious to her. She drew him to one side and the pair agreed to work together, keeping apart when not actually working, and then planning their expeditions meticulously, often to the extent of disguising her as his footman. All the time he kept up the pretence of being a gentleman of leisure, always paying his bills on time, and not keeping late hours. Former companion James had by now seen the error of his ways and retired to a monastery in Westphalia.

The year 1775 saw one of his most daring escapades. Count Gregory Orloff, once a favourite of Catherine the Great, was touring Europe, and on 26 October he attended the Covent Garden theatre. The count was given to ostentatious displays of wealth and was known to possess a golden snuff box encrusted with diamonds, which was said to be worth £40,000. Barrington was determined to have it, and, unbelievably, he did, but not for very long. The count felt his loss and raised the alarm. Barrington was seized but had managed to slide the box back to the count once he realised that there was no escape. He was, nonetheless, taken into custody and kept for several days before appearing in front of Sir John Fielding, the blind magistrate. Orloff, who could not speak English, did not appear. Barrington professed to be a respectable Irish surgeon, brought forward a number of character witnesses, and the case collapsed. Once more, his name was kept out of the newspapers, but in such a closed society, rumour and gossip did the job and his friends began to desert him.

His next plan was even more audacious. On 19 January 1776, the queen's birthday, he disguised himself as a clergyman and gained access to the Royal Levee at Saint James. His target was the Earl of Mexborough, an Irish peer. As part of their regalia, those of the Orders of Knights of the

Garter, Bath and Thistle wore their insignia of enamelled gold and diamonds on the outside of their coats, suspended by a ribbon. This time Barrington was successful in cutting the prize free and spiriting it away. A haul valued at around £800 was safely delivered to a fence from Holland – the crowning event of his career. For some reason, rather than enjoying his normal rest period and presumably huge payday, he continued to work, which resulted in more court appearances and more acquittals, but his unwanted reputation was growing. He was arrested for uttering threats, and as he had no one to stand bail for him, was confined to the Tothill Fields Bridewell, being eventually bound over to keep the peace. This time the damage to his reputation was well and truly done; he was exposed as an impostor and common pickpocket. A short while later he was caught stealing some cheap studs, worth 3s 6d and a half guinea, from a Mrs Dudman at a theatre and this time he was unable to talk his way out of trouble. He was sentenced to three years' hard labour in 'ballast – heaving', and after a brief stay in Newgate, he arrived, in January 1777, at the *Justitia* in Woolwich.

Barrington still had one friend left. Miss West missed him and was depressed at his capture. She endeavoured to send him two guineas per week and visited as often as possible, but it was not to last as she was caught stealing a watch in February and sentenced to a year in Newgate. Barrington had lost one dear friend, but another old acquaintance was soon to join him.

David Brown Dignam

Another of the aristocrats of crime was David Brown Dignam, who appeared in court at Bow Street in March 1777, charged with receiving £1,200 from a Mr Clarke after promising to make him the Clerk of the Minutes in his Majesty's Customs House in Dublin. Although he brought the case, Clarke was not entirely innocent. He had not the slightest interest in the position, except as a means of providing him with an income for doing nothing. Dignam was further charged with receiving £1,000 from Josiah Brown, promising him that he would be a writer on the *London Gazette*. In both cases the dupes had been presented with impressive warrants embellished with the forged signatures of the Home Secretary and Lord Weymouth.

Dignam would appear to have been something of a fantasist, at one time passing himself off as a member of the Irish Parliament and accusing the distinguished French dramatist Beaumarchais of being a spy. He also disclosed to Lord Suffolk details of a fictitious conspiracy to shoot

King George, which implicated various members of Parliament. His origins are obscure; contemporary reports suggest that he was the son of a reputable Irish gentlemen and had received a liberal education before being employed by one of the secretaries of state. His personality matched that of Barrington, and like Barrington he was described in court as 'a very gentlemanlike man'.

Nonetheless, he got five years in the hulks. Unlike Barrington, he was unable to reconcile himself to convict life and attempted to bribe one of the turnkeys to let him escape, and when that failed, he tried to hang himself. An article in *The Scots Magazine* for July 1777 records that, whether through ignorance or sheer bravado, upon entering his new home he hired a boat for a guinea a week and directed his black servant to use it to attend upon him. On his first day, he ordered a dinner to be brought to him from Woolwich. This was intercepted by Captain Erskine, who ordered the servant to take it back and give it to the first poor person he met.

So great did their celebrity become that they were sketched together for the May 1777 issue of *The Gentleman's Magazine*. Dignam and Barrington drew crowds to Woolwich hoping to catch sight of them at their labour as they,

> presented themselves to view with the rest of the criminals, wheeling ballast to the skreens. Barrington, from an appearance the most genteel, is become an object of commiseration, his behaviour is mild humble and patient. Entertains a just sense of his dishonest course of life and performed his lot with all possible industry in a state of true contrition; and it is hoped that, if set at liberty, he would make a proper atonement to the public for his offences by becoming a useful member of society.

Dignam spent a lot of his time in the sick bay before being moved from the hulks to Newgate prison at the beginning of January 1780. He wasn't there very long. On 6 June that year the prison was burnt down during the Gordon Riots and the prisoners escaped. There is an extremely brief account in the *Norfolk Chronicle* for 11 November that reports: 'The celebrated David Brown Dignam, whose punishment previous to the late insurrections in this city, was changed from ballast heaving in the hulks at Woolwich to imprisonment in Newgate, took the benefit of the insolvent act of their High Mightinesses the mob, and has since not been heard of.'

With that he disappears from history, his end as obscure as his origins.

Above: A vagrant being
whipped through the streets.
16c woodcut. (CC)

Right: Hanging of Guy
Fawkes 1606. Cruickshank.
(CC)

Tobacco being loaded for export at Chesapeake Bay 1751. (CC)

Old Newgate prison. (CC)

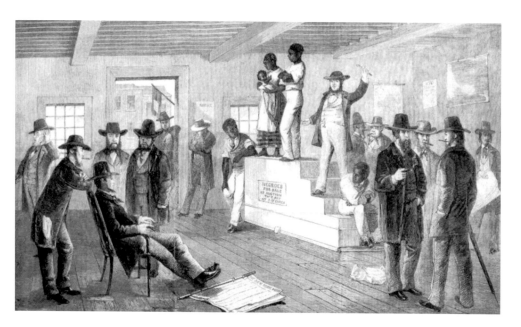

Above: A Slave auction. Virginia convicts were sold in the same way. (*Illustrated London News*)

Right: The hangman John Price being arrested for murder. (Newgate Calendar)

Bampfylde Moore Carew.
(Wellcome images)

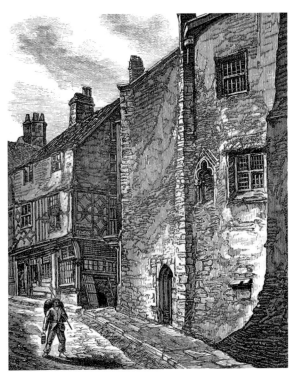

Old Newgate prison,
Bristol. (Wikipedia)

Execution at Tyburn. Hogarth. (Wellcome images)

Elk-Ridge Landing, *May* 15, 1765.

THE Subscriber, understanding that many false Reports have industriously been propagated, relative to the Loss of the Ship *Dolphin*, *Dougall McDougall* Master, who sailed from *Patapsco* in *November* last, takes this Method of acquainting the Gentlemen, who shipp'd Tobacco in her, that he has received Letters from Messieurs *John Stewart* and *Campbell*, importing that the said Ship, after some Days excessive Storms (during which Time many Ships of great Value were lost) was forced on Shore in *Mount's-Bay*, near the Land's End.——That the Tobacco would be lost, but that the Shippers thereof were insured at Six Pounds Sterling *per* Hogshead, agreeable to their Request. WILLIAM LUX, Attorney in Fact (4ʷ) for Messrs. *John Stewart* and *Campbell*.

Loss of the Dolphin, 1765.

Left: Duncan Campbell, merchant. (Wikipedia)

Below: Woolwich 1746, John Rocque. (CC)

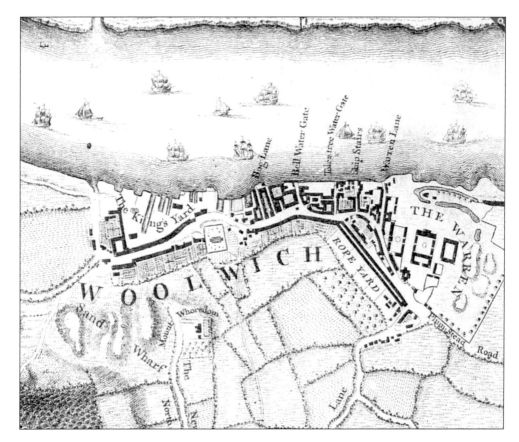

Right: Sir Charles Bunbury
6th Baronet 1740–1821.

Below: Convict leg irons.

Execution of Richard Parker, 1797. (CC)

Convicts at work, Woolwich Reach. (*London Magazine*, 1777)

Right: Digham and
Barrington, 1777.
(*London Magazine*, 1777)

Below: Arrival of the First
Fleet 1788, Watkin Tench.
(CC)

Botany Bay, 1788. (CC)

Hulks in Portsmouth Harbours c.1814. (Ambroise Garneray)

Picking pockets, 1818, Cruickshank. (CC)

The hulk *Discovery* at Deptford 1820s. (CC)

Left: Thomas Muir
by Alexander
Stoddart.
(CC BY-SA 3.0)

Below: Ireland
Island, Bermuda, in
1848. (CC)

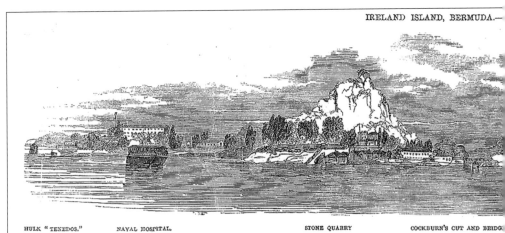

IRELAND ISLAND, BERMUDA.—

HULK "TENEDOS."   NAVAL HOSPITAL.   STONE QUARRY   COCKBURN'S CUT AND BRIDGE

The *Warrior* at
Woolwich, 1846.
(*Illustrated London
News*)

Right: The 'cages' below
decks, 1845. (*Illustrated
London News*)

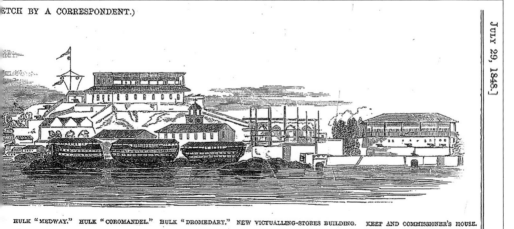

ETCH BY A CORRESPONDENT.)

JULY 29, 1848.]

HULK "MEDWAY." HULK "COROMANDEL." HULK "DROMEDARY." NEW VICTUALLING-STORES BUILDING. KEEP AND COMMISSIONER'S HOUSE.

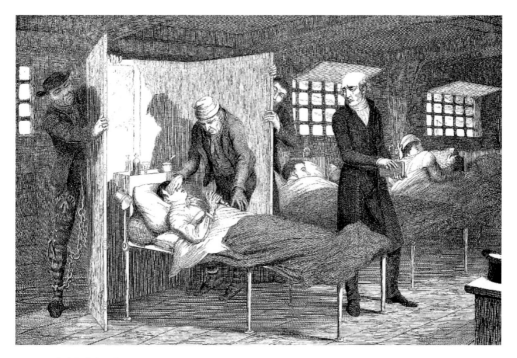

Above: Death
of a convict on
board the *Justitia*,
1848. (George
Cruickshank)

Left: Miles Confrey,
1854. (*Punch*)

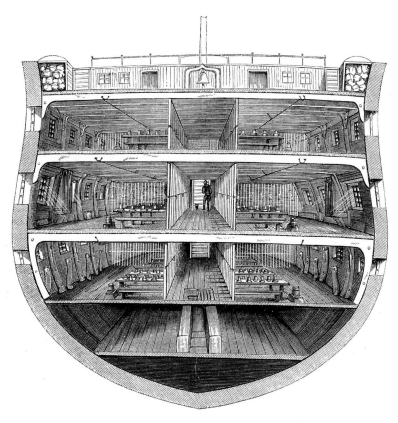

Sectional view of the interior of the *Defence* hulk. (Meyhew & Binny, 1849)

Woolwich 1850s. (Meyhew & Binny)

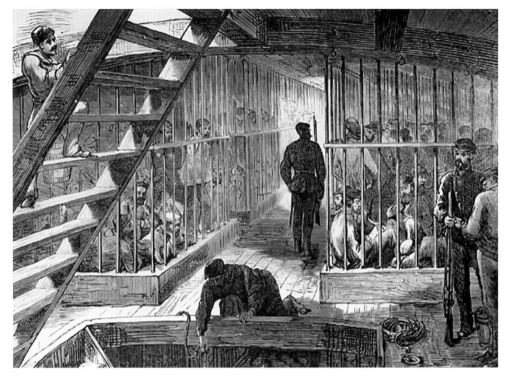

Below decks. (*Illustrated London News*)

Convicts returning to the hulks at the Arsenal. (Meyhew & Binny)

George Barrington Reformed

Barrington became a model prisoner and many a visitor could not understand what such a gentleman was doing there among the dregs of society. Despite his notoriety, he came to be regarded as a youthful first offender who was capable of reform. He was released at the beginning of 1778 having served less than a year of his sentence. He was soon back at work, but with a twist. With his society friends gone and respectability a fading memory, he decided to target churches, but was spotted attending a sermon by a well-known preacher in Holborn and caught with some items in his clothing. He was taken to Newgate and then to court where he blamed his arrest on a notoriety stirred up by the press and the vindictiveness of a particular constable. His eloquence and histrionics were to no avail on this occasion and he was sent back to the *Justitia* for another five years. To add to his woes, Elizabeth West had been caught again and died of jail fever while serving a sentence of three years in Newgate.

His attitude to this second sentence in the hulks was different and he tried several times to escape. It is possible that he was involved in the attempted breakouts of 7 June 1778 and September of that year. There is no proof that Barrington was involved, but his despair seemed to deepen and he stabbed himself in the chest with a penknife, a wound that took a long time to heal and his general health grew worse. In the early part of 1782 someone of influence took pity on him and he was released on 30 April, having been granted the King's Pardon on condition that he left the country and never returned. Barrington went back to Dublin and carried on much as before. Unfortunately, he was almost as infamous there as he was in England and a series of arrests and acquittals followed. He moved to Scotland but found the constables there a little more industrious than he was used to and he returned to London, in breach of his pardon. Inevitably, he was soon recognised and arrested, detained at the insistence of Duncan Campbell for having violated the terms of his pardon, and appeared at the Old Bailey on 18 January 1783. Despite much pleading and whining, the facts were clear, but some of his old charm remained and instead of being returned to the hulks he was allowed to serve out his sentence of eleven months in Newgate prison.

He emerged a free man at the end of 1783, but he was still well known as the 'noted George Barrington'. Though he became more cautious, he was taken several times into custody, his eloquence saving him time and time again. Still a comparatively young man at the age of 28, and better dressed than any of his contemporaries, he was not out of the game yet. He tried his luck on Sir Godfrey Webster MP, lifting more than ten guineas in gold and a fifty guinea note at the Opera House. Possibly, Barrington was losing his touch, his hands roughened by manual labour and his wits dulled as Webster felt himself being robbed and pursued the thief out into the street. He was caught and appeared once more at the Old Bailey on 25 February. He again blamed the publicity and prejudice against him, and as crucial evidence was lacking, he was acquitted once more.

Things did not improve. On another occasion he was caught and locked up in a public house named the Brown Bear in Bow Street until he could be taken to court the following morning. He escaped during the night, but this was not his best move as he now had the sentence of 'outlawry' pronounced upon him in the Kings Bench, which meant that if he was ever caught he could be sentenced to death automatically without further trial.

He fled London and spent the next eighteen months moving around the country, even joining a company of comedians in Glasgow, but this did not last long and he was soon back at work. He was arrested in Newcastle upon Tyne and returned to Newgate where his fellow malcontents raised £100 in his support so that he might employ counsel. His only chance was to appeal against being an outlaw, and after much legal argument his efforts were rewarded, which still left the original charge of theft from Godfrey Webster. Amazingly, he managed to talk his way out of that one as well.

In what may have seemed like temporary retirement, he moved to a small holding in Hampshire with a recently acquired wife and child, but this was short lived. At Enfield Races a very wealthy man named Henry Townsend was missing £20, a gold watch and some seals. Barrington was recognised and arrested, resulting in another appearance at the Old Bailey and a conviction. Judge Chief Baron was in no mood for leniency this time, declaring that this should have been a capital indictment and admonished him for wasting his many talents. Barrington was sentenced to be transported for a period of seven years.

At the end of January 1791, 319 convicts made their way from Newgate to Blackfriars Bridge and then to Botany Bay. It was the fifth batch of convicts to set sail since the First Fleet in 1787, this time consisting of 1,878 men and women. Opinions and records differ as to which ship took him to the other side of the earth – by his own account it was the *Albemarle*. Once again, his luck held and one of the few friends he had made sure that he was to be treated differently to everybody else by not having to wear irons and being allowed to share a cabin with a carpenter and second mate.

During the voyage a very serious revolt broke out and an attempt was made to seize the ship. According to Barrington's own account, he played a very large part in defeating the revolt, having finally worked out where his best interests lay. Barrington was given the run of the ship for the rest of the voyage by an incredibly grateful captain. Upon reaching Australia, he was recommended for 'favourable consideration' to the governor of the colony. His remarkable abilities, other than stealing from pockets, were recognised and he was made Superintendent of the Convicts and High Constable of Parramatta. Those who had judged him throughout his criminal career had often spoken of giving him the chance to use his talents responsibly and this time he took it.

Barrington was credited with the writing of three books, or at least his name was used to sell these early accounts of the colony. None of these works was written by him; they are most likely compilations of journalists from official reports and earlier published writings. *A Voyage to Botany Bay* was first published in London in 1795, followed by *A Sequel to Barrington's Voyage to New South Wales* in 1801 and *The History of New Holland from 1616 to the present Time*. The latter was published in 1808 some years after his death.

He continued to be held in very high esteem by all who met him, but his health became very poor and he died, possibly of TB, on 27 December 1804, at the age of 49.

Gentleman Harry Sterne 1778

Another of the 'flash mob' was Henry Sterne, better known as 'Gentleman Harry', who appeared in April 1778 before Sir John Fielding charged with 'several daring and cruel burglaries'. Like Barrington and Dignam, he gave every appearance of being a gentlemen, having had 'a most liberal education he was able to converse fluently in both French and Italian'. According to one report, he was 'clerk to a House of Eminence on the Thames Side until the year 1774 when forming improper connections, he experienced the effects of evil communications'.

Sterne, it emerged, had a private lodging at Walworth, where he went by the name of McMurdo. According to the press, he was part of a group of thieves accused of a large number of high-profile burglaries in Finchley, Kentish Town, Cripplegate, and other parts of the capital. They seemed to be particularly brutal: in one case at Enfield during 1778 a servant girl was badly wounded with a knife; in another a gentleman was viciously cut. Two of the gang were hanged at Tyburn but somehow Gentlemen Harry remained free. He was mentioned in the press a short time later, pushing a cart full of furniture stolen from Long Acre. Again, he seems to have escaped any sort of punishment and does not appear again until November 1782 when he was arrested in connection with the burglary of Dr Miller in Essex, who was badly wounded. His co-defendant, James Grant, was tried for the offence but, 'Sterne was sent to Justice Wilmot at whose office several informations were lodged against him. He is a remarkable smart young fellow, dresses gay, beyond suspicion, and his education he told a person present, cost more than he and his family were ever worth. Indeed, except Barrington, there has not been a more genteel collector upon the town for many years.'

Once more, he seems to escape without trial or punishment, and one wonders if his miraculous escapes are due to certain information that he might have passed on (in the time-honoured fashion). Another four years pass until in June 1786 he is mentioned once more in the following strange report:

> The noted Barrington was on Monday night at Vauxhall; he made no doubt, a good harvest without detection – many of his brethren were on the road and at the door, but he and Gentlemen Harry were the only two pickpockets that attempted admittance. These noted pickpockets have established a club, where all business in their trade is scientifically transacted, they hold it at a public house in the neighbourhood of Lincolns Inn Square.

His finest hour came on 4 June 1787, the birthday of King George III, when his grace the Duke of Beaufort attended a gathering to celebrate the event at St James's Palace. As was customary, he was wearing The Order of St George suspended by a ribbon around his neck. Normally referred to as a 'George', it was made of gold and silver set with diamonds and worth around £500. Possibly inspired by Barrington's success many years before, Sterne was determined to try for it. Upon leaving the event and waiting for his carriage, Beaufort was jostled by two men and almost instantly realised that the George was missing. He shouted for his servants, who saw Sterne and an accomplice making their way out. One, thought to have been George Wakeman, ran off, but Sterne was caught and searched, and the George emerged from his pocket. A few days later he was in front of the magistrates, who asked the prisoner to what profession he was bred and how he had been educated. Sterne replied that it was of very little consequence to his worship and begged him not to ask any questions that did not apply to the case, for it was, he observed, only wasting his worship's precious time to answer them. The magistrate, irritated at this 'consummate effrontery', told him that he was 'As great a rascal as any in England!'

'That,' replied Gentlemen Harry, 'is language that at once betrays your ignorance as a magistrate and your illiberality as a man, and if you were younger than you are, and not sitting on that Bench you should meet me as a gentleman for such unparalleled conduct.'

'I don't want to meet you anywhere,' replied his worship, 'for I am persuaded you would rob me if you had in your power.'

'You might make yourself easy on that score,' replied the prisoner, 'for I believe you have nothing to lose.'

The bench told him that he had better be silent or he should suffer for his insolence, to which he replied, 'I am persuaded that you will show me no favour, and I will not suffer you tamely to insult me in this unfortunate to predicament.'

Sterne was committed for trial, the newspaper report concluding that 'Henry Sterne is a very old offender that belonged to the famous or rather infamous Finchley Gang in the time of the late Sir John Fielding.' At his trial at the Old Bailey the jury was asked to choose between two charges, the first being highway robbery, which is 'a taking from the person either by actual force and violence applied to the person who is robbed, or by putting him in such fear as induces him to part with his property'. Second, and in relation to the particular charge,

> stealing the same property *privately* from the person of the Duke of Beaufort, which is always so laid as not to be perceived; it therefore clearly excludes all idea of a highway robbery; for it is either taken by force, or the effect of fear, that necessarily supposes that the person must perceive the violence, or the impression of fear, and must see the person that takes the property; and the evidence most clearly and unquestionably applies to the latter; for there is no circumstance of violence whatever spoke of by his Grace the Duke, or any of the witnesses, and to be sure the evidence which appears to have been very correctly given, does certainly prove that whoever was the hand that took the George from his Grace the Duke of Beaufort, stole it privately, and therefore it comes within the second charge of this indictment.

The second charge was a capital offence, and it would be reasonable to assume that was the one upon which he should have been convicted. The judge certainly thought so in his summing up. The jury had other ideas and found him not guilty of highway robbery but guilty of stealing *but not privately*, thereby saving him from the gallows. His sentence was one of seven years' transportation.

How well these various gentlemen of crime knew each other and cooperated is an interesting question. In June of 1787 Barrington and Sterne were certainly in contact. According to one newspaper, Sterne announced his intention to publish his memoirs, receiving, in response, from Barrington the following:

> What the deuce can tempt you to turn author? Are there no kennels to sweep; no shoes to black; no girls to flash for; no quack doctors bills to deliver; if you must turn honest to gain a subsistence, do it without turning author, which is the worst and last profession a wise man can or would follow! An Author! Why, you have forgot that an author is the only *pickpocket* that *starves* by his *profession.*

We shall never know whether Harry heeded these wise words or what a fascinating tale he would have told had he, indeed, 'turned author'. He died in Newgate in March 1788.

David Battie

Another presumed associate, David Battie, also described as 'remarkably handsome with a very genteel address and always well dressed', was present at Saint James's on the king's birthday when, to his extreme embarrassment, he was arrested for stealing nothing more than a pocket handkerchief. According to reports, it was Battie who had once picked the pocket of the Right Honourable Charles James Fox as Lunardi made his first balloon flight on 15 September 1784, and attempted to rob the Duke of Queensbury while he was in conversation with the Prince of Wales at Ascot in 1786. For this latter offence he was seized upon and 'docked of a fine head of hair, horsewhipped and exposed on the ground with a halter around his neck'. The story goes that he had once lived at the Hampshire Hog, a public house in Piccadilly, and was involved in running E & O tables (Even or Odd, an early form of roulette), but when this enterprise failed he fell in with Barrington and Sterne. One report continues:

> It is incredible the number of pickpockets that were under the management of these men, as regularly carried their stolen property to a house in Drury Lane well-known at Bow Street, where 20 of a night might be apprehended. Battie on his trial

might be compare it to Macheath [The handsome villain in *The Beggar's Opera*] for there were no less than four of his girls in the court during his trial and sentence, by no means destitute of beauty; there was one in particular seemed almost frantic when sentence was passed for Botany Bay.

Battie was held in Newgate until November 1789, after which he was moved to the *Justitia*. As he does not appear on any of the ship's lists for Australia we can assume that he served his time on that hulk.

Wakeman and Dew

There were two further members of the Finchley Gang. George Wakeman was thought to have been involved in the stealing of the 'George' with Gentleman Harry. He and Alexander Dew were arrested in December 1795 for stealing a pocketbook containing £500. They were convicted at the Old Bailey and sentenced to be transported for seven years. Wakeman was 36 and Dew 30. Wakeman had been convicted in 1790 of stealing a watch and was sentenced to seven years' transportation. Dew is listed as being transported to New South Wales on the *Barwell* in September of 1797, but Wakeman does not appear on the list of deportees.

Thomas Muir: The Scottish Martyr, 1793

Thomas Muir was a Scottish lawyer dedicated to political reform. At the age of 22 he became leader of 'The Society of the Friends of the People', a radical group campaigning for parliamentary reform influenced by the ideals of the French Revolution. They advocated universal suffrage, annual parliaments and the writings of Tom Paine. Under his influence, parliamentary reform societies were established all over Scotland. Muir visited France, arriving in Paris in January 1793, the evening before the execution of Louis XVI, with which he strongly disagreed, arguing, correctly, that it would be very bad for future reform movements.

During the following six months he was in close touch with many of the leading French revolutionaries. Charged with sedition at home and in his absence, problems with his passport delayed his return to England to contest the charges, resulting in him being declared an outlaw. Muir was tried in Edinburgh on 30 August and found guilty, with others, of having created disaffection by means of libel and seditious speeches. He was sentenced to fourteen years' transportation. The Scottish Martyrs, Muir, and fifteen other activists were brought from Leith in November 1793 in the *Royal George*, a revenue cutter, and delivered to the hulks. Overseer Duncan Campbell (a fellow Scot) appears to have had some qualms about holding Muir and his fellow seditionaries. Quite possibly he was afraid of the effect that a group of revolutionaries would have upon the other prisoners by stirring up trouble and inciting revolt. It is also possible that he felt uneasy about having to imprison people for their political views. He was likely to have prepared himself for some controversy over the reception of these prisoners, but as a bureaucrat he had little choice other than to take the Scottish prisoners.

Campbell wrote to the Home Office on 6 January 1794 expressing concern about the effect of hard labour on Muir's health. He was told that no distinction should be made between Muir and other convicts, and so he was placed in irons and sent on board the *Prudentia* at Woolwich. Muir and Thomas Fyshe Palmer, a fellow revolutionary from Bedfordshire serving seven years, were languishing in the prison hulks by night and being forced to labour in a chain gang on the banks of the Thames by day. An attempt to ship them out to Botany Bay in the convict transport *Ye Canada* had failed when her timbers were found to be rotten. Efforts on Muir's behalf were made in Parliament, with Fox and Sheridan speaking for him, but to no avail. He was taken onboard the *Surprize* and left the country on 2 May 1794, arriving in Sydney with others transported for the same offence on 25 October.

Upon arrival, the authorities were possibly uncertain what to do with their new charges. They did not regard them as convicts but as men banished from their country. Muir's time there appears to have been fairly uneventful. As political prisoners, and men of talent and education, Muir and his associates were accorded far greater freedom of movement than ordinary convicts. Before their departure from Portsmouth, each had received a considerable sum of money raised as a subscription on their behalf among the wealthy London Whigs. They were able to sustain themselves without recourse to the official colonial stores, and kept free of the compulsory manual labour normally demanded from all dependents. Muir bought land in a secluded spot near the coast, which enabled him, in February 1796, to escape in an American ship named the *Otter*, which had possibly been sent by admirers in the United States. The ship arrived in Vancouver Sound on 22 June 1796.

Learning that he was in danger from British ships in the vicinity, he determined to find passage to Cuba. There are many stories about his adventures during this time, including one claiming that he was wrecked on the west coast of North America and lived with an Indian tribe for three weeks before making his way to Panama and eventually Havana *en route* to Spain. It was during this part of the trip that tragedy struck. Near Cádiz his vessel was attacked and taken by an English Man-of-War. Muir was severely wounded by a piece of shrapnel to the left side of his face, which removed his cheek bone and destroyed his eye. As he lay for two months in a hospital at Cádiz, reports reached England that he had been killed. He was offered French citizenship and invited to spend the remainder of his life in France. He arrived in Paris on 4 February 1798 in a very weak state, addressed the Directory with the tale of his adventures, and solemnly declared that he adopted the Republic of France as his native land. In the short time remaining to him he campaigned tirelessly among his new compatriots in favour of a Scottish republic, constantly in touch with events in his native land. Leaving Paris for fear of British agents, he moved to Chantilly where he died suddenly on 29 January 1799, probably from infection in his facial wound.

Chapter 7

Aaron Graham
1802–1814

After the retirement of Campbell, the new superintendent was the 49-year-old London magistrate Aaron Graham, by all accounts a most remarkable man whose life and career are worth investigating. Graham was born in Gosport, near Portsmouth harbour, and had grown up amid the inspiring sight of His Majesty's fleets as they sailed in and out of port. Little is known about his early life, but he was greatly encouraged towards a naval career by Captain Thomas Pasley, a bluff, straight-talking Scotsman then approaching 60 who had been at sea since he was 14 and had seen much action against the French and in the West Indies. According to Graham's obituary, they met in 1767 when Graham was 14 and sent on board the *Seahorse* off the coast of Africa. Pasley was greatly impressed with his abilities and took an interest in his career. Graham moved on to other ships, including an appointment as secretary to a flagship, before accepting employment on the Newfoundland Station, a bleak and remote outpost of British jurisdiction. Despite his early seagoing experience, he excelled in clerical and organisational matters, and this is where his future lay.

His time in Newfoundland resulted in him being secretary to four successive governors, but his gift for bureaucratic work ensured that he had many unofficial duties and ran the station in all but name. He was quiet and unobtrusive, the perfect subordinate who mastered any task or crisis, and upon whom his superiors came to rely. As secretary to Admiral Edwards, Graham superintended all things afloat, handling the paperwork and legal issues. As well as these duties he organised theatrical events, and was an agent for prizes, thereby obtaining a share of all that was captured by the station during the American war. When the island was threatened with invasion he mustered the forces onshore, organised the fisherman and inhabitants, and acted as their commander. Graham presided during several consecutive seasons as Chief Justice of the island and contemporary witnesses attributed the success of the governors in large measure to his skill, describing him as an admirable aide. He seems to have maintained some mercantile connections; in 1782 he owned the *Maria*, which brought in supplies, and it seems that another of his ships was lost or captured on its voyage out with a cargo of salt. One report says that he was appointed purser to the *Bellerophon*, grappling with the accounts as it was being built in 1784.

He had married by licence Sarah Dawes (1761–1837) in 1776, at St Dunstan's Stepney, with the consent of her widowed mother as she was only 18 at the time and therefore a minor. Sarah was first cousin to Sir Henry Tempest, a dissolute and money-grabbing baronet who appears again later. Their marriage produced three sons and two daughters. His first son, Henry, born in 1778, was given the middle name Pasley.

Late in 1791 Graham returned to England and took up an appointment as a London police magistrate under the Middlesex Justice act of 1792. This established seven police offices, each staffed by three stipendiary (paid) magistrates and up to six paid constables. These were set up at Bow Street, Queen's Square (Westminster), Great Marlborough Street (Westminster), Worship Street (Shoreditch), Lambeth Street (Whitechapel), Shadwell, Union Hall (Southwark) and Hatton Garden. Graham was based at the latter and was recalled as 'rather under the middle size, neat in dress and person, with inoffensive manners, and insinuating in his address'. He was constantly employed, it would seem, in helping superior officers, with money, advice and any assistance they might require.

Mutiny on the *Bounty*

The following year, Graham, accompanied by Stephen Barney, a barrister of the Inner Temple and former town clerk of Portsmouth, was involved in the defence of one of the mutineers from Captain Bligh's *Bounty* in a court martial. The proceedings opened on 12 September 1792 on HMS *Duke* in Portsmouth harbour, with Vice-Admiral Lord Hood, the 67-year-old Commander-in-Chief, presiding. (The irony here is that the niece of Alexander Campbell, Graham's predecessor, was Elizabeth Betham, married to Captain Bligh.) Bligh was not present at the proceedings.

The main charge was under the Articles of War section XIX: 'If any Person in or belonging to the Fleet shall make, or endeavour to make, any mutinous Assembly upon any pretence what so ever every Person offending herein, and being convicted thereof by the Sentence of the Court-Martial, shall suffer Death.'

The causes of the mutiny are uncertain and endlessly debated. Bligh was not thought to have been unnecessarily harsh and had known some of the prime movers of the rebellion for many years. Although a magnificent sailor technically and practically, Bligh was a poor manager of men with an inflated idea of himself, probably suffering from a personality disorder. He lost his temper frequently and had no capacity for empathy. One possible contributing factor is that having spent time in the relative paradise of Tahiti, the crew were unwilling to return to the iron discipline on board ship. All involved gave different versions of events at the time. (They may have landed in what seemed to them like paradise, but they took their British view of the world with them, along with venereal and other diseases, introducing the indigenous peoples and their feuding tribes to firearms and crime. It has been said that their one positive introduction to the island was a pregnant cat, which eventually led to a great reduction in the rat problem.)

Graham's client was Peter Heywood, nephew to Captain Thomas Pasley, a young midshipman of only 16 when the mutiny occurred and who came from an old, well-connected but financially embarrassed family on the Isle of Man. His family had managed to engage the services of Graham at the instigation of Pasley, who wrote to Heywood: 'A Friend of Mine, Mr Graham who has been Secretary to the different Admirals on the Newfoundland Station for these twelve years, and consequently Judge Advocate at Court-Martials all that Time, has offered me to attend you […] He has a thorough Knowledge of the Service, uncommon Abilities, & is a very good Lawyer.' Graham volunteered his services in August, and on 5 September Pasley made his way over to barrister Francis Const's chambers in the Middle Temple, off Fleet Street, to meet Const and Graham. The outcome of that meeting seemed very positive and Pasley wrote to Heywood: 'I have every Reason to think you may look forward with pleasing Hopes, I refer you to my Friend Mr Graham for Information.' He had seen Graham's fabled skills at work and could not refrain from praising this 'intimate & very particular Friend'. It was a great help that Graham had seen most of the evidence before the meeting as part of his preparation and it was rumoured that he had bribed the boatswain to give perjured evidence in Heywood's favour. He had also interviewed a number of the witnesses to make sure that the evidence they were about to give was the most helpful version.

From his great experience of human nature and familiarity with a wide range of people passing through his court as a police magistrate, from gentlemen in straitened circumstances to the most disreputable thieves, there were few better qualified than Graham to plead for his client. Francis Const might have been a good barrister, but Aaron Graham knew not only the law but also what people in naval circles expected from it.

The survivors of Bligh's open-boat journey gave evidence against their former shipmates. On 18 September six defendants were found guilty of mutiny and sentenced to death by hanging, with recommendations of mercy for Peter Heywood and James Morrison 'in consideration of various circumstances'. On 26 October they received royal pardons from King George III and were released. Joseph Muspratt, the cook's assistant, won a stay of execution by filing a petition protesting that court-martial rules had prevented his calling two witnesses in his defence. He was still awaiting the outcome when able seamen Thomas Burkett, Thomas Ellison and John Millward were hanged from the yardarm of HMS *Brunswick* in Portsmouth dock on 28 October. There was some unease expressed in the press – a suspicion that 'money had bought the lives of some, and others fell sacrifice to their poverty', and that 'in the end it was class, relations or patronage that made the difference'. But in an age when you could be hanged for stealing many trivial items, surely an example had to be made in the case of something as serious as mutiny. In December, after what must have been a tense few weeks, Muspratt was reprieved, and on 11 February 1793 he, too, was pardoned and freed.

The relationship between Graham and Heyward did not end there. Heyward came to stay with Graham and his family at his house in Great Russell Street, Bloomsbury. They were visited by Heywood's sister, Nessy, who, in a letter home, said of Graham, 'he has the most prepossessing countenance with eyes in which are strongly pictured the sympathetic worth and goodness in his heart.' It is a great pity that no portrait of him has been discovered. With Graham's assistance and connections, Heyward was able to resume what was to become a respectable naval career.

Captain Anthony Molloy

In 1793 Graham was called to testify before a committee of the House of Commons, appointed to enquire into the state of the trade to Newfoundland, and in the spring of 1795, he became part of the defence team in the court martial of Captain Anthony Molloy. Molloy was attached to Lord Howe's fleet, hunting for French convoys during the Atlantic Campaign of May 1794. When the fleet was sighted Howe ordered an attack, with Molloy in the *Caesar* instructed to lead the column into battle – which he failed to do, preferring to stand off and fire from some distance. Despite this, *Caesar* claimed casualties of eighteen men killed and seventy-one wounded. In the aftermath, Molloy was strongly criticised by Howe for failing to obey orders to break the French line and a court martial was convened aboard HMS *Glory* at Portsmouth on 28 April 1795. Molloy was charged with 'failure to cross the enemy's line, in obedience to the signal of the admiral', and 'that he did not use his utmost endeavours to close with and defeat the enemy'. Speaking for the prosecution was Rear-Admiral Sir Roger Curtis, captain of the fleet during the battle. Molloy argued that the ship had been thrown into confusion after a ball had struck the stern-beam and left her unmanageable, but after three weeks of deliberations the charges were found to have been proved. The court tempered the findings with the observation that his courage was unimpeachable, but nevertheless he was sentenced to be dismissed from his ship and resigned from the service before dying in 1814.

The Spithead Revolt

In 1796 Graham is listed as a magistrate at Hatton Garden with a salary of £400 per year. The following April saw yet another change in the career of this remarkable man. Graham was engaged as a government spy by Secretary of State, the Duke of Portland. A serious seaman's protest at Spithead over issues of pay and conditions was causing grave concern. Suitably attired, he toured the inns and boarding houses frequented by seamen around Spithead, Gosport and Portsmouth, interviewing sailors, dockworkers, innkeepers and the like, keeping his ear to the ground in an attempt to gauge the general mood and find out who was behind it all. He sometimes had to pay for information and wrote to his boss, 'I assume I can spend money freely.' He got no cooperation from the local authorities, who were wary of anyone from London, and wrote to Portland, 'The police of this place is in so weak a state that government can hope but for little assistance from it. There is to be a meeting of the shipwrights to consider an application for an addition do their pay in time of peace. They are to appoint delegates.'

He investigated strong and continuing reports that the radical London Corresponding Society orator John Thelwall was stirring up the action, which he discovered to be untrue, but he did find radicals aplenty with red cockades, subversive literature and seditious talk. And talk it was, as he reported to Portland, 'I mix with and converse a great deal with the seamen upon the beach and it is no small degree of consolation to me under the misfortune which they have brought upon the country (but which I am persuaded they do not sufficiently understand to be sensible of) to find that there is not a man in the fleet whose attachment to the King need be doubted or who would not rejoice in an opportunity of meeting and fighting the enemy.'

The month-long strike was eventually settled through negotiation with Admiral Lord Howe, and some of the men's demands were met, including the reassignment of some unpopular officers, a pay rise and a royal pardon for all crews.

Inspired by this success, a far more serious mutiny broke out at The Nore, an anchorage in the Thames Estuary, on 12 May. This time the demands were far more radical and included an end to the war with France, which led to suspicions that events were being orchestrated by Jacobin agitators and revolutionary groups like the London Corresponding Society – whose meetings Graham had attended undercover – or even the United Irishmen. The mutineers blockaded London and were led by Exeter seaman Richard Parker, but the movement failed as lack of food and water caused the ships to slowly disperse. The end came when Parker seriously misjudged the mood of the men and ordered all the ships to sail to France to join the revolution. They refused to follow and the revolt collapsed.

Portland sent Graham over to perform the same service as he had at Spithead, but the mutiny had fizzled out the day before he arrived. He found the place, 'in a state of absolute siege', the fleet delegates still 'going at large about the town', and the Admiralty 'at a loss to know what to do with prisoners who are continually coming in from the different ships'. About 500 men were being held on the charge of mutiny at the time. He wrote to Portland: 'The captains are very apprehensive of serious consequences from so many being put into confinement and suffered to remain there without any plan being laid down for disposal of them.' He found the situation so dangerous that he used his powers as a magistrate to issue a proclamation forbidding strangers to enter Sheerness. He arrested three seamen who were haranguing some townsmen about the injustices that the sailors were suffering, but as every available space in the town jail was full of captives already he had to transport them to Maidstone jail himself. It was eventually decided that there was nothing to charge them with and they were released. As luck would have it, while Graham was in Maidstone the mutiny's leader, Richard Parker, was brought in charged with 'piracy and high treason', civil offences that gave jurisdiction to Graham and his boss, Portland. Graham and a fellow magistrate spent three hours questioning Parker in his cell, hoping to trace civilians who had aided the mutiny and thereby reinforcing the civil case, but Parker denied knowledge of anyone ashore.

It is clear from Graham's final reports that he believed, once more, that most of the suspicions entertained about subversive elements being involved were without foundation:

> no such connexion or communication ever did exist and were
> without serious foundation. The mutineers at Nore at one
> time had London at their mercy. They were in possession
> of thirty of the King's ships and had effectively stopped the

navigation of the River Thames and Medway, and might have starved the capital, yet they had done no more than rifle a few ships to fill their own stomachs. Had their policy been born of revolutionary ideas, they would certainly not have let slip such a decisive opportunity.

To account for the pandemonium, it was thought that the seamen were bored to distraction after two years at the Texel and wanted to get into battle:

> capable of no other mischief than was to be apprehended from a want of the fleet to serve against the enemy. [...] the want of beer and fresh beef prompted them to revenge and that and nothing else induced them to interrupt the trade of the river, it was done on the spur of the occasion and with a view of obtaining a supply of fresh provisions.

Parker and at least twenty-nine men were hanged from the yardarm, a fate far worse than a normal land-based execution as the victim was hauled up on the rope and strangled slowly without the possibility of an instantaneous death that a sharp descent would have given. What could have been Graham's contributions to naval history, the depositions of the *Bounty* mutineers and the interrogation of Richard Parker, have been lost.

A Nasty Incident at Sheerness

In April 1801 Graham was involved in a very serious incident at Sheerness. A crew member was dismissed from his ship by the Commissioner Resident, the navy's chief representative at the dockyard, for some minor incident, but the same representative caused him to be impressed and sent on board a ship at The Nore. He must have been very popular as the following day hundreds of dockyard workers seized the commissioner, roughed him up considerably and extracted from him a promise that the man should be released, which was done. A contemporary report continues:

> Not content with obtaining the avowed object of their tumultuous meeting, this inflamed, irritable and misguided rabble, pursued the commissioner and Mr GRAHAM (the Police Magistrate) into the dockyard, grossly abusing and insulting them. Mr Graham, therefore, solicitous to quell this

lawless tumult by the Civil Power alone, and anxious to avoid the necessity of shedding a drop of blood, though the military were willing and ready to assist, had their interference being required, judged it proper to read the Riot Act; in doing which, subjected to a very great and shameful abuse and personal danger. A little before 9 o'clock the people dispersed and went to their respective employment in the dockyard, though, as the weather did not admit to the impressed man's demand return till yesterday, they appeared unsettled and dissatisfied, but were appeased by his being brought on sure about noon yesterday.

The same afternoon about 5 o'clock a man who had been active in the riot was taken into custody in the dockyard by two constables without any disturbance or interference of military power. He was connected to the police magistrates office in the garrison and after examination was committed to Maidstone jail and immediately sent off a post-chaise escorted by upwards of 20 of the Sheerness Volunteer Cavalry. In passing the gates at the end of the town some feeble attempts to rescue the prisoner were made by a numerous mob who are quickly dispersed by the cavalry after this charging a body of stones by which one of the horsemen was cut in the face but no other mischief was done.

This morning all the different classes of people went very peacefully and orderly to work, except one man who was apprehended, and a few who, it is supposed have absconded on account of the late alarming and disgraceful riot.

Not willing to let the matter rest, Graham offered a reward of £100 for the apprehension of two of the rioters. The outcome is not recorded.

Cobbett

The following April, Graham was in the news once more. The Treaty of Amiens between England and France had been signed on 27 March 1802 and the population of London were asked to show their enthusiasm for this by illuminating their windows. William Cobbett, the well-known radical publisher, author and orator, was opposed to the treaty and his windows remained resolutely dark, giving an assembled mob cause to break them.

As his views were no secret and he was expecting trouble, he had applied to magistrate Graham for some protection, which resulted in a patrol being sent from Graham's office. Despite this, windows were broken and attempts made on Cobbett's front door. Graham attended in person and arrested three of the mob himself, but at Clerkenwell court the miscreants turned out to be clerks at the post office, one of them barely 16, and all from respectable backgrounds. They were charged with riotous assembly, and despite the defence claiming that Cobbett had brought it on himself by provocative acts of opposition to the treaty, they were convicted, with the jury recommending mercy. When Cobbett was asked if he agreed his reply was, 'Certainly not Sir, I came here for justice not for mercy.' Mercy is what they got, however. The three received substantial fines but were set free.

Inspector of Hulks

Despite what was already a very busy career, and continuing unknown problems with his health, Graham was offered the post of Chief Magistrate of Bow Street, which would have included a knighthood. It seems that his health would not allow him to take on the extra duties and he had to decline the offer. He did, however, accept the post of Inspector of Hulks from January 1802 after the government assumed direct control and administration of them. He was the first to hold the newly created post and was officially appointed on 25 March 1802 with an initial salary of £273 3s 10d, and in April he personally selected 200 convicts from the hulks and removed them to the *Calcutta*, which was to sail for New South Wales in a few days.

The change of convict management from the private contractors to this new officer made no practical difference to the administration and life on the hulks as such, but it did enable the Crown to engage Campbell as an inspector as recommended by Bunbury many years before. He was to visit each place of confinement in person, at least once in every quarter, to examine the behaviour and conduct of the officers, the treatment and condition of the prisoners, the amount of earnings in every place of confinement, and of the expenses attending it. He was to report to both Houses of Parliament at the commencement of every session. These were all the new duties imposed and he was to receive a salary not exceeding £350 per annum for himself, plus payment for a clerk, his travelling expenses, and all other charges incurred in the execution of his office. This was, of course, in addition to his £400 salary as a magistrate. He was also to superintend the fitting-up of proper vessels, recommend officers and servants, draw up rules and regulations for their conduct and treatment of the prisoners, keep an audit of all the expenses of the establishment, and to exercise all powers of superintendence and management. The Secretary of State for the Home Office was now the senior official responsible for the hulks and the Middlesex JPs relinquished their involvement. Aaron Graham presided over the passage of the hulks from the private enterprise sector into the domain of public accountability, a great advance in the administration of justice for the time. During the first twenty years, the hulks had accommodated about 8,000 convicts, about one in four of whom had died on board.

When Graham took over, the hulk establishment consisted of the *Retribution* stationed at Woolwich, housing 450 convicts, *Captivity* at Gosport, with a similar number, the *Laurel* at Portsmouth docks, with about 300, and the *Portland* in Langston Harbour with about the same again. The *Prudentia* had just been retired from Woolwich and the newly acquired *Zealand* was stationed at Sheerness with around 450 convicts, making the Medway a permanent hulk station. The new inspector began to make reforms immediately, and had rations increased by rooting out some of the corrupt contractors and insisting that none of the hulks' facilities were to be used for personal gain. Graham had large-vaulted chapels constructed on the *Captivity*, *Zealand* and the *Portland*, which must have been a source of bemusement and anger to the poor souls crammed into the rest of the ship. He tried to restructure further soon after his appointment, in an attempt to separate different categories of prisoner by closing the main companionways and installing separate ladders to each of the decks, which although well-meaning, was unsuccessful. When attempts were made to convert one of the hulks by separating the decks and building a chapel, the carpenters turned up one morning to find that all their work had been torn down by the residents during the night. They packed up their tools and left.

Outside of his criminal work, Graham had a keen interest in the arts and, in December 1803, became a trustee of the Drury Lane Theatre and was elected to the Theatre Board of Management. He was variously described as one of the principal shareholders, manager, superintendent and supervisor of affairs. While there, he made the acquaintance of a young actress named Harriet Mellon (1777–1837), who had attracted the attention of the wealthy banker Thomas Coutts. Graham was apparently acting as go-between and helping to facilitate their relationship; his discretion was beyond question. Harriet married Coutts in 1815 when she was 37 and he 79. His death, at the age of 86, in 1822 made her the wealthiest woman in England. To add a title to her fortune, in 1827 she married the 9th Duke of St Albans, twenty-three years her junior. One of Graham's other duties was close attendance upon the owner, playwright and MP Richard Brinsley Sheridan, to which he applied his usual administrative brilliance – so much so that Sheridan presented him to the Prince of Wales in 1806.

Graham gave employment to William Bridle, the later notorious governor of Ilchester jail, who, in 1822, was dismissed for the unlawful, cruel and oppressive treatment of prisoners in his care. Bridle served for six years as second mate on the *Justitia* and left with glowing references from his former employer.

The Holford Committee of 1811

The Penitentiary Act of 1779 had outlined strategies for the building of new prisons, as proposed by philanthropist John Howard, Jeremy Bentham, and others, but although it had passed through Parliament little had happened.

In 1811 a select committee was established under George Holford, the MP for Lostwithiel in Cornwall, to re-examine the organisation and design of proposed central prisons that would replace or supplement the hulks and limit transportation. It sought the opinions and ideas of many who had been active in prison reform over the past few decades. That the government would fund imprisonment was no longer in doubt and two models were considered. First, Bentham's Panopticon, which he had begun to design in the 1780s, saw the prison as a machine to reform its inmates based on a system of continual observation and supervision. Bentham was very keen on the idea that prisons should pay for themselves and introduced the idea of prison labour to this end. The plan was rejected by the committee, which disliked the idea of prison as a commercial enterprise, partly because prison labour would be in competition with the free market and not really advisable in times of great poverty. In 1803 the then Prime Minister Henry Addington refused to fund the building of the Panopticon and ten years later, as Home Secretary, he finally rejected the scheme altogether. The committee favoured a rival proposal, taking as its model the Gloucester Penitentiary, built in 1792, with a regime based on ideas of solitude, labour and religion.

The committee did not recommend that the hulks should be discontinued; on the contrary, they were of the opinion that existing problems could be lessened, if not entirely removed. They were aware that these floating prisons possessed two great advantages over every other place of confinement: they were much cheaper than any building that could be erected on land; and they were, in theory, mobile and could be towed from place to place. A vessel, which would not be worth more than £3,000 or £4,000 to break up, could be converted to house some hundreds of prisoners for £5,000 or £6,000 more, totalling around £8,000 or £10,000, whereas the construction of a prison would cost a great deal more. The capability of being transferred to any port or place accessible by water was also a convenience of great potential benefit. As regards the employment of the convicts, there was always a demand for labour in the neighbourhood of the navigable rivers and harbours of the country, particularly the public works carried out by the Naval and Ordnance Departments.

Holford spoke at great length to the Commons on 22 June 1815 'On the motion for going into a Committee on the Bill to amend the Laws relative to the Transportation of Offenders', and expressed his disappointment that little had changed with regard to the well-being of its inmates, but he remained generally optimistic about future reforms and his detailed and informative speech is worth quoting at some length:

> In the year 1811, (the latter of the two years to which the inquiries of the Committee of 1812, were particularly directed) the number of convicts on board the Hulks at Portsmouth, Sheerness, and Woolwich, was 1,564; and the average number employed at those places during, that year (on the days on which convicts worked) was only 831; so that 733 were left in the hulks without employment; a much larger proportion of the whole number than can be supposed to have been sick, or infirm, or wanted for ship's duty, on board the four hulks. It should also be observed that every weekday is not, with the convicts, a working-day; for, as there is no employment found for them under cover, they are prevented from working by bad weather; and from some of the hulks it is not thought safe to send them on shore in dark and foggy days. The fact, that the most is not made of the labour of the convicts, is put beyond all doubt-by the statements given in the Report of the Committee of 1812, concerning the estimated value of their services during the year 1811, founded on returns, made to that Committee, from the several places where Hulks are stationed. According to these returns, the total value of the earnings of the convicts at Portsmouth, Sheerness, and Woolwich, in that year, was £24,447 of which sum, the earnings of the convicts

at Woolwich alone, (480 only in number) amounted to no less than £14,751 leaving £9,696 for the earnings of the 1,564 convicts belonging to the four Hulks stationed at Portsmouth and Sheerness. Or, to consider this matter in another point of view, if we take from the aggregate expense of the hulk establishment, in 1811, the value of the earnings of all the convicts in that year, (according to the accounts furnished to the Committee) and divide the remainder by the whole number of convicts, we shall find the charge of each man to be about £18 but if we take the expense of the Hulk at Woolwich, for the same year, separately, and deduct its separate earnings, the convicts at that place will have cost only about £2 a head. It will of course be asked, how it happens that the earnings of the convicts at Woolwich should have amounted to above £5,000 more than those of three times their number, employed at Portsmouth and Sheerness. This circumstance was entirely owing to the attention paid to the Woolwich convicts by Lieutenant-Colonel Pilkington, the officer in command of the Ordnance department at that place, who took great pains to turn the labour of these men to account; for this purpose, he gave them increased allowances, and provided additional guards and keepers to look after them while at work. The expense incurred, by lieutenant-colonel Pilkington, on these heads, during the year 1811, amounted to £2,055 but it was, even in a pecuniary point of view, money well bestowed. I should observe that the sum of £14,751 mentioned above, was not the gross value of the men's earnings, but the net amount, after these out-goings were deducted.

I contend, that Woolwich furnishes an example, upon this occasion, which might be followed with advantage, at other places where hulks are stationed. It may, perhaps, be said, that we shall not easily find men of equal talents with those of Pilkington, to superintend the employment of convicts; and that, if we had such persons to undertake that duty, we could not give them the advantage of being at the head of the public department, in the yards where the convicts are to be employed; a circumstance which must have greatly facilitated lieutenant-colonel Pilkington's exertion. But, allowing all due weight to this observation, and admitting that, for these reasons, it may not be practicable to make the labour of the convicts as productive, generally, as it has proved in this particular instance, I think that what has been done at Woolwich affords a reasonable ground of expectation, that the burden of the convicts upon the state might be materially diminished; (while a great improvement would, undoubtedly, be made in their habits) by connecting with their labour the attention of an intelligent person, at each, place where a hulk is stationed; by making it their interest to be industrious; and by placing over them as many guards as may be necessary to see that they work properly, and to allow of their being divided into as many companies as the nature of their employment may require.

The arrangements here alluded to must be made upon the spot; they must be different at different places, where convicts are to be employed, having reference to local circumstances, and to the particular kind of work which the men are to perform; they must be made in concert with the officers of the several yards; and, above all, to have their full effect, they must be executed under the observation of a regular superintending officer, constantly at hand, and competent to see that they are adhered to; and not under the occasional inspection of a person who is to come, four or five limes in each year, from London for that purpose.

The class of persons from which a deputy superintendent might most conveniently and properly be selected, seems to be that of the lieutenants of the navy upon half-pay, among whom may be found many a meritorious individual, rendered unfit for the active pursuit of his profession by the loss of a limb, or by some wound or injury received in the service of his country, but qualified for the superintendence of a concern of this nature, by a clear head, strict principles of honour and integrity, and habits of discipline and command. The commissioner of a dock yard would not think it beneath him to communicate freely, upon all points relative to the convicts, with a person of this description; who would, in that case, be treated, by the other officers of the yard, with a degree of respect and consideration, that would be of great use to him in the execution of his office.

It has been apprehended, by some persons, that any attempt to procure actual accounts of the convicts' earnings will be attended with much inconvenience. It is admitted, that there will be no more difficulty, or trouble, in keeping these accounts, than in the case of common labourers; but it has been surmised, that although the officers of the different yards are willing enough to accept of the work of these men, while it goes for nothing, and the value of it does not enter into the calculation of what is spent in the yard, the employment of them will be disliked, and endeavours will be made (at least in some of the yards) to get rid of them altogether, if their services are to be estimated, and their earnings brought to account. I will not undertake to say, that some practical difficulty may not occur, in framing proper arrangements upon this Lead, from the cause here stated; but the House will, I am sure, agree with me in thinking that difficulties of this nature are not to be submitted to as insuperable, but should be encountered and controlled by the authority of Government; and will be ready to vest powers in any quarter, in which they may be required, for that purpose. I must here remark, that, if there be any ground for such an apprehension as that to which I have now alluded, it strongly fortifies the arguments in favour of the expediency of appointing deputy superintendents at each of the places where there are hulks, as it constitutes of itself a sufficient reason for the residence, at every such place, of an officer of a higher description than that of a captain of a hulk, or an ordinary clerk, to see that justice is done to the public and to the convicts.

I know that, in the opinion of many gentlemen, there can be nothing less likely to succeed, no project more visionary, than an attempt to produce amendment on board the hulks. We cannot, indeed, give to the offender, in these prisons, the advantage, which would be afforded to him in a penitentiary, of reflecting, in a separate cell, without interruption, on his past life and future prospects; but with the means of inspection and separation, which experience has shown to be attainable in the vessel, and with due attention to the convict on shore, we shall at least be able to keep him from the commission of fresh offences against law or good order, during his imprisonment; from stealing – from gambling and swearing – from drinking and quarrelling – from the use of indecent or profane language, and from vicious conversation of every kind. Will it be contended, that the prevention or interruption of these practices, for seven or fourteen years of a man's life, will have no influence on his future conduct and character?

Can it be supposed that the evil propensities of men, which are invariably confirmed and nourished by habitual indulgence, will not, on the other hand, be weakened, in some degree, by long restraint? Will not employment, though on compulsion, create a habit of industry? Are not the habits of mankind, in general, formed by a course of discipline and education, not adopted from choice, but imposed, for their benefit, by the will of others? But to lay aside, for a moment, all question of amendment and reform, it will be a great point gained, if we only prevent the offender from becoming worse on board the Hulks, and redeem this establishment, in some measure, from the obloquy which is now attached to it (and justly) in the public mind. The objection now felt, to employ a person who has lately quitted the Hulks, is not that he has been criminal, but that his crime has been punished; it is not that he committed an offence seven or fourteen years ago, but that he has passed seven or fourteen years of his life in the pestilential air of an ill-regulated prison. Let these places of confinement be put upon a proper footing, and the convict will not experience the difficulties, which he now finds, in. procuring an honest livelihood on his discharge; nor can I see any reason why, after this shall have been done, arrangements may not be formed for giving employment to such of the convicts leaving the hulks, as may be inclined to accept it, not in a separate establishment for that purpose (which might, perhaps, be objectionable, as pointing out these persons too much to the notice of the public), but among the numerous labourers and manufacturers employed in different works by Government. To this point, also, the attention of a deputy superintendent might possibly be directed with advantage.

The utmost effort would, however, be made to improve the arrangements in the hulks; and with that view it was intended to construct seven or eight different compartments, among which the prisoners would be distributed by the governors, with the approbation of others, according to the degree of their crimes, the actual or probable reform of their morals, and the decency of their manners. Thus, he hoped that provision would be made to guard against the general contamination which was justly to be apprehended from the indiscriminate intercourse of different descriptions of prisoners. He could assure the House that nothing was neglected that promised to benefit the system of imprisonment under consideration. In order to encourage the reformation of prisoners in the hulks, it had been for some time the established practice to make a quarterly report to the Prince Regent of such prisoners as were thought deserving of royal clemency, which was never refused to proper objects; and the release of such persons must naturally have the best effects on the conduct of other prisoners.

Another important improvement, too, was intended, and it formed a part of the Bill before the House, namely, that all prisoners transmitted to the hulks should bring with them an account of their conduct at the prison from whence they came, also of the offence of which they were convicted, together with their trial and convictions. Thus, the governor of the hulks would be at the outset enabled to form a judgment how to class each prisoner so as more effectually to provide against improper intercourse. The right hon. member, after replying to the observation that prisoners in the hulks cost the country more than those confined in the penitentiaries, by stating, that the former must have an allowance of beer from the much harder work in which they were employed, added, that such improvements as were in contemplation, he hoped, would be productive of a satisfactory result.

Sir Samuel Romilly strongly objected, not merely to the details, but to the principle of the Bill under consideration; because by that Bill it was proposed to perpetuate a system of transportation, which was found utterly ineffective for the purpose it professed. The rational object of all punishments, short of death, was obviously to reform the offender. But those who suffered transportation were generally initiated in new crimes, introduced to worse habits, and in every respect disposed to much more mischief to society; than they were inclined to, or qualified for, before their transportation. The question, then, for the House to consider on this occasion, was, whether a system, found so defective, ought to be continued; for the Bill under discussion referred to transportation as well as to the hulks. With respect to the latter, he saw no reason why any large number of prisoners should be confined together in one vessel; but he objected to the system of the hulks altogether, whether they were to be used as a place of punishment, or for the temporary confinement of persons meant to be transported.

In either case these hulks were exceptionable, especially as no provision was or could be made in such places to prevent that contaminating intercourse, which served to introduce prisoners to vices with which they were before unacquainted, to teach them new sources of villainy. This was particularly to be deplored with regard to those unfortunate persons of tender years, who were so often confined in the hulks. There were at the present moment on board the hulks some children of the age of 14, 13, 12, and even 11 years of age; and it was a fact, that within the last four years no less than 105 children, under 16 years of age, had been transported to Botany Bay; yet it was notorious, that crimes had continued to increase; and did not such increase prove the radical deficiency of our system of police? That system ought, therefore, to be inquired into, and peculiarly deserved the attention of Parliament; for as it was the object of all punishment and criminal law to prevent offences, the system which failed to answer that end ought to be corrected. The House could hardly imagine the extent to which the progressive increase of crimes had gone of late years. But he had to state, from authentic returns, that while the number of committals, in London in the year 1806 amounted only to 849, they reached in 1813 to 1,278; so that in the former year those committals were one-third less than in the latter, and this extraordinary increase of crime had taken place, let it be observed, in a period of war; although whatever calamities belonged to war, it had generally been remarked to have the effect of producing a diminution of crime, from the number of persons which it required for the army and navy. With this statement, then, before the House, he hoped that he should not say in vain that our system of police ought to be inquired into, and especially that a mode of punishment ought not to be tolerated, which, instead of reducing, operated to augment criminality.

For what a serious responsibility would the House incur if it overlooked the subject, especially with regard to the poor child, who, probably from want of education, was led into delinquency, and consigned to a species of imprisonment which only served to qualify him for the worst crime, until at last the law exacted his life as the penalty of that contamination which its own injudicious exercise created. Thus, punishment, instead of effecting reform, rendered those who were the objects of it worse than before. He attributed a great part of the existing evil to the defective state of the police of the metropolis. By the present system, the police officers had the strongest interest not to put down young offenders, but to allow them to go on until their crimes became so enormous, as to be very profitable. It was the most serious duty of the House to inquire into all these circumstances, and most especially into the disgraceful fact of the great increase of crimes. He wished that the Bill might be stopped in its progress. If not, he implored the House to do no more in the present session than pass a temporary Bill for a twelvemonth, and in the meantime institute an inquiry into the various circumstances to which it related.

The committee of 1811 could have put paid to the hulks for good, but once again matters came down to a constant reassurance that everything was absolutely fine onboard, and that any alternative would have been prohibitively expensive and there were wars to finance.

It was 1812 before every ship had its own chaplain, with varying degrees of interest and influence. They established a school on the *Captivity* at Portsmouth in 1813 – which did not last long – and libraries were established, though, as can be imagined, their contents were not much sought after and did little to 'reclaim the prisoners from habits of vice'. The reports of the chaplains, which accompanied those of Capper (see next chapter), did a great job of promoting the view that everything was as good as could be expected, which is just what the authorities wanted to hear.

Graham retired as a magistrate, and from control of the hulks, due to ill health. The last report to bear his name was delivered by his assistant, John Henry Capper, in November 1814. During the last three years of Graham's rule more than 900 men were pardoned from a population of about 2,000. To give this some context, about 500 pardons were granted during 1824 from a population of about 3,000.

Graham died on 4 December 1818 at 56 Great Queen's Street, at the age of 64, having suffered from what was described as 'a very severe indisposition for upwards of five years which rendered him too weak in body to be capable of any exertion'. His hearse was drawn by six horses and his remains were deposited in a vault under St George's Church, Bloomsbury. The remaining lease of twenty-seven years on his house was put up for sale, along with his furniture and effects the following March. He was survived by two sons: Edward Lloyd Graham, born in Hendon, who joined the Royal Navy and became captain of the frigate *Vestal* in 1802 (Edward died at the age of 38 in 1820); and Henry Elliot Graham, born in Colwall, Herefordshire in 1793, who became a vicar in Cornwall and died 1855, at the age of 62.

In a bizarre twist, Graham's wife, Sarah, had left him to live with her first cousin Sir Henry Tempest (1753–1819) as his common-law wife (by all accounts he was a 'thoroughgoing rogue'). Aaron Graham's daughter, Ellen Tempest Graham (1793–1834), left with her mother and adopted the name of her stepfather as her middle name. Graham does not seem to have been too upset and left his errant wife his estate – as did Sir Henry Tempest. Sarah died in 1837, at the age of 80.

Aaron Graham had been a brilliant administrator, an expert on naval affairs and financial matters, an experienced manager of men, and had a taste for the arts. Could there be a better man to manage the floating criminality on the Thames? On paper probably not, but, in reality, he was already greatly overstretched as a magistrate and lawyer, involved in the preparation of various reports and enquiries. He frequently had to give evidence at the Old Bailey and had been in bad health since at least 1806, when he was unable to accept the post of chief magistrate. There are no records of his day-to-day involvement with the hulks, and despite several accounts of him in the press, this part of his career is barely mentioned. It seems as though much of the day-to-day running was left to his staff, and underlings like John Henry Capper, who we shall consider next.

Chapter 8

The Capper Years
1814–1847

John Henry Capper – 1774–1847

John Henry Capper was born in Chelsea on 21 September 1774 to Peter Capper and Mary Pitts. As with the previous office holders, little is known about his early life or career. There is a possible marriage between a man of that name to Frances Amelia Hill in Bermondsey in October 1796, when he would have been 22, but there are no further details. His obituary notices state that he had been in the 'Home Department' for fifty-three years, taking us back to 1799, when he would have been 25, but nothing further has been discovered. He had a brother, Benjamin Pitts Capper, born in 1772, who served in the Royal Lancashire Militia as a young man, but by 1811 he was described as '3rd assistant clerk of passports in the Alien Office, Crown Street, Westminster'. By 1818 he had become head of the Alien Office, sometimes described as the forerunner of MI5 and the secret service.

John Henry had been clerk to Aaron Graham, but for how long is not known. He was called to give evidence before a Parliamentary Select Committee in 1812 on the process of transportation, and though nothing has been found linking him to the hulks before that date, he must have been involved for quite some time. As part of his testimony, he was asked how convicts were selected for transportation and outlined the process thus:

> When the hulks are full and the convicted offenders in the different counties are beginning to accumulate, a vessel is taken up for the purpose of conveying a part of them to New South Wales. A selection is in the first instance made of all the male convicts under the age of 50, who are sentenced to transportation for life and for 14 years; the number is filled up with such from amongst those sentenced to transportation for seven years, as they are the most unruly in the hulks, or are convicted of the most atrocious crimes; with respect to female

convicts, it has been customary to send, without any exception, all whose is state of health will admit of it, and whose age does not exceed 45 years.

It made practical sense. A growing colony needed young, fit people to labour and produce the next generation; the old and infirm would merely become a burden. Capper took over from Graham officially as 'Superintendent of the Hulks' on 12 July 1815, at the age of 40, with a healthy salary of £400 pa. This was something of an elevation in title as Graham had been styled merely 'Inspector of Hulks'.

From his time in office, it appears that Capper lacked all the qualities that had defined Campbell and Graham. He was a career civil servant; obedient, subservient, bureaucratic and dull, lacking any entrepreneurial spirit or desire to institute improvements. His only real qualification was having worked with Graham for a number of years, and, in many ways, that is all that the establishment required, someone to reassure them that everything was fine, and that officers and convicts were working together harmoniously. At a time when the country was in a period of unrest, with serious social problems, they would have been most grateful not to have to worry about the wellbeing of a few thousand criminals. Having said that, when he first took charge he seems to have taken his duties seriously and was a good organiser, working out costings and estimates, but careful to avoid expressing an opinion on anything controversial. Despite his new appointment, Capper was still a Home Office functionary who had to file reports and carry out tasks that would take him away from the hulks. Like his two predecessors, the position was not one to which he could give his full attention. The government regarded him as an expert in the field of imprisonment and sought his views on the costings of the first modern penitentiary at Millbank, then undergoing construction twelve miles upstream from Woolwich. Such faith was quite possibly misplaced as, despite Capper's input, the enterprise was described as badly planned and extravagantly built.

During his first year in office he visited every hulk in the fleet, perhaps making sure to impress Lord Sidmouth, the Home Secretary. The *Justitia* lay at anchor off the Woolwich Warren with about 470 inmates; in Portsmouth Harbour there was the *Captivity*; the *Laurel* was at Gosport and the *Portland* at Langston Harbour. In total they held about 1,200 convicts. Initially, Capper visited one or other of the depots monthly, spending around twenty-four hours inspecting everything for himself, listening to complaints from the convicts as well as his officers. Part of his job was to submit regular reports and for the first of these he reported that the total number of inmates as at 1 May 1815 was 2,038, of which 112 were under the age of 19. The total cost for the two years ending 31 December 1814 was £144,542. Profit made from the labour of the convicts for the same period came to £38,992, calculated at1s 6d per day for an artificer, and 1s for a labourer, rates that had been fixed thirty years ago.

One of the government's major concerns during the winter of 1815, as the Napoleonic wars came to an end, was the return of an estimated 15,000 convicted felons who had been conscripted into the army and navy. Churchwardens and local police were asked to pay particular attention as 'the greatest exertions will be necessary to restrain depredations and murder'. The recruitment of those convicts willing to serve had worked well in the short term, but there was no plan for the resettlement of a battle-hardened army of desperate men looking for employment and somewhere to live.

Despite many tales of abuse below decks, assault and 'unnatural practices', particularly against the young by predatory elders, there are very few authenticated instances of this in the records. It is possible that accounts may have been made up or exaggerated in letters to relatives and friends in the hope of exciting some compassion from the authorities. Again, self-regulation would have played its part. Crime covers a vast range of activity and a man imprisoned for stealing a purse is just as likely to be opposed to predatory attacks on the young or vulnerable as any magistrate. Nonetheless, it was undeniable that assaults and crime did take place below decks. One way to combat this was to increase surveillance.

Capper's priorities included putting into practice the reforms recommended by the committee of 1811. One of these involved dividing the different decks within the vessels into separate caged compartments with a supervisory passage down the middle, enabling constant surveillance, though free association was allowed until bedtime. This adaption was first carried out on the *Dunkirk* in Plymouth and the design was adopted by other vessels. The separate cages allowed much improved inspection of the prisoners during the time that they were confined below. At Sheerness the newly remodelled *Retribution*, which had begun its refit at the end of Graham's tenure, now held about 450 men in separate bays, each with eight to sixteen men behind a grill, which enabled the guards to see everything that went on within. On the *Retribution* Capper was faced with the problem of ventilating the ship, which, it has been said, he carried out in a manner all of his own, perhaps symbolic of his period in office: 'I did not fail to give due consideration to the state of ventilation on board this ship, I found it necessary in order to admit free circulation of air to place at one end of each of the two upper decks an iron bar door opening into the chapel, and also one in the hall orlop deck communicating with the steerage, which have added materially to the ventilation.'

He had, in effect, achieved very little, as no fresh air was admitted, but the iron doors did allow closer surveillance of the prisoners. The restructuring organised housing for the convicts on three decks. The bottom, or orlop, had eighteen secure bays, each 9ft long, fronted by an iron grill with each side separated by a 5-ft-wide corridor with a bulkhead separating one bay from another. The deck above the orlop, known as the lower deck, was similarly arranged, except for the addition of the ship's companies' quarters. The bays amidships were 15ft by 18ft and intended to contain no more than eight prisoners, but from the beginning they had to take ten or twelve. The upper deck had twelve bays and in the stern were the storerooms and cabin for the chaplain. The captain's quarters were to be found at the stern of the spar deck. Most of the basic improvements were completed by 1815, which, although resulting in greatly increased security, did nothing to address the overall conditions of extreme overcrowding.

As the number of inmates continued to increase, platforms were erected along the sides of the deck. Six men slept on each, with a rug covering each couple. The space allotted was 6ft in length and not more than 20in in width. In contrast, the official naval allotment of sleeping space for each seaman was 14in. The platforms could be used as tables during the day or placed upright against the walls to create more space and put back for sleeping at night.

The problem of controlling such a large number of people was not helped by a shortage of wardens, who, though largely illiterate, were expected to follow written instructions, resulting in confusion and conflicting ideas over what the various procedures should be. However, some progress was made. The days of 11 and 12-year-old boys being locked in all night with career criminals of every description without supervision came to an end under Capper. He also introduced a 'character book', which was updated every three months, grading each convict from very good to very bad in six categories. The different classes were not allowed to mix, but with improved behaviour they could rise to the highest class, and, having served more than half their sentence, one out of 100 might be considered for parole. In the early days, some were selected on condition that they worked as guards on the hulks or agreed to join the navy. The prospect of a pardon had an excellent effect on conduct and morale was said to be much improved.

Capper filed biannual reports, giving the average number of prisoners on the hulks and a general overview of the situation, which were produced as parliamentary papers. In his report to the Home Secretary for 1815, he felt able to declare: 'The separating of the prisoners of indifferent character from those who are orderly disposed, has produced so great a change that I have been assured by all the officers that their duty in governing the convicts has been made comparatively easy to what it was formerly.'

During 1815 the *Portland*, which had seen service as a hulk at Langstone Harbour for thirteen years, was in a bad way and not worth repairing. As a replacement he acquired the seventy-four-gun, 29-year-old *Bellerophon* and had her fitted out for convict service, after nine months' work at a cost of £1,200. Assuming that similar amounts were spent on fitting out the *Retribution* and the *Leviathan*, the total expended on refitting the old naval ships would have come to about £3,600. All the inmates had been transferred from the *Portland* by January. The *Captivity* and the *Laurel* were also fitted out but to a lower standard due to a lack of funding.

Known to seamen as the 'Billy Ruffian', the *Bellerophon* had served at Trafalgar, escorted Nelson's body back to England and seen Napoleon's surrender the previous year. This once-proud and magnificent ship was now reduced to a hulk in the convict service and stationed at Sheerness. She was renamed *Captivity* in October 1824 to allow the *Bellerophon* name to be used for another ship, a common and confusing naval practice (there had been a previous *Captivity*, which became a hulk in 1796, named the *Monmouth* before that, and broken up in 1816). In April 1826 the 'Billy Ruffian' moved for service at Plymouth and was finally broken up for scrap in 1836.

In his report of August 1817 Capper informed the House from his office in Great Queen Street that 'the number of convicts received at Woolwich, Sheerness and Portsmouth have exceeded all former times, consisting of over 1,000'. All, he says, 'have been both orderly in their conduct on board and on shore at labour. The convicts have been quiet and industrious.' He described the general health of the convicts as very good and trotted out the usual tale that the twenty who had died in the last six months were ill long before they became his responsibility:

> The officers have been attentive to the duty and on all occasions treated the prisoners with great humanity. The public works have furnished daily employment for nearly the whole of the prisoners confident to work, but many of them are totally unfit for either labour or transportation and from either age or infirmity are unable to execute even the ordinary duties of the ship so they remain a complete burden on the convict establishment. Arrangements have been made for drafting as many as possible to the vessels at Gosport where public labour is least required.

Capper expressed his continuing concern about the number of boys on board, which, in the last eighteen months, totalled 129 aged 16 or under. Some seventy-one had been transported to New South Wales, leaving fifty-nine in the various convict ships and, considering their previous lives, he had 'received the most satisfactory accounts of their behaviour which he put down to great extent to then being divided from the main population'. Despite an outbreak of smallpox, only four had died from it during the previous year, his report continued. Dysentery at Woolwich in 1816, he claimed, was 'not confined to the hulks alone'. On 1 January 1817, on the various hulks, there were 2,364 convicts received from the county jails in England, Wales and Scotland: of these, 1,790 had been transported to New South Wales, forty-five had died, one escaped and 437 had been either discharged or moved to other places of confinement. On 1 January 1818 there were 2,132 prisoners.

As regards expenditure, Capper reported that the amount spent between December 1816 and July 1817 was £41,830, from which sum was deducted the earnings of labour at £17,218, making the actual expense £24,611 for the care and maintenance of an average of 2,159 prisoners. The expense of attending the establishment had exceeded former periods by about £4,000, which was spent on clothing the prisoners received on board and those sent to New South Wales, plus keeping the ships in a proper state of repair. Attached to this report was another by Samuel Watson DD (Doctor of Divinity) stationed at Woolwich Arsenal, who testified that 'the extension of Royal Clemency to those distinguished by regular obedient and industrious behaviour had not failed to stimulate even the sullen and careless, having a very beneficial effect against the general despondency'.

Thomas Price, chaplain of the *Retribution* at Sheerness, reported:

> the *Retribution* hulk continues in a state of the greatest order imaginable. A prison inmate of a superior class made applications not to be sent to the hulks but to be kept there until he could be removed on board the ship that was to take him to New South Wales. He came down here and afterwards expressed himself thus to a gentleman in London, "instead of the most shocking scenes of depravity and the most domanial uproar and confusion as formally pictured to us, I believe without exaggeration one is greeted with cleanliness, order, impropriety. I could not have believed it possible that amongst 500 men of such varied and bad characters so much peace and quietness might be enjoyed or much security from plunder and pillage."

Edward Edwards, chaplain of the *Bellerophon*, was pleased to say, 'above four fifths of the convicts on board the *Bellerophon* conduct themselves in an exemplary manner; amongst them there are doubtless hypocrites; but having made this concession, I feel satisfaction in stating my conviction to be that many of them are sincere and reclaimed. The school has 250 scholars, all the boys attend and generally improve beyond any expectation. The captain has of late no cause to reprove any of them.'

Samuel Watson, chaplain of the *Justitia*, reported: 'the partitions of the ship into divisions as numerous as due regard to cleanliness and ventilation would allow, has by means of classification afforded facilities for observing the conduct of individuals which were unattainable while the men were congregated into two large masses; and the hope of promotion from a less eligible to a more comfortable quarter of the vessel has a most powerful influence on the minds of many. In the hospital I see nothing but a studious attention to the comfort of the sick and infirm.'

A report was sent in by William Tate, chaplain of the *Laurel*, and the first *Captivity* hulk at Portsmouth, which stated that the present condition of the convicts was so satisfactory as to call for few observations, 'they are, with remarkably few exceptions, respectful to their chaplain and obedient to their officers, orderly in their awards, diligent in the school and attend to the reading of evening prayers with the most praiseworthy decorum'. Capper would attach to his reports the views of his chaplains, which were always fawningly faithful to the image of tranquillity that he liked to portray. How the chaplains were selected is a mystery, but none raised a criticism of anything they saw on board. A report from 1812 states that their salaries are considerably lower than the amount paid to those in county prisons – from £250 down to £150 for the hulks – and this differential is unlikely to have changed in the intervening years.

As time went on, Capper diversified into having the convicts load and unload vessels, paint ships, clean cables, carry timber, and perform a range of menial tasks, against a background of increasing resentment from free labourers who found their available work reduced by convict labour. They were, of course, forbidden to form organisations in their own interests and had no way of combating the cheap labour. In October 1815 there was not enough work for the convicts to do at Langstone Harbour, where they had been developing the arsenal at Cumberland Fort, just east of Portsmouth. By the 1820s things were better organised and convicts were regularly at work on dockyards, and at river work along the Medway and the Thames, moving from one to another as the labour was required.

Another report from January 1819 begins: 'The prisoners recently received into the hulks have brought with them the most infamous characters, but their behaviour since their arrival on board has been orderly and I can assure your lordship that by far the greater part of these prisoners who have been confined upwards of 12 months have conducted themselves in a very becoming manner complying with regulations both on board and labour on shore. In the dockyard at Sheerness about 800 prisoners have been for a considerable time employed in a very advantageous matter.' Capper continues that the *Justitia* at Woolwich had received many prisoners from the county jails and that nearly 1,000 had been transported to New South Wales:

> A great many of the juvenile offenders waiting to be transported, now separated from adult prisoners, have been transformed from the shocking state in which the first appeared. Generally very quick and clever, they have been brought into a very good state of discipline considering that several of them are but boys and some merely children. Some are learning the trades of shoemaker, tailor and bookbinder, others carpenter, cooper and smith. The provisions furnished by the contractors have been good and wholesome and instances of complaint on the part of the prisoners have been very rare.

Not all the young apprentices, however, were happy learning a trade. In November that year one of them 'plunged a knife into the breast of the person appointed to instruct him in the art of shoemaking'.

The figures for the end of the year 1818 were: 2,131 on board all ships, a total of 3,044 had been received, 2,187 had been transported, 433 discharged by pardon or otherwise, five had escaped, fifty-seven had died and 2,493 remained in the hulks. It continued like this year-on-year, portraying the hulks as healthy schools of reclamation and contentment. It is perhaps a wonder that the entire labouring class of London was not queueing for a place in such an ideal environment.

Not all were deliriously happy. During 1820, 'an attempt was made by a gang of convicts employed in the Royal Arsenal at Woolwich to affect their escape by swimming across the Ordnance Canal, but they were immediately secured'. On 1 January that year there were 2,837 on board the hulks, with 2,996 received from different jails during the year, making a total of 5,833, of which 2,758 were transported, 448 discharged by pardon or transferred to other places, sixty-six had died and six escaped, leaving a total of 2,555 for January 1821. In one of his reports in July 1823 Capper states: 'Sir, I have the honour of reporting to you that the prisoners on board the respective convict ships have, since my last report, continued to behave in a very orderly manner, (with the exception have a few convicts at Woolwich who attempted to escape), and that they have fulfilled their tasks of labour when on shore to the satisfaction of the persons under whom they have been employed.' There were no deaths from typhus in 1821 at Woolwich or Portsmouth and over the year as a whole there was 'considerably less mortality than was contemplated'. Other deaths were often due to 'a previously existing condition'. And so it went on.

Robert Pitts Capper

Capper was initially without his own clerk, but in 1823 he obtained permission to employ one, and chose his 22-year-old nephew, Robert Pitts Capper, at a salary of £270 a year, appointed officially by Sir Robert Peel. While occupying this position, Robert also had a tea and grocery business with his brother in the Strand and was living at 87 York Road in Lambeth. His father, Benjamin, was a powerful man in the civil service who had compiled a Topographical Dictionary of the United Kingdom and may well have had some influence in securing the position for him. By all accounts, Robert was a very bright lad and Capper senior began to give him more and more responsibility, so much so that as he grew older the younger man took over virtually the entire superintendence. He visited the hulks in place of John Henry and his signature was recognised by officers and contractors as carrying the authority of the superintendent proper. For John Henry, Robert was an excellent choice; he unwaveringly followed his uncle's lead in presenting the sunniest possible view of life aboard the hulks.

When first appointed, John Henry had been living in Lambeth Road and had his office at home, for which he received an allowance of £131. He was eventually given a room at the Home Office but continued to take the allowance until his retirement. It did not occur to Capper to relinquish any part of his £400 per year income merely because advancing years and ill health prevented him from carrying out his duties. Gradually, his interest waned, and he carried out the bare minimum of inspection, leaving it to Robert to compile the reports and carry out the inspections. It was claimed that other perks of the job included the employment of convicts to do private work for him often without payment.

The year 1823 began with the execution of Robert Hartley on Penenden Heath, Maidstone, for the stabbing of Captain Owen on board the *Bellerophon*. The black-hearted villain had been involved in housebreaking pretty much full-time since the age of 9 and confessed to at least two murders. He was

25 years old. Capper reported 3,031 prisoners present in the hulks on 1 January; 1,470 of them had been transported to New South Wales during the year and five had escaped. The total expenditure for the year was £91,038, with earnings amounting to £48,422. During May eight convicts sent down to Woolwich from Aberdeen 'conducted themselves in the most violent and outrageous manner maintaining a long and bloody conflict with those in charge of them and the constables who came to their assistance, found necessary to lash them to ring bolts on the deck in which situation these desperate characters were carried to sea'. There was some fun in Plymouth when the convicts were set loose with a diving bell, which was 'employed with a steam engine machine' to gobble up a mass of loose shingle, sand and mud before discharging it into a swampy morass, 'the noxious exhalations from which have often proved extremely prejudicial to the health of the inhabitants and troops of the garrison [about 150 yards distant]'.

As we have seen, the Hulks Act was periodically renewed, and in June 1823, under the Labour of Convict's Bill, Parliament authorised the use of hulks in any British colony, resulting in them being established in Bermuda in 1824 and Gibraltar in 1842. In both locations the convicts were involved in the levelling of land, constructing roads and the building of dockyards. By the end, in 1863, Bermuda had received some 9,000 convicts. At Millbank Penitentiary, in the latter part of 1823, there was a spate of dysentery and a large outbreak of 'sea scurvy', despite the cure having been known for many years. This was put down in part to the cold weather and reduction in the prisoners' diet. Furthermore, the huge new prison had been built on a swamp, making it extremely damp, and its foundations were sinking into the mud. At least thirty inmates died during the period, and in a hastily drawn Act of Parliament, 400 convicts on board the Woolwich hulks were sent off to New South Wales. Sir Robert Peel made the navy ships *Ethalion* and *Dromedary* available at Woolwich as hulks and they took on board a total of 467 men. The *Narcissus* and *Heroine* accommodated 167 women and it took several weeks before the evacuation was complete.

Naturally, disease accompanied the prisoners on to the hulks, but a report in April 1824 said of the ex-penitentiary convicts now onboard that 'since their arrival they have experienced a great improvement in their health being "well fed, healthy and robust"'. Despite, or possibly because of this renewed vigour, they were mutinous and argumentative, becoming more so as their health improved, with many attempting to escape. A few of the male convicts were employed in moving timber cables and rubbish, but the vast majority had nothing to do all day, which led to the trouble. The women were also subject to poor health and in March 1824 twenty of the

167 were in the shipboard infirmary with their spirits described as 'broken'. Most of them were pardoned rather than being returned to Millbank, as were a number of the better-behaved men, with many being released in that year. The remainder were moved back to Millbank in the summer, despite it having been reported that the penitentiary was to be immediately demolished (it was in fact whitewashed and restocked).

By January 1824 all the adult prisoners on the *Bellerophon* moored at Sheerness had been transferred to other hulks, leaving it available exclusively for 320 boys, many of whom were aged 14 or under. They were, in the main, convicted of minor crimes, and many were illegitimate or had been disowned by their families so that upon release they had nowhere to go and carried on with a career in crime. During their time on board, according to Capper's Commons Report of January 1826, they had produced 6,000 pairs of shoes,15,500 garments and numerous other articles. This situation continued until the end of 1825 when they were transferred to the former thirty-four-gun frigate *Euryalus*, which had been specially fitted out with workshops but was overcrowded from the start. The vessel was eventually to house 383 juveniles, but without any classification that would separate the bad from the vulnerable. Even Capper was eventually forced to admit in 1828 that '8 out of 10 that have been liberated have returned to the old courses'. Discipline was very lax with below decks largely ruled by a set of older bullies who controlled the food supply. The whole enterprise was judged to have been a failure. Capper was questioned about the situation on board and described it as 'quite melancholy to see some of them, they can hardly put their clothes on. Some from Manchester deemed incorrigible are obliged to be dressed by others.' 'Are they allowed to play games?' he was asked. 'There are no games allowed,' was the reply.

Perhaps even more distressing is that, unlike their elders, the young lads never left the ship from the moment they arrived until they were discharged. Their only respite from the relentless religious onslaught of the chaplain, Henry Dawes, was a walk around the deck in silence. Transportation must have come as a huge relief to some. In November 1838 168 boys were dispatched to Van Diemen's Land onboard the *Pyramus*, the most juveniles ever dispatched at one time.

The roll call continued. On 1 January 1824 the total hulk population of England consisted of 2,953. A further 2,801 were added to this number, including 410 who had arrived from Millbank. Some 1,885 of these had been transported 542 discharged by pardon or otherwise, fifteen had escaped and eighty-two had died, leaving a total of 3,230. The total cost of the stations at Portsmouth, Woolwich, Sheerness and Chatham during

1824 was £33,767, and the earnings of convict labour to be deducted came to £30,096. By 1828 there were 4,446 convicts in the ten English hulks, at a cost of about £73,000 that year, or around £17 per convict. There were fears that large numbers of convicts would be released back into society within seven years, whereas for less than twice that sum they could all be conveyed to New South Wales where the great demand for labour continued.

There was still the general feeling that the employment of convicts on public works was denying work to honest labourers and the question was raised in the Commons. Peel agreed but said that it was unavoidable as the expense of sending those serving short sentences to transportation was not viable when they could be employed profitably at home. Fraternisation between free labourers and convicts was also a worry as it could allow letters out and various contraband in. One newspaper, writing in 1825, calculated that one in every 500 of the population had been deprived of their liberty as a consequence of crime, imprudence or misfortune. Enlisting in the armed forces was still an option, and in April 1824 eighteen convicts from the *Leviathan*, stationed at Portsmouth, were pardoned on condition that they joined the Colonial African Corps, an infantry regiment consisting mainly of deserters, condemned men and Africans, and sent to the Gold Coast.

Bermuda 1826

About 3,500 miles from Woolwich lay the island paradise of Bermuda, where it was decided to send the most violent and destructive inmates of the English hulk system to work as stonemason's labourers building the docks. The first hulk, *Antelope*, was established in the government dockyard on Ireland Island. Four more joined shortly after: the *Dromedary* in 1826, followed by the *Coromandel*, the *Medway*, the *Weymouth* and hospital ship *Tenedros*, raising the compliment to between 1,400 and 1,600 convicts. The climate was perfect – for tuberculosis, yellow fever, ophthalmia and sun blindness. The intense heat meant that conditions on board were as bad as, if not worse than, they were in England. Capper played little to no part in the management of these hulks many miles from home, and even though he was ultimately in charge, his reports contained only statistics and the usual endorsements from the chaplains. The overseers reported to the colonial governors, who were pleased to have the use of convict labour, and there is no evidence to show that those in Whitehall took any interest at all.

Among those on board, there were many convicts from Ireland, some driven to crime through famine, others through attempts at, or mere contemplation of, political insurrection. Among them was John Mitchel, who recorded his experiences in his *Jail Journal*. Escape attempts were commonplace, but largely unsuccessful as there was nowhere much to go other than to hide on the island and try to intimidate the locals into giving food and shelter. Escape by sea was pretty hopeless. Those who tried were normally picked up by English patrol boats, returned and punished. A devastating epidemic of yellow fever swept through the island and the hulks during 1853, claiming more then 650 victims, 160 of them on board the ships.

The last hulk in Bermuda was deactivated in 1862, five years after their abolition in England. All that remained was an outpost in Gibraltar, the *Owen Glendower*, established in 1842 to construct Wellington Fort, with the transport ship being converted into a hulk upon arrival. Eventually the convicts – at one time numbering 900 – were moved to purpose-built prison cells within the dockyard and the hulk was used as a prison ship until it was realised that the whole enterprise was costing more than it would to employ free labourers. In May 1875 the scheme was abandoned after thirty-eight years.

The Middle Years

At Chatham on 16 October 1829 the *Dolphin* snapped its moorings and began to sink into the mud. Initial press reports claimed that up to 200 men had died but in fact it was only four: three had drowned and one was accidentally bashed on the head by a fellow convict. The near sinking was caused by a scupper hole being left open on the lower deck, but she was soon brought upright with very little damage and returned to service.

Capper's reports continued. At the beginning of 1830 he reported that there were now ten hulks stationed at Portsmouth, Sheerness, Chatham, Woolwich, Plymouth and Deptford, containing a total of 4,250 convicts, many under the age of 20. He was also proud to announce that earnings of the convicts amounted to £31,646, whereas expenditure was £37,626. His report was followed as usual by those of the chaplains, which had by now become so routine that the press didn't bother to report them, although, on this occasion, it was remarked that 'their moral behaviour is generally favourable doubtless less a consequence of moral improvement than the discipline in which they are kept'. There were, at this time, three convict ships in Bermuda containing 1,000 men and the proportion of earnings to expense was nearly the same, £13,000 as against £15,300. It was also reported that all the horses employed in Portsmouth dockyard, forty in number, had been removed and that the work was to be performed by convicts from the hulks – ten men to replace one horse.

An unnamed man who served time on the *Retribution* at Sheerness during 1826 gave evidence before a select committee on secondary punishment in 1832, describing an evening on board, during which they indulged in singing or smoking, dancing, brewing kettles of tea and fiddling with instruments from the chapel, with officers occasionally joining in and giving encouragement. Female 'friends' were allowed on board, contraband was traded, and bladders filled with spirits were secreted down a trouser leg or under a skirt. On another occasion he remembers dining on pheasant with beer, and other meats sent in by friends. All of which, if true, must have been a rare exception to the usual activities on board. He also describes how contaminated meat was served to the men while the good stuff was retained for inspections, and the same with bread, and clothing, which was supposed to be changed every six months, but he had spent eighteen months in the same slops. Upon discharge, the captain would present the prisoner with a book that he had to sign saying that he had received so many suits of clothes, shoes, stockings, etc., none of which had, in reality, been issued. Others examined described constant pilfering among the cons, a lack of washing facilities, fighting, and drunkenness. Upon the committee's recommendations, tobacco and visits from friends were no longer allowed and the hours of labour were increased. Before 1832 the men had been allowed to buy small quantities of tobacco, but for some reason the authorities decided to ban it, causing much dissatisfaction and disturbance and a corresponding massive increase in smuggling.

In June 1832 there was a serious outbreak of cholera at Chatham, with more than eighty cases, sixteen of which were fatal, including a nurse and Mr Conway, the surgeon. The disease was very little understood at the time and was facilitated by the filthiness among people crammed together in a debilitated state. It soon spread to Plymouth and Portsmouth.

October saw a most ingenious escape. Captain Beazely had been 'out for the evening' and told one of the convicts to make sure that his clothes were brushed ready for the morning. The felon had a much better idea: he dressed himself in the captain's clothes and walked smartly out of the gates. Unfortunately, we are not given his name or ship and therefore do not know if he was ever recaptured. Another cunning plan, which was uncovered before it could be put in place (at least on this occasion), was to send in some money inside a stone ink bottle. This seemed to be surprisingly simple. First, empty out the ink, then put in as many sixpences as you can afford, followed by some melted pitch to keep them in place, then the ink is poured back in on top, being very careful to check the weight doesn't exceed that of a full bottle of ink.

As regards remuneration for their work, the *Public Ledger* during December 1832 reported: 'out of each shilling earned for the government by the convict he is entitled to one penny which is carried to his credit; but of this he receives only one third weekly, the reminder being left in hand to accumulate until the end of his sentence, thus it sometimes happens that a man who has been six or seven years at the hulks on his discharge is put in possession of £10 or £15 added to which he is supplied with an additional sum of money to defray his travelling expenses home, be it ever so remote.' Remuneration differed between the hulks: at Woolwich, for example, there was an allowance of up to 4½d per day; at Gosport prisoners had an allowance of 1d per man for biscuits, tobacco and beer. Articles of clothing and sums of money given to the convicts upon discharge also varied greatly between locations.

Returning once more to statistics, on 1 January 1833 there were 3,898 convicts left in the hulks after transportations and the usual deductions, which included a total of 110 deaths from cholera during that year. Four more deaths occurred when sixteen convicts in Woolwich out on a working party ate what they thought was a nourishing patch of wild celery. Unfortunately, it was hemlock, and they were quickly seized with nausea, stupor and vomiting before being carried off to the infirmary at the Arsenal.

The following is a rough guide from various sources to show the daily routine of the convicts during Capper's time. Obviously, things varied from time to time and place to place, and from ship to ship, but it gives some idea.

3am	Cooks rise to prepare prisoners' breakfast, heating up several gallons of cocoa in a giant copper pot.
5.30am	All hands called by the ship's bell.
5.45am	Convicts muster on deck, stow bedding, visit the 'heads' to relieve themselves. Breakfast of coarse bread and cocoa eaten in silence. One of the three decks is washed, which is done every morning alternately.
6.45am	Ship's bell sounds nine bells. Proceed to labour. Taken ashore in two longboats about 100 men to each. On leaving the hulks their irons are examined by the guards, who also search their persons to prevent anything improper being concealed [...] in the event of anything being afterwards

found upon a prisoner the guard who searched him is made responsible. The prisoners are divided into sections of ten, each of which is then subdivided as the work requires. They may be delivered into the charge of dockland labourers or overlooked by the first and second mate who patrol the yard not only to prevent them from escape but also to make all parties attend strictly to their duties.

7.30am	Convicts begin work on the dockyards.
11.45am	Mustered and counted to make sure there are no escapes and searched to prevent any public stores being brought out of dockyard.
12 noon	Prisoners return for dinner, meat and potatoes. Dinners are served by officers and the prisoners are locked up in their wards to eat it. A watch, consisting of an officer and half the ship's company, is on watch where they remain until 12.40 when the other half relieve them. (On the board that *York* at Gosport and later at Woolwich convicts dined in sheds on shore.)
1pm	Prisoners return onshore for labour as before.
5.45pm (4.00pm in winter)	Return to the hulk, irons are examined and their persons searched as before.
6pm	Supper, 6oz of bread and a pint of gruel, a thin porridge made from oatmeal, sometimes augmented by a pint of soup or some meat and potatoes.
6.30pm	School commences. The drive for education came from the belief that it could prevent reoffending, but learning to read and write after a day of back-breaking labour in the dockyards was hardly relished.
7pm	Half an hour or so of relaxation. Reading or conversation.
7.30pm	Prayers in the chapel, not compulsory but popular as a break from the tedium.
8pm	Men mustered one last time before being locked in their wards for free association for about an hour.
9pm	Bedtime, lamps extinguished and hatches locked.

There were libraries on some ships The one on board the *Defence* contained such gems as *First Sundays at Church*, *Reflection on the Works of God*, and *The Rights and Worship of the Jews*. Dickens' *Household Words* and similar items were not to be seen as the chaplain objected to them.

On *Justitia* from around 1829 the weekly bread ration was lifted from 5 to 7lb. The supply of meat was still 'enhanced' by the daily delivery of ox heads from local abattoirs, but supplies of green vegetables were rare, which meant that scurvy was a constant problem despite the ease with which it could be fixed.

On Saturday evenings every prisoner would have to wash and shave in preparation for Sunday morning when they were inspected to make sure that their linen was clean and in proper repair. This was followed by church. The process of loading, unloading and marching convicts to work twice a day generated criticism. An 1831 Select Committee report pointed out that so much time was lost in the process that convicts actually worked two hours less than free labourers every day. Unlike their counterparts in land prisons, convicts in the dockyards were able to converse with fellow workers on the site. Efforts were made to keep them apart, but interaction was near impossible to avoid due to the nature of the tasks. Without communication, work could not be carried out effectively, and many men suffered terrible injuries when safety was compromised. The falling of stone and timber resulted in broken arms, legs and amputations. Death was not uncommon and was often covered up by officials. Prisoners were prevented from working in bad weather as it was thought unsafe to send them onshore on dark and foggy days. Furthermore, escape attempts were feared, and men were routinely searched by overseers. Mayhew observed, 'Here the officers proceeded to search under the men's waistcoats, and to examine their neckcloths, so as to prevent the secretion of clothes about their persons, which would enable them to disguise themselves, and to escape among the free labourers. No less than seventeen such attempts to escape had taken place among the *Defence* convicts in one year, though out of these only three got off.'

From around 1835 the system of rewards for good behaviour was refined. Upon arrival, a man would sleep on the lower deck, which was dark and stiflingly hot, and, if his behaviour was good in the opinion of the officers, he would be moved first to the middle and then upper deck; each deck was airier, drier and less crowded than the one below.

The great cholera outbreak of 1832 was 'attended with much loss of life', but, 'the proportion of deaths compared with the number of cases has been far less than the average in society at large.' There are no comprehensive statistics on the death rate during Capper's time. In the last quarter of the eighteenth century roughly one in three prisoners died and by the mid-nineteenth century things had greatly improved, despite the continued prevalence of vermin throughout. One convict stated that that he well remembered seeing the shirts of the prisoners, when hung out upon the rigging, so black with vermin that the linen appeared to have been sprinkled over with pepper. At other times the marshes or the state of the river itself were blamed for the various outbreaks of fever. The surgeons had, in some sense, taken on the role of the chaplains in their reports to authority and it was to be hoped that their scientific training would lead them to a more critical view of matters. However, it should be born in mind that any statistics from this period will be distorted by the fact that young and able-bodied men would have been selected for work in the colonies, leaving only the old and feeble. Nonetheless, as with the chaplains, there was a pressing need to keep a lid on anything detrimental to the status quo.

Despite his failings, not everyone was dismissive of Capper's efforts. During 1834, 'a unanimous desire was manifested throughout the whole service to present John Henry Capper Esq. the Superintendent, with some token of their regard.' A subscription was taken up among all the officers and guards to purchase 'a splendidly chased salver, and most elaborately finished centrepiece, each bearing an inscription bearing the universal sentiments of the whole service'. A dinner was given on Friday, 26 September at the Freemason's Tavern in Chatham, with speeches and toasts, and 'passed in the upmost harmony and conviviality'. Capper was on the committee of the South London Dispensary based at Melina Road, Westminster, a charity founded in 1814 for the relief of the sick and poor in Lambeth, Christchurch and Newington. He became treasurer in 1837 and chairman in the following year. He was also a director and trustee of the grandly named 'Australasian, Colonial and General Life Assurance and Annuity Company', based in Bishopsgate Street. Despite his lackadaisical attitudes, he couldn't have been all bad as he is shown to have been paying an annual two guinea subscription to the Marine Society, a seafarers' charity.

As a further indication that Capper was regarded with some respect, in 1835 he was asked to appear before the House of Lords Select Committee on Gaols for his views on using Dartmoor prison as a replacement for Millbank; his view was that Dartmoor should be used as a distinct place of punishment rather than as a replacement for the penitentiary. The committee recommended that the number of boys on the *Euryalus* be reduced, and some space was made for them at Parkhurst and Dartmoor prisons, reducing the total number of inmates to 140 by the following year. The number rose again in subsequent years, and over the next three years hundreds of older boys were transported to Australia. Eventually, those who would have been marked for the hulks were sentenced to terms in Parkhurst or Dartmoor and the *Euryalus* went to the breakers yard in 1843.

Also in 1835, there was a change in law that meant that Parliament agreed to pay the cost of transporting convicts sentenced to transportation from the various county jails to the various hulks, thus relieving the pressure on the local rates. In his report of March 1837, Capper mentions a great increase in the number of convicts during the last two or three years, which he says is due to the number of soldiers who were to be transported for various offences against military discipline and also, 'the continued arrivals in this country of numbers of the black population from the West Indies who are now convicted in the colonies and sent to England to be transported, ninety three in the previous year'. He also describes the situation in Bermuda as being excellent, 'costing less than one shilling per day per man who are mainly occupied in stone quarrying'. Further in his report, Capper gives a very interesting breakdown of convicts received during the year 1837; 1,366 were known to have been previously convicted, 1,862 were supposed first offenders, 836 were above 30 years of age, 1,897 were between 20 and 30 years, 1,130 between 15 and 20 years, 116 between 13 and 15 years and one prisoner under the age of 10. Of 110 military prisoners seventy-seven were received from British colonies, thirty-three from regimental depots in England and sixty prisoners were also received under sentences of the civil authorities in the colonies. Of the total received 3,341 were natives of England, fifty-nine natives of Wales, 271 were Scottish, 214 Irish, fifty-four natives of British colonies and thirty-one were foreigners. In 1838 the cost of maintaining the convicts in New South Wales and Van Diemen's Land came to £236,000.

The topic of transportation had often been debated in the House of Commons and in 1837 the government appointed yet another select committee, chaired by Sir William Molesworth, to consider the matter. Their findings are considered later. The question arose as to whether, now that New South Wales contained so many free and freed people, it was desirable for transportation to continue there. According to a press report in May of 1839, the Secretary for the Home Department was seriously considering the abolition of the hulks, which were admitted to be 'great nurseries for the most atrocious crimes', and considered by the police 'a sort of university for plunderers, where the science of depredation is taught in all its branches'.

In 1839 the government reduced the number of convicts sent to New South Wales and on 22 May 1840 an order in council ended transportation there for good. At the end of 1842 Newgate was so crowded that all those found guilty in November and December had to be crammed into the hulks, 'excepting those who have been selected as the first inmates of the model prison at Pentonville'. The female convicts would probably remain in Newgate until after the provincial Lent Assizes when 'they will be joined by other women under the same sentence of transportation'. This class of 'unfortunates', ran the report, 'are not what are designated "abandoned women", some of them are persons of superior education, but have become dupes to systematic villains'. The early Victorian period saw the growth of people and organisations interested in society's poor and unfortunate, mainly from religious motives. The 'benevolent ladies' who visited the women hoped to 'qualify them for the various graduations of domestic servitude according to their capacities, as persons of this description are anxiously sought after in the colonies, provided that they could carry out with them certificates of recent good conduct'.

On 5 September 1840 Capper married Elizabeth Forbes at Millbrook in Hampshire. He was 65 years old. No record has been found of any previous marriage or children and Elizabeth was sole executor and beneficiary under the terms of his will.

The year 1843 seems to have seen a deterioration in the health of the convicts, with even Capper reporting to the Commons, 'there are a great number of prisoners who are so totally disabled by disease as to render it generally impossible to carry their sentences into effect.' A Mr Risk reported that the diseases most prevalent are scrofula (Lymphadenopathy), phthisis (TB), pneumonia, fever and various bowel complaints. Of most interest is the evidence of Peter Bossey, the surgeon responsible for Woolwich, who again blames most illness on the convicts being delivered from various prisons: 'many are brought in in a state unfit for embarkation in consequence of various diseases, and so in enfeebled by the effects of imprisonment that they can scarcely support the labour of the dockyard till their strength has been restored by the cheering influence of regulated association and a solid animal diet. I conclude that the air, exercise and diet afforded during their stay in the hulks is of great service in recovering their powers and preparing them to prepare for their future voyage.' Bossey also noted that most of the men who died were housed on the lower or middle decks, which were permanently damp, poorly ventilated and evil smelling.

Attitudes were beginning to change. Towards the end of 1843 there were reports that the hulks were no longer to be used as convict establishments but only for housing men before they were sent out of the country. This was seen as a victory for those who not only opposed the hulk system but also wanted the manual labour performed by the several hundred unemployed free men. In Portsmouth the Admiralty gave orders for 100 extra labourers to be employed to replace convicts. Capper's Report for that year stated that of 3,954 convicts in the hulks, seventy-one had been previously transported, 1,154 could neither read nor write, and there were only four Jews. The following year it was stated that Millbank prison was to be the general depot for all convicts under sentence of transportation and that the hulk system was to be entirely superseded. On 31 December 1844 there were 3,160 in the hulks, 2,202 in England, 1,338 in Bermuda, and 313 in Gibraltar. There were eleven hulks in total: six in the home ports, four in Bermuda, and one at Gibraltar.

In June 1846 Robert Capper admitted to having been in full command of the hulks when ill-health caused John Henry to take to his bed in Lambeth Terrace. His long reign came to an end, with a pension of £240 per year. He took his nephew Robert with him into retirement, in receipt of a pension of £130 per year. His main achievement during thirty years was to keep a lid on the sometimes appalling conditions on the hulks, and the decision taken in 1817 to retrofit the hulks with secure separated housing below deck. In the census of 1851 Capper is aged 76, a 'retired clerk, secretary at Home Office', with wife, Elizabeth, aged 70, living at Sidmouth Lodge, Lower Tulse Hill, with three servants. He died on 1 November 1852 at Manor Park, Streatham, aged 78, and is buried at Norwood Cemetery, Lambeth.

The Williams Enquiry of 1847

Just before he retired, Capper was called upon to explain his management of the hulks to yet another committee. William Mawman Brown, a convict occupied as a nurse on the *Warrior* at Greenwich, contacted the reformist-minded MP for Finsbury, Thomas Duncombe, with graphic details about the appalling situation on board. Capper resigned before the enquiry began as he was too ill to take part.

One of the few ways convicts could communicate with the outside world was by having messages smuggled out, and, in 1846, this is what happened, with notes being passed hand-to-hand until they reached Duncombe. On 28 January 1847 the MP reported to the House of Commons what he had been told. The notes concerned the conditions suffered by the inmates, mainly at the hands of Peter Bossey, the hulk surgeon. Bossey was accused of taunting a dying old man who begged to die at home, laughing at him and telling him that he would die where he was. Among several horrific stories, he was accused of throwing freezing water over a man having an epileptic fit and threatening to flog him if it happened again, having men chained to their beds and lying in their own filth, punching a man with a grossly enlarged liver to 'break loose the collected fluid', and ordering a consumptive prisoner back to work, causing his death within hours.

The complainant, Brown, was an American prisoner doing twelve years for forgery, whose main evidence concerned the situation in Woolwich. A prison inspector, Captain William Williams, was called upon to investigate, and conducted his enquiry from mid-March till the end of April 1847, during which time he interviewed ninety-eight witnesses, sixty-four of them convicts. Williams was disappointed that he could not question Capper in person due to his ill health and had to content himself with Robert, who, it was said, emerged in a 'crestfallen' condition due to there being no doubt of the part he had played in general slackness and petty incompetence. Williams' general conclusion was that conditions were 'utterly disgraceful to a civilised and Christian country'. It had all been heard before, but this time it was without the obfuscation and distortions of Capper and his cronies.

When it came to Bossey, Williams found that many of the allegations against him were unfounded but had been reported in good faith. Williams thought it wrong that Bossey should be running a private practice with his brother in Woolwich, creating a conflict between his business interests and his duty to those on board. His record-keeping was loose and inaccurate, and his treatment of the dead was a reprehensible disregard of common decency, causing distress among the convicts. He was also using his post as surgeon to the hulks to engage in what must have been a very lucrative sideline training apprentices. Large numbers of autopsies were performed – giving the students ample opportunity to improve their anatomical knowledge – and they had a (literally) captive population upon which to practise. The inquiry found that Bossey was using the hulks as pseudo-teaching hospitals, visiting convict patients with groups of students to discuss symptoms, often accompanied by his brother. According to Williams, it was a great impropriety that they were 'left in charge of the hospital in the absence of the assistant surgeon, and [...] prescribing medicines, and performing such operations as bleeding, and passing catheters, the latter requiring much experience with manual delicacy and dexterity'. Bossey was allowed to retire on an excellent pension of £400 a year.

Among his other findings: punishment was excessive and largely unrecorded, despite regulations to the contrary, and no exception was made for those of obvious unsound mind; defective ventilation with the water closets inconveniently placed and imperfectly constructed with no vent to the exterior and effluvia flowing between the decks; imperfect light, making it impossible to read or even see distinctly without candles. Many of the officers were incapable of performing their duties satisfactorily due to age or infirmity, and others were so ingrained in a system of corruption and employing convicts to work for them privately that it was recommended that the whole system should be reorganised.

By far the worst of his findings was the utter filth that he found on *Justitia* and the hospital ship *Unite*: 'the great majority of the patients were infested with vermin, and their persons, in many instances, particularly their feet, were begrimed with dirt.' No regular supply of body linen had been issued and many had been five weeks without a change, and no record has been kept of when the sheets were last changed. When new patients arrived at the hospital ship old ones were turned out and new arrivals installed with no change of bed linen. Convicts were not supplied with a means of washing themselves and there was an extraordinary omission of green vegetables. Much of the oatmeal gruel was thrown overboard by the convicts themselves as inedible, in spite of their extreme hunger. Despite the terrible things that he uncovered, Williams stopped short of recommending the abolition of the hulks. Possibly he thought that the dismissal of Bossey and the Cappers was enough for things to gradually improve.

The casual approach to the disposal of the dead was another of the accusations that had led to the enquiry. It was claimed that a convict who had been taken onboard the *Warrior* in May of 1846 died a few days later and there was an immediate post-mortem whereupon his entrails were taken from the body and thrown into the river 'where dozens had gone before'. This in direct contradiction to the Anatomy Act, which stipulated that a body could not be dissected until forty-eight hours after death. It was reported that many prisoners believed that medical treatment was purposefully deficient so that they would die and their bodies sold for profit.

Captain Williams found that dying on board the hulks was a public affair, lacking in dignity. If a convict died in the night, his clothes and bed were ransacked by fellow prisoners. If they died after 8am, the nurse looking after them was entitled to their rations. When a death occurred at night, convicts in the sick bay shouted up to guards upon deck, and the corpse lay in full view until morning. The body was then carried in the under sheet of the bed and laid on the floor by the door of the hospital where it was scrubbed with warm water and soap, often attracting a crowd of other patients. It took time for a coffin to be delivered, and the body would lie under a sheet at the far end of the deck until it was collected. A burial ground did exist in the marshes near the hulks at Woolwich, but it was not consecrated. In 1841 the Inspector of Anatomy wrote to the Undersecretary of the Home Office, advising that interring dissected bodies of convicts in any parochial burial ground in London was a controversial topic. First, a double fee was required as the body came from outside the parish; second, the fact that these were bodies of convicted men could lead to an outright refusal from the directors. In a quarter of a mile stretch close to the marshes, their corpses were buried along the bank in shallow, sandy, unmarked graves.

In 2016 the remains of more than 200 people were found on 'Deadman's Island', off the Isle of Sheppey, in the mouth of the Swale and near the old hulk station at Sheerness. The remains were exposed due to rising sea levels and coastal erosion over the years, which is slowly washing away their final resting place, leaving wooden coffins and parts of skeletons sticking out of the mud. Any scientific analysis of the remains has yet to be made public, but it is thought that they date from the 1820s and 30s. It is possible that many were buried after a cholera outbreak on *Retribution* on the 1830s.

After Capper 1847–1857

In 1847 hulks were still stationed at Portsmouth/Gosport (the *Stirling Castle*, *Briton* and the *York*), and Woolwich (*Justitia*, *Warrior*, *Wye* and *Unite*), holding a total of about 1,400 convicts unsuitable or too ill to be transported and not fit enough to be housed elsewhere. Chatham, Sheerness and Devonport were no longer in use and since 1843 no convicts scheduled for transportation to Australia had been sent to the English hulks. The whole system was overhauled, diet was improved, the number of guards increased, corporal punishment diminished and an award for good conduct was instituted. This new broom was wielded briefly by Captain Herbert J. Voules, who, after a year, gave way to the Lieutenant Colonel Sir Joshua Jebb, whose aim from the start was to abolish the hulks entirely and house the prisoners onshore. Despite good intentions, things did not go well. The *Justitia* was by now falling apart from old age and was soon replaced by two small ships, the *Wye* and the *Hebe*, presumably to save money on refitting. The inmates were no longer classified but all shoved together on one deck, as they had been many years before. New guards were brought in, interfering with the largely self-regulating lives of the convicts, disrupting supply chains for contraband and the accepted pecking order. An increase in the quality and quantity of food meant that Voules thought it wise to stop paying the convicts' earnings regularly as there was no need for them to buy extra food. Again, this disturbed many established practices on board.

After the Williams Enquiry and the installation of Herbert Voules as inspector, rules and regulations were expected to be followed, and this did not go down well. On board the *York* at Gosport in 1848 ten convicts exercised almost complete control, inducing a general spirit of insubordination and rebellion, leading to fifty-three of the worst troublemakers being moved to Millbank. In June of that year, on board the same ship, convict William Atter smashed in the head of James O'Connor, one of the guards, who had had him flogged previously. Atter was hanged for murder in August.

It was quite understandable that few of these improvements were appreciated, and for some time the convicts were described as being in a state of 'sullen insubordination'. The *York* in Gosport was in a state of almost open mutiny over a long period. Attacks on staff became common and a number of serious mini-riots took place. In June 1848 a guard was murdered, resulting in a number of prisoners being transferred to land-based jails and the hulks in Gibraltar and Bermuda, with most of the ringleaders being transferred to Millbank. Things became fairly quiet for a while, until 1850 when trouble flared up again on the *Stirling Castle* at Portsmouth and the *York* once more. The authorities increased the number of guards, but it was by now recognised that the hulks were totally unfit for purpose. Public antagonism had increased, as had the views of most of the Commons. Added to this was the fact that they were increasingly expensive to fit out and maintain.

The policy of transporting the most hardened offenders was abandoned, as was the practice of allowing well-behaved prisoners to work out half their terms in the hulks before being recommended for free pardons. In its place healthy prisoners who behaved themselves were sent to Australia with 'tickets of leave', which, by the 1840s, opened up exciting prospects of a vast improvement on their miserable lives in England. Inevitably, many were dissatisfied, having had hopes of regaining their freedom at home dashed. There was a large outbreak of cholera on board the *Justitia* in 1848. Examination after the convicts had been removed established that she was beyond repair and her thirty-four years of service as a hulk came to an end. In similar vein the *Warrior* at Woolwich was fit only for the breakers yard. At long last those in power came to realise that it might be cheaper to build shore-based prisons rather than carry out costly repairs to rotting ships. Jebb, in his report, concluded, 'on reviewing the whole subject and the entire experience which has been gained concerning the occupation of the hulks, we cannot too strongly recommend that immediate measures be taken for abolishing them and building convict prisons onshore both at Portsmouth and Woolwich.'

In 1853 prison sentences were substituted for many convicts hitherto marked for transportation. In 1856 the government was able to abolish the use of hulks as temporary facilities to hold prisoners destined to serve their sentences abroad, except for hardened offenders whose crimes rendered them beyond redemption. Irish political prisoner John Mitchel, writing in the 1850s, believed that some Englishmen purposefully committed crimes to exploit the hulk system, declaring that 'hulking, as a profession, is as yet confined to England; [and] it will become a more favourite line of business there, as the poverty of the English poor shall grow more inveterate'. When men grew destitute and faced the workhouse, life as a convict was measured out against the negatives of offending. After all, prisoners were provided with three meals a day, and they mastered trades and learnt to read and write. When released, they were even given a little money. Nevertheless, government officials made every attempt to make life on board as punitive as possible.

The prison at Portsmouth had been finished in 1852 and the two hulks there were handed over to the Admiralty to be broken up, leaving only the hospital ship *Briton*. The convicts themselves were employed to tear apart the *York*, which they did with great relish. In 1855 the passage of the Penal Servitude Act substituted transportation for specific terms in land-based prisons. All that remained were the *Warrior, Defence* and the *Unite* hospital ship. On 14 July 1857 fire broke out on the *Defence* moored off Woolwich Arsenal, and the remaining 171 persons on board were safely evacuated to the *Unite*, thence to the invalid prison at Lewes. All that remained of an eighty-year 'temporary experiment' were those moored at Bermuda and Gibraltar. The prison hulk system was wound down and officially disbanded in 1857 after an eighty-year tenure, but their legacy as dark, terrifying places lives on.

Chapter 9

Case Histories III

The nineteenth century was no less fascinating in its collection of social outlaws and misfits as previous centuries, and again there is enough to fill many volumes. This is just a small taste of some of the more interesting cases.

Henry Phanton, 1826

On 15 April 1826 the *Northampton Mercury* reported that Henry Phanton, a brush maker from Birmingham, aged 15, John Andrews, 15, and William Andrews, 14, had been sentenced to death at the Warwick Lent Assizes. The three boys were convicted of 'burglariously entering' the workshops and warehouse of William Rostill in Birmingham and stealing ten boxes. Rostill was a dealer in tortoise shells, turtle shells and ivory boxes. The boys were spared the noose and their sentences were commuted to transportation for life, but before leaving England, they spent a year on board the prison hulks *Justitia*, *Retribution* and *Euryalus*, moored at Woolwich, Sheerness and Chatham. Henry Phanton lived for four months on *Euryalus*, specially fitted for juvenile convicts in 1825. More than 400 boys, ranging in age between 8 and 17, were packed into the ship. The chaplain, Thomas Price, lamented his charges' lack of moral and social restraint and reported that his efforts to combat their 'depravity' were hampered by the lack of a system of separating boys into different categories to assist with discipline. With such levels of overcrowding, disease spread quickly: scurvy and ophthalmia were two common complaints. The boys were employed in making clothing for the convict establishment and had to do so in the strictest silence. Only two hours' exercise was allowed daily and on Saturdays the boys were scrubbed all over with tepid water and soap. Relatives were allowed to visit under supervision, and escapes were rare.

The daily routine for *Euryalus* was as follows:

5am	Wake-up call. Ports opened, hammocks lowered. Boys washed and examined.
5.30am	Chapel – hymn and prayers.
6am	Breakfast.
6.30am	Elder boys report complaints to be investigated. Ship cleaned.
8am	Work in silence.
9am	Commander hears complaints and decides punishments – e.g. stopping dinner; caning 'moderately'; solitary confinement on bread and water.
12 noon	Dinner.
12.30pm	Air and exercise on deck in silence.
1.30pm	Work.
2pm	One third of boys sent to chapel for lessons in reading and writing.
5pm	Stop work. Boys clean ship and wash themselves.
5.30pm	Supper, air and exercise on deck.
6.30pm	File up and take hammocks down.
7pm	Chapel.
8pm	Muster. Hang up hammocks.
9pm	Absolute silence throughout ship.

On 22 March 1827 the three lads and 187 others set sail on the *Guildford* to start life in New South Wales. In November 1845 Phanton was reported as having absconded from the district to which he had been assigned and charged with cattle stealing. Nothing is known about the ultimate fate of the two Andrews.

The Howarth Bros 1827

Soon after midnight in the early hours of Monday, 6 August 1827, two young men were retiring to their lodging in Frome, Somerset, when they observed three men: one in a timber yard and two others standing nearby. Bravely, they approached the men, who ran off. The boys woke the owner, who grabbed a lantern and carving knife and the three made their way towards the wood store, where they found that the door had been broken open and a considerable amount of timber had been stacked outside ready to be carted away. They heard a rustling in the garden adjoining and Oxley, the owner, discovered a very powerful, ill-looking fellow with a drawn sword in his hand. The villain gave Oxley a tremendous blow on the head and stabbed him in the side, but he fought back, and a fight ensued, until the fellow cried for mercy and threw down his sword.

The arrested man turned out to be a millwright named George Howarth, and when the constables searched his home they found it crammed with stolen articles of every description among which were: elegant dresses, books, barrels of gunpowder, pistol bullets, Bath stove grates, a dog house, iron bars, new beams, sets of scales, new timber boards, chains, bags of hops, casks, velvet pulpit cloths and cushions, nails, screws, blocks, every kind of labouring and gardening tool, silver spoons, a tanned cow hide, leathers, earthenware, new brooms, servants' liveries, bags of feathers. Later, the house revealed yet more surprises. Secreted under floors in large recesses plastered over, and under the roof, were nearly 200 yards of fine cloth and a number of blankets stolen some time ago from the Parish Blanket Manufactory. There were curiously contrived swords for wearing under trousers, a quantity of cooper's timber stolen on a previous occasion from Mr Oxley, carpets, sheepskins, skeleton keys, etc.

The culprit was afterwards taken to the Blue Boar public house in Frome Market Place for the purposes of having his wounds attended to, but he managed to escape on Tuesday night or early Wednesday morning by leaping from a high window into the river below and gaining the opposite bank.

Howarth was described as: 'about five feet ten inches tall aged about 55 of strong muscular form; dark complexion with rather coarse prominent features and several wounds on the head, the hair of which is shaved off; a stab wound on the left side; and a cut across the upper part of the nose. He has an imperfectly cured fracture of his left leg slightly above the ankle which has made his leg slightly crooked and his gait slow, his feet are about 12 inches long and proportionately large, he weighs just over 12 stone, with dark hair turning grey, regular features; he has hazel eyes with thick bushy eyebrows nearly meeting over the nose, he speaks with a North Country dialect and is by trade a millwright like his brother but has worked as a sawyer, and a ships carpenter.'

A reward of fifty guineas was offered immediately for his recapture and was soon doubled to 100. He was later seen at Pen Pitts Woods, near Bourton, in Dorset. The *London Evening Standard* of 28 August takes up the story:

> He called at a lonely cottage by the wood in a near exhausted
> state one day last week and entreated the woman who occupies

it to bring him some water. At that moment he saw a person on horseback coming up the lane close by and immediately fell flat in the ditch until the person had passed; he then crossed into the wood in a very weak state and beckoned to the cottager to bring the water to him. She became alarmed at his extraordinary appearance and hesitated for some time what to do, but never having heard of Howarth's depredations, she charitably placed a jug of water within a short distance of him and then had the opportunity of observing him particularly. He still continued without hat coat or shoes, had the black plaster placed by the surgeon and the cut on the upper part of the nose and was in a very weak and deplorable state. When the woman returned to fetch the jug Howarth was gone but had left a part of his cravat with which he had been bathing his wounds. As soon as the above intelligence was communicated to Mr. Culverhouse, the constable of Frome Woodlands, he proceeded to the spot and was joined by all the respectable inhabitants of the neighbourhood when a general search was made but hitherto without effect. The pursuit is still going on and although the miserable fugitive is in that part of the ancient forest of Selwood where he can travel for nearly ten miles, want of food and clothing must prevent his proceeding much further without being apprehended, especially as hand bills offering 100 guineas reward and giving a full description of his person have been carefully delivered to every cottager in the neighbourhood.

Howarth was recaptured and placed before the magistrates on the following charges:

1. Stealing oak planks from the store room of Mr Oxley.
2. Cutting and maiming Mr Oxley.
3. A robbery at Christ Church in Frome.
4. The theft of thirteen blankets from the parish manufactory at Frome.

Local reports describe the appearance of 'the wretch' as really quite appalling: 'when the disguising cap was put on him, which he usually wore during his depredations, it covered the head to the top of his nose, leaving eye holes, and was really horrible.' Howarth was committed to Ilchester Gaol to take his trial at the next assizes on 13 September 1827.

The local papers had a field day with their new-found celebrity. Originally from Cheshire, Howarth was married, unable to read or write, and for about sixteen years, he and his brother had been in the constant habit of committing robberies of the most daring nature without awakening suspicion. Sheep and calves have been stolen from fields, joints of meat from butchers' shops, cloth from factories 'and even sacrilege has been committed by them [...] Frequently, innocent persons have been arraigned on suspicion of committing these crimes. They maintained the respect of those who knew them to such an extraordinary degree that to have spoken a word against their good name would have been considered an insult.'

Meanwhile, younger brother Ralph, 49, was also in trouble. He too lived an outwardly respectable life as a master millwright and member of the Methodist Church. Stolen goods were found on his premises, and he was tried and sentenced at the Bridgewater Assizes during August 1827 to two terms of seven years' transportation for stealing a gun and a sack, along with other items. Ralph was sent to the prison hulk *Captivity* at Devonport on 17 September 1827 to await transportation to Australia.

The Howarths did not plunder through want; they were clever as millwrights, seldom without employment and frequently earned three guineas a week each. Despite being journeymen mechanics with no other means of support than the wages of their labour, their neighbours were surprised at how they were able to afford such a profusion of good things and it seems that their generosity was equally astonishing. It was not uncommon for them to give away joints of meat. They had so much that they were in the habit of salting and drying joints of lamb, mutton and beef. The brothers' contempt for the established church was also clear: George's wife had a gown made from the clergyman's surplice, and Ralph's wife had a bonnet made of velvet made from the pulpit cushion. Also, 'When the church was robbed of these articles, the sacrament wine was drunk, and an indecency committed in the flagon which had contained it!'

While awaiting trial, George would not discuss any of the robberies but would readily answer any inquiry about his escape and recapture. After he left Knutsford Gaol he was taken to Birmingham and housed in the prison there. He boasted to the other prisoners that if he did not have such heavy irons on his legs he would get through the roof in ten minutes, and claimed that if he had two knives, he could cut the irons from his legs by 'hacking the knives against each other and making them into saws'.

Howarth's trial at the assize court in Taunton took place on 3 April 1828. He appeared dejected and stood with his arms crossed in a 'declining posture', with his head held very low. When asked to plead, he raised his head slightly and said in an almost inaudible voice, 'Not guilty'. He appeared very different from the fearless, muscular brute that many expected. In fact, such was the awe that Howarth inspired by his reputation that lithographic prints of him and his former residence were exhibited in many of the stationers' shops in Taunton.

The prisoner was asked if he had anything to say and replied that he did not but hoped for mercy. He asked the jailer's permission to sit down, which was refused, so he burst into tears and continued weeping for a short time. The jury found him guilty of the Oxley fracas, the theft of twenty-eight blankets from the parish to a value of £28, and of stealing timber on previous occasions from Joseph Oxley. The theft from Christ Church had occurred six years ago and the judge was of the opinion that the goods could have passed though many hands during that time and ordered the jury to acquit.

George was sentenced to be transported for a total of fourteen years on the burglary charges, but the matter was not over yet. One of the counts against him was that he had been in a garden 'for an unlawful purpose and that then and there, in order to prevent his lawful apprehension, he maliciously cut and stabbed with intent to murder'. His defence counsel raised several objections to this charge on a matter of law, and Justice Littledale ruled that it should be considered by a higher court.

The act in contention was Lord Ellenborough's Act, or the 'Malicious Cutting and Stabbing Act' of 1803, which carried a death sentence on conviction, if it could be proven that the cutting and stabbing had been carried out to resist lawful arrest while in commission of a crime. The defence's point was that Howarth had moved on, unobserved, from the scene of the crime, was no longer committing it, and that being in someone else's garden was not a felony. In which case Howarth was quite justified in defending himself and could not be convicted of that charge. The law was considered by nine judges and the trial judge. They unanimously decided that from when he was first seen in the wood store until he was captured in the garden using the sword to wound Oxley to avoid capture came within the meaning of the act as he was still in contemplation of the felony. The learned judge did not mince his words:

> Under these circumstances, said his Lordship, your life is forfeited to the laws of your country and from what I have ascertained of the catalogue of your offences you have certainly been a wicked and desperate character; the sentence of death must therefore be recorded against you; whether

you will suffer the penalty due to your crimes depends on the recommendation to be made to His Majesty. I would not have you flatter yourself that your life will be spared, but prepare yourself to meet the contrary event. If however the former should be the case it will be for the purposes of ridding this happy country of you for the term of your natural life.

Sentence of death was recorded against Howarth, but despite his strong words, it seems that Justice Littledale 'humanely interposed on his behalf', presumably seeing some good in him. He received a reprieve and was sentenced to be transported for life.

His brother, Ralph, who had been convicted of the theft of a gun and a sack received fourteen years and was moved to the hulk *Captivity* at Devonport on 17 September 1827. He boarded the *Claudine* on 19 August 1829, arriving at New South Wales on 6 December 1829. He died in 1859.

On 8 September 1828, at the age of 58, George Howarth was also moved to the *Captivity* to await transportation, which occurred when he boarded the *York* on 25 April 1829, arriving at Van Diemen's Land on 28 August. Presumably, the brothers were reunited on the *Captivity* for six months or so between 8 September 1828, when George was sent there, and 25 April 1829, when he was shipped out. They were transported on different ships to different destinations 1,000 miles apart and probably never saw each other again. George's fate has not been traced.

Tolpuddle Martyrs 1834

In 1833 six men from the village of Tolpuddle in Dorset founded the Friendly Society of Agricultural Labourers to protest against the gradual lowering of agricultural wages. They refused to work for less than ten shillings a week, at a time when wages had been reduced to seven shillings and were due to be further reduced to six. The Society's rules show that they operated as a trade-specific benefit society, led by George Loveless, a local Methodist preacher, and met in the house of Thomas Standfield. In 1834 James Frampton, a magistrate and land landowner in Tolpuddle, wrote to Home Secretary Lord Melbourne complaining about the union, recommending that Frampton use the Unlawful Oaths Act 1797 – an obscure law enacted in response to the Spithead and Nore mutinies that prohibited the swearing of secret oaths – to have them arrested. The Society's members – James

Brine, James Hammett, George Loveless, George's brother, James, George's brother in-law, Thomas Standfield, and Thomas's son, John – were arrested and tried together before the judge, Sir John Williams, in the case *R v Lovelass and Others*. All six were found guilty of swearing secret oaths and sentenced to be transported to Australia.

James Loveless, the two Standfields, Hammett and Brine sailed on the *Surry* to New South Wales, arriving in Sydney on 17 August 1834. George Loveless was delayed due to illness and left later on the *William Metcalf* to Van Diemen's Land, reaching Hobart on 4 September. Of the five, Brine and the Standfields were assigned as farm labourers to free settlers in the Hunter Valley. Hammett was assigned to the Queanbeyan farm of Edward John Eyre, and James Loveless was assigned to a farm at Strathallan. In Hobart, George Loveless was sent to the farm of Lieutenant Governor, Sir George Arthur.

In England they became popular heroes and 800,000 signatures were collected for their release. Their supporters organised a political march, one of the first successful political marches in the country, and all were eventually pardoned in March 1836, with the support of Lord John Russell, who had recently become Home Secretary, on the condition of their good conduct. When the pardon reached George Loveless some delay was caused in his leaving due to there being no word from his wife as to whether she was to join him in Van Diemen's Land. On 23 December 1836 a letter was received to the effect that she was not coming, and he sailed home on 30 January 1837, arriving in England on 13 June 1837.

In New South Wales there were delays in obtaining their return journey due to the authorities having to confirm their good conduct with the convicts' assignees and then getting them released from their assignments. James Loveless, Thomas and John Standfield, and James Brine left Sydney on the *John Barry* on 11 September 1837, reaching Plymouth on 17 March 1838. A plaque next to the Mayflower Steps in Plymouth's historical Barbican area commemorates the arrival. Although due to depart with the others, James Hammett was detained in Windsor, charged with an assault, and did not arrive back in England until August 1839.

Upon their return from transportation, the Lovelesses, Standfields and Brine first settled on farms near Chipping Ongar, Essex. The five later emigrated to the town of London, Upper Canada (in present-day Ontario), where there is now a monument in their honour and an affordable housing co-op and trade union complex named after them. George Loveless is buried in Siloam Cemetery, on Fanshawe Park Road East, in London, Ontario.

James Brine died in 1902, having lived in nearby Blanshard Township since 1868, and is buried in St Marys Cemetery, St Marys, Ontario. Hammett returned to Tolpuddle and died in the Dorchester workhouse in 1891.

Richard Wiltshire Loader, 1848

It all started well enough. Richard Wiltshire Loader was born in Stapleford, Wiltshire, in 1803, son of a grocer, and married Elizabeth Perry Morgan, the daughter of a yeoman farmer from Hampshire, in 1824. In 1832 their son Richard was born, and he and daughter Elizabeth were baptised at Fisherton Anger in Wiltshire. Both parents are described as publicans, living at Quidhampton, Wiltshire. By the census of 1841 they had moved to Balcombe in Sussex. Richard, now aged 38, with four children, had become Superintendent of Police for the district. He was apparently governor of Horsham Jail until that was closed in 1845, upon which he was given a handsome remuneration for his loss of income. He joined A Division of the Metropolitan Police, covering Whitehall, and rose to the rank of inspector.

On 1 February 1847, upon the highest recommendation, he was appointed Overseer of the hulk *Justitia* at Woolwich with a salary of £200 p.a. One of his duties involved paying the men and various tradesmen, for which he would put in an invoice before collecting and cashing a cheque for the appropriate amount. In May 1847 he collected a sum totalling £750. Mr Knowles, the quartermaster on board the hulk, remembers Loader coming back with the money in the evening, saying that he felt ill. In the morning he had gone – and so had the money. It emerged that he had been in the habit of borrowing money from subordinate officers and not repaying it, and that when he fled, he took with him a watch and gold chain belonging to one of the prisoners (this had been placed in Loader's safekeeping, along with all the valuables belonging to many other convicts during their confinement).

In June 1848 adverts appeared in the papers offering a £50 reward of information as to the whereabouts of Loader, who had 'absconded with upwards of £400 of government money'.

Nothing more was heard from him until shortly after 7am on Tuesday, 3 April the following year when there was a knock on the station house door in King Street, Westminster, which was answered by one of the constables. Loader explained that he had come to give himself up. Inspector Otway of A Division, Loader's old work colleague who had known him for about sixteen years, came into the room and the prisoner burst into tears. He began apologising for not giving himself up before, saying he was 'very much oppressed'. When asked about the money, he said that he had been all over the country and that it was all gone, apart from 12s 2d.

Loader was taken before the magistrate at Bow Street and admitted to all the charges in a very distressed state. He was remanded in custody until his appearance at the Old Bailey on 9 April 1849, where he again pleaded guilty. He was given a sentence of seven years' transportation, upon which he collapsed in the dock. He was taken to Newgate on 2 May where he is described as aged 46, weighing 14st 11lb, and bizarrely named as a 'hulk overseer and grocer'. His health and behaviour were described as good. Because of his guilty plea there was no examination in court, and we are denied any further information about his motivation or mental state, but it is probably safe to assume that he had a severe mental breakdown, which caused him to destroy an exemplary career and wreck his family.

On 11 June 1850 he was moved to Portland prison, where he is described as a grocer aged 48. It is possible that he was allowed to disguise his true profession for his own protection and adopted his father's occupation. He wasn't there for long as, on 24 October, he was visited by wife, Elizabeth, and son, Richard, in Pentonville, and again on 22 May 1851. On 14 July he was granted a conditional pardon. The authorities must have taken pity on him as he served little over a year in prison. There is a letter from the Home Office, dated 19 April 1853, in response to Elizabeth Loader asking for a free pardon on behalf of her husband. The response is: 'I am to say to you that your husband has already received a greater degree of indulgence then the gravity of his offence would have in entitled him to expect, Lord Palmerston does not feel justified in advising her Majesty to interfere further in his favour.'

On the census entry for 1861 he is listed as a lodger living at 28 Surrey Street, Brighton, aged 57, and 'formally a brewer and grocer'. Head of the house is William Baily, a coffee-house keeper, but the surprise is that on the entry below is Sophia Loader, 'wife', aged 46, marked as deaf and from Lambeth, and also listed as a retired brewer and grocer. We know that his wife, Elizabeth, was still alive, so Sophia is either a common-law wife or in a bigamous marriage. All we know about the rest of his life is that Richard Wiltshire Loader was buried in Darlington, Durham, towards the end of 1863, when he would have been aged 60.

In the 1851 census Elizabeth is aged 46 and a school mistress at the Union House (Workhouse) in Yeovil, with daughter, Sarah Maria, now 11 and a scholar. Ten years later she is following the same occupation at the Stockbridge Union Workhouse, Hampshire. She died in 1868 and was buried in South Norwood, presumably having retired to stay with one of her children.

Miles Confrey, 1854

Miles Confrey was convicted at Portsmouth on 23 October 1852 for stealing four pairs of trousers – his third conviction for a felony – and received a sentence of ten years' transportation. He was described in the *Police Gazette* as originally from Manchester and aged 23, 5ft 6in tall, light brown hair, grey eyes, fresh complexion, slightly made, single, and 'of bad character'. After a brief spell in Portsmouth jail, he was sent to the prison hulk *Defence* at Woolwich on 8 November 1853, from which he escaped on 20 October 1854, never to be seen again. His occupation was given as 'tailor' but his tattoos make sailor more likely. On his right arm he had a crescent moon and seven stars – the Pleiades, worn by navigators as a directional symbol – a cross, and a ship. On the left was a 'sailor's farewell scene' of a couple, a mermaid, a boxer and an anchor, standing for hope and security. The work on his chest is hard to interpret, possibly a couple dancing, but what the initials stand for only he would know.

Chapter 10

To the Ends of the Earth

The First Fleet, 13 May 1787

Many of the felons living in horrific conditions on board the hulks hoped for release in one of two ways. The possibility of a pardon, however faint, was entertained by the more compliant inmates who obeyed all the rules, while the more criminally minded, dreaming of a better life away from the slums of their former existence, hoped to be transported across the seas. Few convicts with useful trades or skills were sent with the First Fleet. In fact, the process of selection was rather shrouded in mystery if there were any established criteria at all.

Selection procedures were supposed to be based on the principle that a convict went to Botany Bay if eligible to be transported. No other considerations – possession of skills, good or bad behaviour – were supposed to prevail, and given that these undernourished and desperate people were supposed to construct a new colony from scratch, such a policy seems particularly short sighted and has been described as a 'Noah's Ark of small-time criminality'.

When Capper was called to give evidence much later in 1812, the system was more refined and he claimed that males under the age of 50 sentenced to more than fourteen years were selected first, and then, if there was room on the ship, those facing seven years. Healthy female convicts under the age of 45 were also generally favoured, but Capper denied that this was due to the possibility of marriage and childbearing. In short, those selected had to be useful to the future of the colony, and he also mentioned, almost in passing, that the most dangerous and disruptive felons could also have priority.

In the spring of 1787 the multitude was slowly assembled for the first great adventure across the sea. The exact number of persons on board is uncertain, but there were 775 convicts in total, 582 men and 193 women, including 210 from Woolwich who had been sent to Portsmouth at the end of February 1787 in thirty guarded wagons. In addition, there were around 550 crew, soldiers and family members, approaching 1,400 in total. The numbers arriving had been awaited with much trepidation in the community and as the wagons passed by in dreary procession the town residents closed their shop windows and doors, fearful for their lives and property. The streets were lined with troops as the prisoners passed along to Point Beach, where boats waited to carry them onto the transports. This First Fleet of eleven ships, the largest single contingent to sail into the Pacific Ocean, consisted of two Royal Navy escorts, *Sirius* (flagship) and *Supply*, six convict transports, the *Alexander, Charlotte, Friendship, Lady Penrhyn* (women), *Prince of Wales* and the *Scarborough*, and three store ships: the *Borrowdale, Fishburn* and *Golden Grove*. The total cost was estimated to have been more than £54,000.

The successful tenderer for the shipping was William Richards, a naval contractor who gave a good deal of thought to the health of his passengers. Observers agreed that the food provisions were excellent and 'of a much superior quality to those usually supplied by contract'. Richards had also given some thought to convict behaviour: the potential for quarrels when they had to sleep together four to a berth (he thought individual hammocks would be better); their jealousy when some were dressed better than others (he thought there should be a uniform); the influence that the wicked exercised over the others (there should be three classes of felons, on separate ships). In those days, as now, it was generally thought best to segregate youths from hardened, older offenders. Richards was particularly concerned to teach 'the poor fellows' the virtues of hard work, and to reform them. He believed that the intention of the sentence to which they were ordered was to punish them for their former deeds, and turn them from their bad companions, working at a moral reformation.

Despite this high-minded attitude, it was, of course, no pleasure cruise. Surgeon John White was horrified to realise that for months, all the convicts had been fed on salt meat, the poorest diet possible for a long sea voyage, and immediately improved the quality of the food. The surgeons had to try to stem the jail fever raging on *Alexander*, the first ship to embark prisoners, in what was almost a running battle beyond their medical capability. Conditions differed from ship to ship depending on the captain, but, in general, convicts were confined below decks in the stifling heat and stench day after day. Rats, bedbugs, lice, cockroaches and fleas made a meal of all on board. The bilges became foul with an overpowering smell and the chief surgeon reported that forty-eight people died on the journey, about three per cent of the total, though there were also twenty-eight births.

As with any new enterprise, it was beset with problems. Insufficient clothing had been provided for the women convicts, there was no small arms ammunition for the marines and their officers, who had to bluff the 500 or so convicts, all rebellious and resentful, until Rio De Janeiro, where it was possible to buy 10,000 musket balls, and to make things worse, an insufficient number of irons had been provided. After 252 days at sea, and 15,000 miles, the first ship, the *Supply*, arrived on 18 January 1788, and the last on 24 January. Since the first European contact by Captain Cook in 1770, seventeen years previously, not a single ship had returned. Convicts, settlers and soldiers were cast upon a totally unknown land. It might as well have been the moon for all that was known about it.

Their reported first contact with the Aborigines was interesting. The indigenous people flocked to the shore, curious, but warily waving their spears and shouting 'Warra, Warra!' as the fleet docked, which, it later emerged, could be politely translated as 'Go Away!' – the first recorded words spoken by a native to a white man. The Aborigines, or more particularly the Eora people, who had lived on the land in isolation for 40,000 years, met the British in an uneasy stand-off at what is now known as Frenchman's Beach at La Perouse. Some reports indicate that the natives were initially perplexed as to exactly what these strange arrivals *were* and largely ignored them. The Europeans, on the other hand, reacted with fear and hostility, particularly when their possessions started to disappear, not understanding that in Aborigine culture items were held in common.

It is easy to underestimate the effect that the settlers had on the local population, who had lived contentedly off the land for millennia. The new arrivals did not understand the environment, nor, in the early years, did they have much success in finding fertile land or growing enough to feed themselves. They brought with them many new diseases, to which the locals had no resistance: smallpox, tuberculosis, influenza and measles. While the exact number of deaths caused by disease is unknown, in less than a year more than half of those living in the Sydney Basin had died from smallpox. Changes to diet also became a source of ill health among the aborigines, and much distress was caused by restricted access to their traditional food. Native land was fenced off and animals shot for sport, along with the introduction of hooved animals such as sheep, which trampled and destroyed local plants that served as staple foodstuffs. The natives' culture was effectively ended; the land had been declared *terra nullius* – no man's land – and European Australia was established in a simple ceremony at Sydney Cove on 26 January 1788.

The commander of the fleet was 49-year-old Captain Arthur Phillip, an experienced seaman who had been at sea since the age of 13, and an old shipmate of former purser, now Home Office Undersecretary, Evan Nepean.

Phillip was appointed by Lord Sydney and became governor-designate of the new colony. They first anchored at Botany Bay but found it to be too shallow and without a large enough supply of fresh water. The land was very poor and the trees were practically indestructible, so they moved five miles further on in search of a deeper anchorage and a more hospitable site. Eventually, they settled on Port Jackson, now Sydney Cove, and established the first colony. Interestingly, the first settlement in Australia was, and still is, referred to as Botany Bay, even though no convict base was ever established there. The initial settlement was a disaster. Convict and marine starved together in a hell of mutual loathing and mistrust, with the majority of marines refusing to help maintain order after disembarkation. The expedition had been short-changed by its suppliers, and primitive attempts at farming failed due to drought, disease, rats, cutworms and hungry parrots. Everyone was so hungry that any produce was stolen and eaten before it had started to grow to any size, and clothing was soon reduced to rags. Supply ships were often not sent, or were wrecked while navigating the eight-month voyage. The supply ship *Guardian* was severely damaged by an iceberg in thick fog off South Africa in April 1790 and never reached the colony; *Sirius*, one of the colony's naval vessels, was wrecked on Norfolk Island on the way to China seeking food. In desperation, the tender, *Supply*, and the colony's second naval ship, was sent to Indonesia for food. Hopes were raised when a vessel arrived in Port Jackson in June 1790; it was not the *Supply*, however, but the Second Fleet delivering over 730 more starving and desperate people, including 222 women.

Many of these new arrivals, described on the voyage as 'humble and submissive', were sick or unfit for work and the condition of the healthy deteriorated with hard labour and poor sustenance. As one convict described it, 'We have to work from fourteen to eighteen hours a day, sometimes up to our knees in cold water, 'til we are ready to sink with fatigue.' The food situation reached crisis point and it was only the arrival of the Second Fleet with its meagre supplies that helped to alleviate the crisis. Somehow, the little community survived, working parties were organised, land was cleared, and a community of sorts was starting to be built under the leadership of Arthur Phillip as first governor.

The experiences of these convicts were to be very different from those of their American predecessors. After landing, they were put to work in a penal environment under tighter control than convicts sent to America. They fell under the direct supervision of the government and were subject to discipline, including the use of chain gangs, convict barracks, slop clothing and forced labour. They could not buy their freedom, as those shipped to

America had. Convict servants in America were essentially treated like indentured servants, enabling them to blend in with the general population. In Australia, convicts and indentured servants were separate entities. Prisoners were considered government property with few rights; most considered the term 'convict' to be offensive and referred to themselves as 'government men'.

Even the precise nature of the new government was undecided. In October 1786 Under-secretary of State Evan Nepean wrote, 'The form of government is not yet settled, though I rather think it will be a military one.' The government had been trying to merge an unstructured community with a military force, resulting in an obvious instability, and it should be remembered that except for George Moore's earlier debacles, transportation was being resurrected after its demise in 1775. A new generation of inexperienced legal officials ran things in London, which is why the story of the First Fleet gives the impression of things being made up as officials went along. Phillip regarded the convicts as servants of the Crown until their full terms had expired and kept them at labour. Back in England many believed that the reintroduction of transportation would mean the end of the prison hulks in the Thames, but that was far from reality.

The Second Fleet, 3 June 1790

The Second Fleet left in December 1789 and became notorious as the most disastrous trip in the history of penal transportation, its human cargo were severely abused and exploited by the private ship owners and former slavers, Camden, Calvert & King. The ships consisted of *Lady Juliana*, *Surprize*, *Neptune* and *Scarborough*. Some were former slave transports equipped with slave shackles, with iron bars placed between the ankles, rather than chains and ankle irons, which prevented even the slightest movement. Seawater often entered the bowels of the ships, soaking all who lay below decks. Reports suggest that the starving prisoners lay, chilled to the bone, on soaked bedding encrusted with salt, faeces and vomit, festering with scurvy and boils. Tales of horror abounded. Starving convicts kept back the bodies of the dead and took their rations until the smell made them give them up. The convict Thomas Milburn wrote the following to his parents: 'I was chained to Humphrey Davies who died when we were about half way, and I lay beside his corpse for about a week just to get his food allowance.' There was enough on board to feed the convicts, but the ship owners withheld the supplies until after the convicts had disembarked, upon which they sold them to the starving inhabitants at an open market on the shore. Of 1,006 convicts, 267 died and 486 were sick from scurvy, dysentery and fever, and 150 perished on arrival, making it the largest death rate of all British convict transports. One hundred and seventy-eight men and eleven women died on the *Neptune* on the passage out. Out of 500 passengers, forty-two were able to crawl from the ship, the rest were carried, and eight out of every ten died at Sydney Cove.

Governor Phillip wished to punish the author of these calamities but doubted his power over offences committed on the high seas. Depositions taken later by the solicitor of the Treasury described the suffering on this voyage as equal to any endured in the slave ships. Before the horrors of the Second Fleet became widely known, the contractors signed contracts for the Third Fleet in great taste. This was due to sail to Port Jackson the following year with 1,820 English convicts and 200 Irish. Despite the outcry in London after details became public, the Navy Board did not impose any financial penalty on the contractors. An enquiry was held but no attempt was made to arrest Donald Traill, master of *Neptune*, who was described as a demented sadist. Traill and his chief mate, William Ellerington, were privately prosecuted for the murder of an unnamed convict, seaman Andrew Anderson, and cook, John Joseph, but after a trial lasting three hours before Sir James Marriott in the Admiralty Court, the jury acquitted both men of all charges 'without troubling the Judge to sum up the evidence'.

The Third Fleet 1791 and Bunbury's Concerns

Between February and April 1791, the Third Fleet arrived at Port Jackson. Those who had survived the voyage were in scarcely better condition than their predecessors. Of the 1,864 convicts, almost one in ten died on the voyage and 576 were sent to the hospital on landing. The survivors were in such poor condition that they became nothing but a burden on the starving wretches already there. During the voyage, convicts on board the *Albemarle* attempted to take over the ship by knocking out the guards and seizing their arms. The attempt was unsuccessful. Two ring leaders were hanged immediately and the others severely flogged.

In 1792 war broke out with France and between 1792 and 1800 only eighteen convict ships went from Britain to Australia as the ships were desperately needed for the war effort. Only eighty-five convicts arrived in 1794, and 353 in 1796. The publicity around the horrific scenes on board the *Neptune* had led to greater precautions to protect the lives and health of the convicts. They were now less crowded, and each ship carried a naval surgeon.

In 1793 Bunbury's concern for the situation of those transported resulted in him delivering his 'Resolutions respecting Convicts for Transportation' to the House. He made six points:

1. That the hulks were now unnecessary due to improvements in local jails;
2. That the confinement felons in Newgate, other jails and the hulks for months waiting transportation is productive of many evil consequences;
3. That a proper prison should be provided for their reception;
4. That the distance of the settlements is so great that it should only be used for those serving fourteen years to life;
5. That a return to transportation to America should be explored;
6. That to preserve those criminals who may hereafter be transported from a calamity similar to that which destroyed the greater part of the unfortunate men of the *Neptune* and to rescue them from the dangers of foul air and famine it seems expedient to allow at least two tons for each person; in addition to regulations already in place, a premium should be given to the contractors, on the arrival of every felon in good health at the place of their destination; and all the provisions on board of the ships hired to carry convicts, should be purchased for the service of government, and the surplus, at the end of the voyage, be deposited in their storehouses.

Bunbury was congratulated by the House. It was commented upon that things were improving and that the question should be considered more 'maturely' at a later date. The matter was adjourned.

As the colony expanded, newly formed companies for service in Australia began to arrive and more farms became established, some started by 'Emancipists', those convicts who had achieved a degree of freedom through pardons or having their sentences reduced. The skilled and hardworking convict could save money to pay for a passage back to England or work their passage back as seamen or carpenters. Slowly, agriculture took hold and the colonist began to look inwards across this vast continent rather than out towards the ocean. There were only three ways a man might gain his freedom: an absolute pardon from the governor, which was very rare and gave him back all his rights including the right to return to England; a conditional pardon, which granted citizenship but no right of return; and the 'ticket of leave', which freed him from his master and forced government labour, enabling him to find his own work, providing he stayed within the colony. These were normally given after four years of a seven-year sentence and had to be renewed every year, but they could be revoked at any time for trivial offences. Generally, wives were not allowed to go into exile with their husbands unless he had obtained his ticket of leave and had shown that he could support a family.

When Phillip left office in 1792 due to ill health, the population of the colony was 4,221, of whom 3,099 were convicts. His place was given temporarily to an army officer, Francis Grose, who unmercifully exploited the convicts and changed a fledgling civilian administration into a military one. A booming trade in alcoholic spirits – most notably making rum – sprang up, making an enormous profit for the officers concerned. They obtained control of the courts, management of the land, public stores and convict labour. After the poor harvest of 1793, Grose cut the rations of the convicts but not those of the Corps, overturning Phillip's policy of equal rations for all. The custom of officers trading in spirits was almost universal and during this interregnum the colony was rife with drunkenness, gambling, licentiousness and crime. John Hunter, another naval man, was the next to take charge, but his attempts to dislodge the Rum Corps, as they had become known, was in vain and he became the subject of a smear campaign that caused him to be recalled in 1800.

The *Lady Shore* Mutiny, 1797

Sometimes, a well-planned mutiny can be successful. Under the command of Captain James Willcocks, the *Lady Shore* sailed from Gravesend, bound for Botany Bay in May 1797, with food, farming equipment and fifty-eight soldiers for the New South Wales Corps, many of whom had been conscripted forcibly, and included former deserters and dissident Irish, none of whom wanted to go to Australia. There were also 119 prisoners and a crew of only twenty-six. Among the prisoners were two Frenchmen who had made two previous escape attempts, Sélis and Thierry. On 28 March 1797 these two, and six other former escapees, were on the *Lady Shore*, bound for Botany Bay. Once aboard, the Frenchmen decided that their only means of escape was to seize the ship, and recruited fellow prisoners, three Germans and one Spaniard.

At 2am on 1 August 1797, after eight weeks at sea, the prisoners crept into the sentries' station while they slept and seized their weapons. They had planned carefully, with each man having a specific task during the takeover, and at the shout of '*Vive la République!*', the mutineers took up their fighting positions: one man controlled the hatch to the women's quarters; two more the hatch of the quarters where the soldiers slept, threatening to kill anyone trying to get out; two covered the deck and were to shoot any sailor or soldier present who would not surrender; two controlled the hatch of the officers' quarters; two were to arrest the captain; two were to seize the three officers on deck and prevent them from giving alarm; and the last one would open an ammunition box, distribute it to his fellow mutineers, and patrol the ship to prevent anyone from outflanking them.

Seeing two armed mutineers, the first mate, Lambert, fired and mortally wounded Delehay, one of the Frenchmen, but was killed immediately. Captain Willcocks received three bayonet wounds and died two days later. Some of the soldiers tried to climb on deck, but the men on the hatches repelled the attempt, sealed the hatches and disarmed the crew. The British officers had to sign a certificate of seizure, as was the custom when a prize was taken at war. The French recruited some of the prisoners – seven Irishmen and four Englishmen – to help sail the ship, and elected Sélis as captain and Thierry as lieutenant. The two wrote a set of regulations, threatening death to any Frenchman colluding with the British or talking of surrender in case of an encounter at sea, with the same to any British man caught with weapons or fomenting another mutiny, and fifty lashes for anyone speaking ill of the republic. These regulations were translated into English and posted all over the ship.

On 14 August, fearing that their prisoners might be difficult to control, the mutineers singled out some of the officers and soldiers, and after having them pledge not to fight against France and her allies for one year and a day, they were provided with navigation instruments and food, and cast adrift in a long boat off the coast of Brazil with their wives, children and four convicts; twenty-nine people in total. They safely reached the shore, 300 miles distant, two days later and eventually made their way England.

Lady Shore sailed on to Montevideo, arriving on 31 August. It hoisted the French colours and saluted the commanding ship with eleven cannon shots, and the harbour with fifteen. Initially, the Spanish contested the validity of the capture, removed all the prisoners, and arrested the three Germans and seven French, but after Sélis and Thierry protested to the Viceroy, and sought support from the French ambassador, the French prisoners were released. The Spanish retained the female convicts, distributing them as servants among the ladies of the city. Some became prostitutes; others had more luck and either married or became otherwise settled.

In November 1799 a Bow Street Officer arrived in London from Portsmouth with Jean Sanlard, alias Provost, who had been captured aboard a French frigate in the West Indies. Provost was recognised and arrested for having assaulted and murdered Captain Wilcox. He was tried and hanged. In 1804 four Englishmen were captured on board several Spanish vessels. Three turned out to be members of the New South Wales Corps, who claimed not to have been part of the mutiny. The ultimate fate of the *Lady Shore* is not known.

The Nineteenth-Century Thomas Bigge

On 6 August 1806 Captain William Bligh, formerly master of the *Bounty*, arrived in Sydney as the fourth Governor of New South Wales, at a salary of £2,000 per annum, twice the pay of his predecessor, Philip Gidley King, who had also tried to reduce the power of the military but without success. Bligh was known as a firm disciplinarian, who, it was hoped, would have the courage to stand up to the Rum Corps, but his confrontational administrative style provoked the wrath of these by-now established and influential settlers and officials. As the colony expanded, new land was needed for farms and the new cash crop of wool, with sheep runs ever increasing in size. Several ex-army and ex-convict businessmen were becoming wealthy by exporting wool to England, and continuing to deal in illegal spirits, in defiance of government regulations that forbade private trading ventures for profit. Bligh tried to put a stop to it, but by 1808 he, too, was out, overthrown in a coup d'état known as the Rum Rebellion, led by a group of powerful but illegal traders. Their corrupt reign could not last forever, and in that same year, the New South Wales Corp was renamed the 102nd Regiment of Foot and recalled to England in 1810.

Between the sailing of the First Fleet in 1787 and the end of 1800, forty-three convict ships had sailed from England or Ireland for Port Jackson. Between them they embarked 7,486 prisoners, 6,040 men and 1,441 women, of whom 705 men and fifty-one women died. The number landed at Port Jackson was 6,634: 5,304 men and 1,330 women.

In September 1819 lawyer and one-time Chief Justice of Trinidad, Thomas Bigge, was appointed by Lord Bathurst, the Secretary of State for War and the Colonies, as special commissioner to examine the governance and operation of New South Wales. His brief was to determine how far the expanding colony could be 'made adequate to the Objects of its original Institution', which he took to be a penal colony, pure and simple. Bigge investigated all aspects of the colonial government, then under the governorship of Lachlan Macquarie, including finances, the church and the judiciary, and the convict system over a period of two years, before returning in 1821. One particular complaint from the leading colonists concerned Governor Macquarie's policy of remediating ex-convicts back into society. His enquiries resulted in a total of three reports, from which it emerged that his views were far from progressive.

The first was published in June 1822, much of it dedicated to criticism of Macquarie's administration, especially his emancipist policy of promoting ex-cons to responsible or government positions, sometimes managing public works or official posts such as magistrates, solicitors and assistant surgeons. He found such appointments indulgent and expensive, giving convicts ready access to alcohol and entertainment. He claimed that the policy diminished respect for these roles as the emancipists had a 'low moral character' and did not have the necessary skills and 'pretensions' for the positions. He argued that the appointments were in fact an 'act of violence' to colonial society. He noted that convicts viewed transportation more as emigration than punishment and recommended that the usual seven-year sentences be increased and that they be assigned as cheap labour to wealthy landholders. He wanted the convicts to have no payment for their labour and advised that they only be adequately clothed, sheltered and fed by the colonists to which they were assigned. He also suggested a crackdown on the number of pardons and early releases and advised that no land grants be offered to emancipated convicts, who should instead form the basis of a future class of landless labourers. This policy would decrease the burden of the estimated £50,000 per annum cost of the convicts to the government and increase the production of British wool.

His second report was published the following year and concentrated upon the judicial system. The third report, published the same year, concerned the state of trade and agriculture and recommended the occupation of extensive tracts of land for sheep grazing. It analysed the farming and grazing systems, and he had particular praise for the methods of John Macarthur. Bigge thought wool growing to be the only clear source of profitable industry for the colony and advocated a policy of providing large grants or sales of land to rich colonists, including a contract of a million acres to a consortium of entrepreneurs known as the Australian Agricultural Company, granting these settlers the use of three convicts per 200 acres.

His reports resulted in the resignation of the liberal governor Lachlan Macquarie and his replacement by Sir Thomas Brisbane, who adopted many of Bigge's suggestions, including the formation of new penal colonies at Port Macquarie and Moreton Bay to serve as dreaded places of isolation and punishment for the convicts. As recommended by Bigge, a designated number of convicts were assigned to the colonists in proportion to the size of their land acquisition. These decisions put an end to the socially progressive policies of Macquarie and reaffirmed strong class distinctions within colonial society.

An unattributed overview of the costs of the colony and its alternatives was published in the *Derby Mercury* for 7 December 1825:

> The entire expense of New South Wales from its settlement in 1788 to December 1821 was £5,301,023 16 shillings and six pence for which 33,155 persons were transported and subsisted and all the civil, naval, military and other expenses of the colony paid. To have kept the same number during the same period in hulks would have cost the nation, including the fitting up of the necessary number of hulks, 40 at least, £7,214,486 and three shillings. And to have subsisted and managed them in penitentiaries, upon the most economical plan, would have cost for superintendence and subsistence only £7,943,221 and the expense of erecting the necessary number of penitentiaries, 40 at least on the least expensive plan yet effected would have amounted to £8,366,640 making the total for penitentiaries £16,309,861.
>
> The labour performed in New South Wales is much more valuable than that of prisoners in hulks or penitentiaries; in fact, the employment of convicts at home where there is a super abundance of free labourers, is of no benefit whatever, but a serious evil, as it must throw out of employment an equal number of free labourers who will come onto the poor's rate for subsistence. In New South Wales the culprit has the chance of becoming an honest and useful citizen; half the number of persons transported up to 1815 had in 1821, become free, and were heads of families, householders and settlers.
>
> This colony is certainly the fruit or the convicts' labour. It now contains a population of more than 40,000 souls who occupy upwards of 700,000 acres of land and possess upwards of 5,000 horses, 120,000 head of horned cattle, and 350,000 sheep. It contains five thriving towns, and several villages, it consumes British manufactures annually of the

value of £350,000, its exports amount to £100,000 per annum it employs upwards of 10,000 tons of shipping, and yields a colonial revenue of more than £50,000 per year.

It appears that the labour of preparing a farm of 30 acres with a three-rail fence, one acre cleared for a garden, and five for agricultural cultivation, with a cot-house 24 feet long 12 feet wide and 8 feet high, weather boarded and shingled could be completed by one convict in one year at an expense including materials of £19. This being the case what an advantage it would be to the labouring poor of England and Ireland and what a relief to the parishes if 5,000 families should annually emigrate from each of the two countries for the reception of whom 10,000 such farms could be prepared by the convicts already there!

In 1825 only seventy-five per cent of freed convicts chose to return to England, presumably finding Australia to have better opportunities than the slums and poverty of Britain. Australia was vast and largely empty, farming was taking off, towns were being built, the opportunity for personal advancement seemed without limit. Many transportees had been sent out for the most trivial of offences. They were not career criminals at all but victims of poverty and circumstance. Once introduced to this environment, they set to work to build new lives for themselves, but not everyone was happy with this state of affairs. It was announced at the end of the year that 'it is in the contemplation of government to render convicts sent to Botany Bay as serviceable as they are in the hulks, for which purpose about 150 superintendents are now getting ready to sail at the end of the month on a salary of about £200 a year.' This was to include several non-commissioned officers on half pay as, 'it has long been notorious that transportation has been for the most part of the convicts, a matter of choice, because on the arrival they become free and at liberty, while on board the hulks at home the labour, on compulsion, is a matter of dread. From this time however, transportation is also to become a real punishment.' Robert Peel seemed in agreement, and upon becoming Secretary for the Home Department introduced stricter measures for new arrivals, keeping them in isolation from the established population for an initial period.

Convict transportation peaked in 1833 when 7,000 prisoners arrived in Australia in one year. Conditions gradually improved and by the mid-1830s only six per cent of convicts were locked up. The vast majority worked for the government or free settlers, and with good behaviour could earn a ticket of leave, a conditional pardon or even an absolute pardon. While under such orders convicts could earn their own living. In 1836 the number of convicts in Van Diemen's Land was 6,475; in New South Wales the previous year the number was 20,207. In the earlier periods the supply of convicts had exceeded the demand and certain concessions were granted to settlers who were willing to maintain them. As the economy picked up, demand exceeded supply and obtaining convict labourers became, to a certain degree, a matter of favour, giving rise to complaints of abuse in the distribution, especially of the more skilled convicts. All applications for convicts were now made to an officer, called, reasonably, the Commissioner for the Assignment of Convict Servants, who was guided in his distribution of them by government regulations.

> Settlers, to whom convicts are assigned, are bound to send for them within a certain period of time, and to pay the sum of £1 per head for the clothing and bedding of each one. An assigned convict is entitled to a fixed amount of food and clothing, consisting, of 12 lbs. of wheat, or of an equivalent in flour and maize meal, 7 lbs. of mutton or beef, or 4½ lbs. of salt pork, 2oz. of salt, and 2 oz. of soap weekly; two frocks or jackets, three shirts, two pair of trousers, three pair of shoes, and a hat or cap, annually. Each man is also supplied with one good blanket, and a paillasse or wool mattress, which are the property of the master. Any articles, which the master may supply beyond these, are voluntary indulgences.

An account of the system of punishments was outlined in 1838: 'For the first act of insolence 25 lashes, for the second 75 or 100 and for the third, sent one year to the iron gangs, guarded night and day by the military and the triangles are always at hand to punish the indolent or insolent. If a convict has served half his time before he is sent to one of these gangs he has to commence a fresh as a new hand.'

Sir William Molesworth's Committee, 1838

By the late 1830s a strong current of opinion, fed by a growing anti-slavery sentiment, was running against Botany Bay and transportation in general. English liberals were hearing more about the system and were shocked by what they were told. It was time for yet another report, this time headed by Sir William Molesworth the 26-year-old MP for the Eastern Division of Cornwall, a friend of John Stuart Mill and a radical opponent of Melbourne's government, whose members he described memorably as 'the miserabilist brutes that God Almighty ever put guts into'.

This Parliamentary Select Committee was to 'enquire into the system of Transportation, its Efficacy as a Punishment, its influence on the Moral State of Society in the Penal Colonies, and how far it is susceptible of Improvement'. It began its deliberations in 1837 and produced its report in August 1838. They studied the moral and economic effects of the system on both Britain and Australia, including whether the threat of transportation was an effective deterrent to crime on the domestic front. Although supposedly objective, the young radical was accused of having been manipulated by Home Secretary, Lord John Russell, and Lord Grey, with the members 'hand-picked for their antagonism towards assignment and transportation and its support of free colonisation', with its opponents describing it as 'a show trial'. The twenty-three witnesses who testified were mainly anti-transportationists who were eager to deliver their testimonies describing rape, sodomy, child molestation, flagellation, and many other horrific vices, crimes and punishments. The aim was to show the colonies in as bad a light as possible. Molesworth and the committee argued that the convict trade to America had been successful because the convicts were merely 'dropped by driblets' into an established society of moral and ethical citizens. In Australia criminals were expected to build the settlements from the ground, creating a colony that was 'composed of the very dregs of society', the consequences of which included 'vice, immorality, frightful disease, hunger and dreadful mortality'. The report openly compared Australia to a slave colony, which anti-transportationists had done years before, describing transportation as 'inefficient, cruel, and demoralising', and the convicts' condition as one of unmitigated wretchedness, involving 'suffering such as to render death desirable'.

It was claimed that there were a very large number of convictions for new offences being committed and the contamination of free settlers by the almost universal criminality of the population surrounding them. Molesworth recommended that convicts should be punished at home in hulks or penitentiaries under the 'separate system' whereby prisoners were kept in solitary confinement to reflect upon their crimes. Transportation was supposed to terrify the criminal class into submission and act as a deterrent second only to the rope, but despite the increased severity of treatment in the wake of the Bigge Report, the threat of transportation was not a significant enough threat to deter crime back in England as most criminals knew very little about the brutal nature of a convict's life in the colony. Although more details of horrible punishments and harsh masters were making their way into Britain by the 1820s and 30s due to the greater availability of newspapers and first-hand reports, many lower-class criminals would have had limited access to these accounts.

In addition, the report claimed that convicts sent to Australia were not redeemed by their time there, but instead were hardened even further in their criminal ways. By forcing even petty offenders to live and communicate with the most callous criminals, 'transportation is not merely inefficient in producing the moral reformation of an offender; it is efficient in demoralising those whom accidental circumstances, more than a really vicious nature, have seduced into crime.' The committee claimed that convicts entering the system were very likely to exit it more corrupt and villainous than ever before. He also found that the system of assigning convicts to private masters was dysfunctional and open to abuse, promoting unequal treatment that had nothing to do with the nature of the offender's crimes.

In a Commons statement, Lord John Russell stated that it was the government's intention to reduce the number transported by discontinuing the use of New South Wales and Van Diemen's Land while extending the penitentiary system at home. In Australia there was a great demand for labour: 10,000 labourers were needed in New South Wales but only 3,000 convicts were likely to arrive in 1838. The aim, in effect, was to clean up Australia and make the Crown lands suitable for sale to young, enthusiastic and respectable emigrants. Decent people were simply being put off from moving there and in consequence land was grossly undervalued.

Aside from that, transportation was costing the Crown between £4 and £5 million annually by 1838, with an estimate that the total outlay between 1787 and 1837 was around £8 million. The expenditure for New South Wales and Van Diemen's Land in 1836–37 was £488,013 for 60,000 convicts. Banishment overseas was ceasing to be the cheap option. Molesworth's portrayal of colonial society as violent and morally suspect outraged colonists, but the report was favourably received by his administration, and although based, at least partially, on exaggerated tales of abuse and rampant criminality, it caused intense debate in the English papers.

In January 1839 a letter was sent from Fox Maule, Under-Secretary of State, to Sir George Grey, Under-Secretary of State for War and the Colonies:

The number of convicts to be employed in the hulks in Great Britain during the present year will be increased to 3,500 and those employed at Bermuda will be increased to 1000, of which 200 will be sent out in the spring and 200 at the end of the year. The number of prisoners in the penitentiary will be 800, an increase of 250. It is not proposed at present to diminish the number of convicts to be sent from Ireland and the probable number to be transported this year will be about 2000. It is proposed to improve the system of punishment and instruction now pursued on board the hulks and build a new prison on the separate system for 500 prisoners. While these changes are taking place at home accompanying alterations must take place abroad.

Instructions will be sent out to prepare the governors of New South Wales and Van Diemen's Land for the immediate diminution and approaching discontinuance of the practice of assignment. Instructions should likewise be sent to prepare buildings in Norfolk Island for the reception of convicts from the United Kingdom and at the government of the island should be entrusted to an officer from home.

The first result of the proposed arrangements will be a material reduction in the number of convicts to be transported during the present year. Instructions already received for the gradual abolition of the system of assignment with a view to its ultimate abandonment will have prepared the colony for this change.

With respect to Norfolk Island, it is the intention of Her Majesty's Government that an essential alteration should be made in the system of punishment pursued there. The healthiness of the climate, the fertility of soil, and its entire separation from intercourse with ordinary immigrants, render it peculiarly fit for the reception of a large number of convicts with little if any increase of expense. A prison will require to be erected capable of holding as many convicts as can be conveniently and profitably employed on the island. In the meantime, you are authorised to incur such expenses as may be necessary for the temporary accommodation of an increased number of convicts in that island and of those who shall arrive in New South Wales in the course of the present year you will send as large a portion to Norfolk Island as you think can be properly received there. The general principles which are to guide the future management of transported conduct are,

1. that a fixed period of imprisonment should, in the first instance, be allotted for the punishment of the crime of which the prisoner has been convicted.
2. that the actual period of imprisonment should be liable to a subsequent abridgement, according to the previous character of the prisoner, the nature of his crime and his conduct during his punishment.
3. that when allowed to leave Norfolk Island he should not be assigned to any individual in Australia, but should enjoy advantages at least equal to those of a ticket of leave.
4. No prisoner is to be detained longer than 15 years.

In order to carry out these regulations it is desirable that Norfolk Island should be appropriated to convicts from the United Kingdom, any persons convicted of offences in New South Wales should be confined in some other part of the colony or employed on the roads. A residence will be for provided for the superintendent and he will receive a salary of £800 a year.

It worked. As a direct result of the numerous concerns raised, an Order-in-Council was issued, removing New South Wales from the list of places to which convicts could be sent, and transportation there was officially halted on 22 May 1840. The last convict ship to disembark in Sydney was the *Eden*, which arrived on 18 November 1840; thereafter, between 1844 and 1853 direct shipments of convicts were sent to Van Diemen's Land and Norfolk Island (a dependency of Van Diemen's Land). As transportation to New South Wales ended the number arriving in Van Diemen's Land rose, peaking in 1846 when around 5,000 convicts arrived. From that year, the transportation system began to be wound down as the Britain government yielded to public pressure for a change in the way convicts were treated. On 30 August 1853 the *Phoebe Dunbar* was the last ship to deliver convicts directly from Ireland, sailing from Dun Laoghaire.

About one third of migrants who went to Australia between 1830 and 1850 paid their own way. Many found that, in comparison to Britain, conditions were very good, and with hard work and determination they could prosper. Some encouraged relatives to come and enjoy the prosperity. Women migrants were also assisted to curb a gender imbalance in the colonies, to work as domestic servants and to foster marriages and childbirth. These migration schemes had resulted in 58,000 people going to Australia between 1815 and 1840. The discovery of gold in 1851 changed the convict colonies into more populous cities with the arrival of many more free immigrants. These hopefuls, termed 'diggers', brought new skills and professions, and contributed to a burgeoning economy.

On 9 January 1868 the convict ship *Hougoumont* arrived at the port of Fremantle in Western Australia with a cargo of 281 passengers, including sixty-two Fenian convicts, and was the last ship to transport convicts to Australia. The ship's arrival marked the end of eighty years of penal transportation to Australia. Between 1788 and 1868 more than 160,000 convicts had been transported.

Appendix 1

The Transportation Act of 1717 (4 George 1 c.11)

An act for the further preventing robbery, burglary, and other felonies, and for the more effectual transportations of felons, and unlawful exporters of wool; and for declaring the law upon some points relating to pirates.

WHEREAS it is found by experience, That the punishments inflicted by the laws now in force against the offences of robbery, larceny and other felonious taking and stealing of money and goods, have not proved effectual to deter wicked and evil-disposed persons from being guilty of the said crimes: and whereas many offenders to whom royal mercy hath been extended, upon condition of transporting themselves to the West-Indies, have often neglected to perform the said condition, but returned to their former wickedness, and been as last for new crimes brought to a shameful and ignominious death: and whereas in many of his Majesty's colonies and plantations in America, there is great want of servants, who by their labour and industry might be the means of improving and making the said colonies and plantations more useful to this nation: be it enacted by the King's most excellent majesty, by and with the advice and consent of the lords spiritual and temporal and the commons, in this present parliament assembled, and by the authority of the same,

That where any person or persons have been convicted of any offence within the benefit of clergy, before the twentieth day of January one thousand seven hundred and seventeen, and are liable to be whipt or burnt in the hand, or have been ordered to any workhouse, and who shall be therein on the said twentieth day of January; as also where any person or persons shall be hereafter convicted of grand or petit larceny, or any felonious stealing or taking money or goods and chattels, either from the person, or the house of any other, or in any other manner, and who by the law shall be entitled to the benefit of clergy, and liable only to the penalties of burning in the hand or whipping, (except persons convicted for receiving or buying stolen goods, knowing them to be stolen) it shall and may be lawful for the court before whom they were convicted, or any court held at the same place with the like authority, if they think fit, instead of ordering any such offenders to be burnt in the hand or whipt, to order and direct,

That such offenders, as also such offenders in any workhouse, as aforesaid, shall be sent as soon as conveniently may, be, to some of his Majesty's colonies and plantations in America for the space of seven years; and that court before whom they were convicted, or any subsequent court held at the same place, with like authority as the former, shall have power to convey, transfer and make over such offenders, by order of court, to the use of any person or persons who shall contract for the performance of such transportation, to him or them, and his and their assigns, for such term of seven years; and where any persons have been convicted, or do now stand attainted of any offences whatsoever, for which death by law ought to be inflicted, or where any offenders shall hereafter be convicted of any crimes whatsoever, for which they are by law to be excluded the benefit of clergy, and his Majesty, his heirs or successors, shall be graciously pleased to extend royal mercy to any such offenders, upon the condition of transportation to any part of America, and such intention of mercy be signified by one of his Majesty's principal secretaries of state, it shall and may be lawful to and for any court having proper authority, to allow such offenders the benefit of a pardon under the great seal, and to order and direct the like transfer and conveyance to any person or persons, (who will contract for the performance of such transportation) and to his and their assigns, of any such before-mentioned offenders, as also of any person or persons convicted of receiving or buying stolen goods, knowing them to be stolen, for the term of fourteen years, in case such condition of transportation be general, or else for such other term or terms as shall be made part of such condition, if any particular time be specified by his Majesty, his heirs and successors, as aforesaid; and such person or persons so contracting, as aforesaid, his or their assigns, by virtue of such order of transfer, as aforesaid, shall have a property and interest in the service of such offenders for such terms of years.

II. And be it further enacted by the authority aforesaid, That if any offender or offenders, so ordered by any such court to be transported for any term of seven years or fourteen years, or other time or times, as aforesaid, shall return into any part of Great Britain or Ireland before the end of his or their said term, he or she so returning, as aforesaid, shall be liable to be punished as any person attainted of felony without the benefit of clergy; and execution may and shall be awarded against such offender or offenders accordingly: provided nevertheless. That his Majesty, his heirs and successors, may pardon and dispense with any such transportation, and allow of the return of any such offender or offenders from America, he or they paying their owner or proprietor, at the time of such pardon, dispensation or allowance, such sum of money as shall be adjudged reasonable by any two justices of the peace residing within the province where such owner dwells; and where any such offenders shall be transported, and shall have served their respective terms, according to the order of any such court, as aforesaid, such services shall have the effect of a pardon to all intents and purposes, as for that crime or crimes for which they were so transported, and shall have so served, as aforesaid.

III. And be it further enacted by the authority aforesaid, That every such person or persons to whom any such court shall order any such offenders to be transferred or conveyed, as aforesaid, before any of them shall be delivered over to such person or persons, or his or their assigns, to be transported, as aforesaid, he or they shall contract and agree with such person or persons as shall be ordered and appointed by such court, as aforesaid, and give sufficient security to the satisfaction of such court, that he or they will transport, or cause to be transported effectually such offenders so conveyed to him or them, as aforesaid, to some of his Majesty's colonies and plantations in America, as shall be ordered by the said court, and procure an authentick certificate from the governor, or the chief custom-house officer of the place (which certificate they are hereby required to give forthwith, without fee or reward, as soon as conveniently may be) of the landing of such offenders so transferred, as aforesaid, in that place whereto they shall be ordered, (death and casualties of the sea excepted) and that none of the said offenders shall be suffered to return from the said place to any part of Great Britain or Ireland by the wilful default of such person or persons so contracting as aforesaid, or by the wilful default of his or their assigns.

IV. And whereas there are several persons who have secret acquaintances with felons, and who make it their business to help persons to their stolen goods, and by that means gain money from them, which is divided between them and the felons, whereby they greatly encourage such offenders: be it enacted by the authority aforesaid, That wherever any person taketh money or reward, directly or indirectly, under pretence or upon account of helping any person or persons to any stolen goods or chattels, every such person so taking money or reward, as aforesaid, (unless such person doth apprehend, or cause to be apprehended, such felon who stole the same, and cause such felon to be brought to his trial for the same, and give evidence against him) shall be guilty of felony, and suffer the pains and penalties of felony, according to the nature of the felony committed in dealing such goods, and in such and the same manner as if such offender had himself stolen such goods and chattels, in the manner, and with such circumstances as the same were stolen.

V. And whereas there are many idle persons, who are under the age of one and twenty years, lurking about in divers parts of London, and elsewhere, who want employment, and may be tempted to become thieves, if not provided for: and whereas they may be inclined to be transported, and to enter into services in some of his Majesty's colonies and plantations in America; but as they have no power to contract for themselves, and therefore that it is not safe for merchants to transport, or take them into such services; be it enacted by the authority aforesaid, That where any person of the age of fifteen years or more, and under the age of twenty one, shall be willing to be transported, and to enter into any service in any persons of the of his Majesty's colonies or plantations in America, it shall and may be lawful for any merchant, or other, to contract with any such Person for any such service, not exceeding the term of eight years; provided such person so binding him or herself do come before the lord mayor of London, or some other justice of the peace of the city, if such contract be made within the same, or the liberties thereof, or before some other two justices of the peace of the place where such contract shall be made, if made elsewhere, and before such magistrate or magistrates acknowledge such consent, and do sign such contract in his or their presence, and with his or their approbation; and that then it shall be same with his lawful for any such merchant or other, to transport such person so binding him or herself, and to keep him or her within any of the said plantations or colonies, according to the tenor of such contract, as aforesaid; any law or statute to the contrary in any wise notwithstanding; which said contract and approbation of such magistrate or magistrates, with the tenor of such contract, shall be certified by such magistrate or magistrates to the next general quarter-sessions, of the peace, held for that county where such magistrate or magistrates shall reside, to be registered by the clerk of the peace without fee or reward.

VI.   And be it further enacted by the authority aforesaid, That from and after the said twentieth day of January one thousand seven hundred and seventeen, if any person or performs shall be in prison for want of sufficient bail, for unlawful exportation of wool or wool-sells, and shall refuse to appear or plead to a declaration or information to be delivered to such person or persons, or to the gaoler, keeper or turnkey of the prison, at the said prison, for the said offence, by the space of one term, judgment shall be entered against him by default; and in case judgment shall be obtained against any such person or persons by default, verdict, or otherwise, and such person or persons shall not pay the sum recovered against him or them for the said offence, within the space of three months after entering up of such judgment, the court before whom such judgment shall be obtained shall, by order of court, cause such offender or offenders to be transported, in the same manner as felons aforesaid, for the term of seven years; and if such offender or offenders shall return into Great Britain or Ireland, before the expiration of the said seven years, he or they shall suffer as felons, and have execution awarded against them, as persons attainted of felony, without benefit of clergy.

VII. And it is hereby declared, That all and every person and persons who have committed or shall commit any offence or offences, for which they ought to be adjudged, deemed and taken to be pirates, felons or robbers, by an act made in the parliament holden in the eleventh and twelfth years of the reign of his late majesty King William the Third, intituled, An act for the more effectual suppression of piracy, may be tried and judged for every such offence in such manner and form as in and by an act made in the twenty eighth year of the reign of King Henry the Eighth is directed and appointed for the trial of pirates, and shall and ought to be utterly debarred and excluded from the benefit of clergy for the said offences; any law or statute to the contrary thereof in any wise notwithstanding.

VIII. Provided always. That nothing in this act contained shall extend or be construed to extend to such persons as shall be convicted or attainted in that part of Great Britain called Scotland.

IX.   And be it also enacted, That this act shall extend to all his Majesty's dominions in America, and shall be taken as a publick act.

Appendix 2

The Hulks Act of 1776
(16 George 3 c.43)

An act to authorise, for a limited time, the punishment by hard labour of offenders who, for certain crimes, are or shall become liable to be transported to any of his Majesty's colonies and plantations.

[Preamble.]

WHEREAS the transportation of convicts to his Majesty's colonies and plantations in America, now in use within that part of Great Britain called England, by virtue of the several Statutes authorising such transportation, is found to be attended with various inconveniences, particularly by depriving this kingdom of many subjects whose labour might be useful to the community, and who, by proper care and correction, might be reclaimed from their evil courses: whereas, until some other more effectual provisions, in the place of transportation to his Majesty's Colonies and plantations in America, can be framed, such convicts, being males, might be employed with benefit to the public in raising sand, soil, and gravel from, and cleansing the river Thames; or being males unfit for so severe a labour, or being females, might be kept to hard labour of another kind within England; be it therefore enacted by the king's most excellent majesty, by and with the advice and consent of the lords spiritual and temporal, and commons, in this present parliament assembled, and by the authority of the same,

[Any male, convicted in England of any crime punishable by transportation to America, may, instead thereof, be kept to hard labour in cleansing the river Thames, &c. for any term not less than three nor more than ten years.]

That, from and after the passing of this act, where any male person shall, at any session of oyer and terminer, or gaol delivery, or at any quarter or other general session of the peace, for any county, riding, division, city, liberty, borough, town, or place, within that part of Great Britain called England, be lawfully convicted of grand or petit larceny, or any other crime for which he shall be liable by law to a sentence of transportation to any of his Majesty's colonies or plantations in America, it shall and may be lawful for the court before whom any such person shall be so convicted, or any court held for the same place with like authority, if such court shall think fit, in the place of such punishment by transportation, to order and adjudge that such person shall be punished by being kept to hard labour in the raising of sand, soil, and gravel from, and cleansing the river Thames, or any other service for the benefit of the navigation of the said river, under the management and direction of an overseer or overseers, to be appointed by the justices of the peace for the county of Middlesex, at their quarter or other general sessions of the peace, for the same term of years as the transportation for the said offence might by law have been adjudged, or for such shorter term as such court shall think fit to order and adjudge; provided that the same shall in no case be less than three years, or more than ten years.

[In case his Majesty should extend his mercy to any male convicted of any felony for which he is liable to suffer death, the judge may order the offender to be kept to hard labour, for the time specified by the secretary of state.]

II. And be it further enacted, That where any male person shall, at any session of oyer and terminer, or gaol delivery, or at any quarter or other general session of the peace for any county, riding, division, city, liberty, borough, town, or place, within that part of Great Britain called England, be lawfully convicted of any robbery, or other felony, for which he shall by law be liable to suffer death without benefit of clergy, and his Majesty shall be graciously pleased to extend the royal mercy to any such offender, upon condition of being kept to hard labour for the term of ten years, or any other shorter time to be specified, in the custody of such overseer or overseers as aforesaid; and such intention of mercy shall be notified in writing by one of his specified Majesty's principal secretaries of state to the judge or justice of oyer and terminer, or gaol delivery, in any county, city, or place, before whom any such offender shall be convicted or condemned, it shall and may be lawful for every such judge or justice of oyer and terminer, or gaol delivery, to make an order for allowing forthwith to every such offender the benefit of a conditional pardon, in the same manner as if there was a pardon under the great seal; and may and shall adjudge, that every such offender shall be kept to hard labour, in the custody of such overseer or overseers as aforesaid, for the time specified in the notification from such secretary of state.

[When any offender shall be ordered to hard labour, the clerk of the assize, &c. shall give a certificate to the sheriff or gaoler,]

III. And be it further enacted, That when any offender shall be ordered to be kept to hard labour, in manner aforesaid, or as herein-after is directed, the clerk of the assize, clerk of the peace, or other clerk of the court by which such order shall be made, shall give to the sheriff, or gaoler, having the custody of such offender, a certificate in writing, under his hand, containing an account of the christian name, surname, and age of such offender; of his offence, of the court before whom he was convicted, and of the term for which he shall be so ordered to hard labour; and the sheriff, or gaoler, having the custody of such offender, shall, with all convenient speed, after the making of any such order, and receiving of such certificate, convey such offender, or cause him to be conveyed to such place within England;

[who shall deliver such offender and certificate to the overseer, &c.]

and also deliver such offender, or cause him to be delivered, together with the said certificate to such overseer or overseers as aforesaid; and the overseer or overseers, to whom any such offender shall be so delivered, shall give a proper receipt in writing under his or their hand or hands, which shall be a sufficient discharge to the sheriff, or gaoler, so delivering such offender.

[Expenses incurred in conveyance of offenders to be paid by the county, &c.]

IV. And be it further enacted, That all expenses incurred by any sheriff or gaoler, in the conveyance of any such offender as aforesaid, shall be paid by the county, riding, division, city, liberty, borough, town, or place, for which the court, ordering such punishment by hard labour instead of transportation to America, shall be held; and the sheriff or gaoler, shall receive the money due for such expenses from the treasurer for such county, riding, division, city, liberty, borough, town, or place, by order of the justices of the peace, at their quarterly, or other general session, who are hereby required to make such order accordingly.

[Overseer to have the same power over offenders in his custody as a sheriff or gaoler.]

V. And be it further enacted, That after delivery of any such offender, as aforesaid, into the custody to which he shall be adjudged, the overseer or overseers, who shall have the custody of such offender, shall, during the term for which he shall be ordered to hard labour, have the same powers over such offender as are incident to the office of a sheriff or gaoler; and in case of any abuse of the custody, or other misbehaviour in discharge of his office, shall be liable to the same punishment as a gaoler;

[Offenders to be kept to hard labour in raising sand and gravel from the Thames, &c.]

and also shall, during such term as aforesaid, keep such offender to hard labour, either in raising sand, soil, and gravel from, and cleansing the Thames, or in any other laborious service for the benefit of the navigation of the Thames, but at such places only, and subject to such directions, limitations, and restrictions, as the master, wardens, and assistants, of the Trinity House, shall from time to time prescribe.

[Offenders not to be employed in delivering ballast to masters of ships, &c.]

VI. Provided nevertheless, That such offenders shall, in no case, be employed in delivering tonnage of ballast to masters and commanders of ships, but only in digging, raising, and taking up, the gravel, sand, and soil, from the shelves and sand-banks of the said river of Thames, and in discharging the same upon the shore, above the high water mark, or in some other laborious service for the benefit of the navigation of the Thames.

[Offenders to be fed with bread, coarse food, and water or small beer.]

VII. And be it further enacted, That every offender who shall be ordered to hard labour, in the custody of such overseer or overseers as aforesaid, shall, during the time of such service, be fed and sustained with bread, and any coarse or inferior food, and water, or small beer, and also clothed; and such offender shall not, during the term of such service, be permitted to have any other food, drink, or clothing, than such as shall be so allotted to them;

[No person to supply them with any other food &c. on penalty of 40s.]

and if any person shall supply any such offender, at any time during the term of his said service, with any drink, food, or cloathing, other than such as shall be so directed or permitted, he or she so supplying shall, for every such offence, forfeit any sum not exceeding forty shillings.

[Offenders who refuse to work, or otherwise misbehave themselves, may be whipped, &c.]

VIII.   And be it further enacted, That if any offender, who shall be so delivered as aforesaid to be kept to hard labour, shall, during the term of such service, refuse to perform any labour authorised by this act, or who shall be guilty of any other misbehaviour or disorderly conduct, it shall be lawful for the overseer or overseers having the custody of any such offender to order such whipping, or other moderate punishment, to be inflicted upon him, as may be inflicted by law on persons committed to a house of correction for hard labour.

[Every offender, at the end of his confinement, shall receive a sum of money, no less than 40s nor more than 5l together with decent cloathing.]

IX.   And be it further enacted, That every offender who shall be delivered to be kept to hard labour in manner aforesaid, shall, at the end of the term of such service, and upon being restored to his liberty, receive from the overseer or overseers, under whom he shall have so served, such sum of money not being less than forty Shillings, nor more than five pounds, together with such decent clothing, as the court into which such returns shall be made, as herein after mentioned, shall appoint:

[His Majesty, on the good behaviour of offenders, may shorten the term of their confinement.]

and if any such offender, whilst confined to hard labour in manner aforesaid, shall, by his industry and other good behaviour, shew such signs of reformation, as shall induce the said court to recommend him as an object of his Majesty's mercy, and it shall be thereupon signified, by a letter from one of his Majesty's principal secretaries of state to the overseer or overseers as aforesaid, that his Majesty thinks fit, in consideration of such good behaviour, to shorten the duration of such offender's term, such offender shall be accordingly set at liberty at the time mentioned in such letter; and shall receive a sum of money from his overseer or overseers, together with clothing, in the same manner as if he had served the whole of the term for which he was adjudged to serve.

[Any person, convicted of any crime punishable by transportation, may be sent to some place of confinement within the county, &c. and there kept to hard labour for not less than three years, nor more than ten years.]

X. And be it further enacted, That where any person shall, at any session of oyer and terminer, or gaol delivery, or at any quarter or other general session of the peace for any county, riding, division, city, liberty, borough, town, or place, within that part of Great Britain called England, be lawfully convicted of grand or petty larceny, or any other crime, for which he or she shall be liable by law to transportation to any of his Majesty's colonies in America, it shall be lawful for the court, in which any such offender shall be so convicted, or any court held for the same place, and with like authority, if such court shall think fit, in the place of such punishment by transportation, to order and adjudge that such person shall be sent to some proper place of confinement within the said county, riding, division, city, liberty, borough, town, or place, to be appointed for that purpose in manner herein after mentioned, there to be kept to hard labour, for such term or number of years as such court shall appoint, not exceeding the term or number of years for which the transportation for the said offence might have been adjudged: provided, That the same shall in no case be less than three years, or more than ten years.

[In case his Majesty should extend his mercy to any person guilty of any felony punishable by death, the judge may order the offender to be kept to hard labour, for the time specified by the secretary of state.]

XI. And be it further enacted, That where any person shall, at any session of oyer and terminer, or gaol delivery, or at any quarter, or other general session of the peace, for any county, riding, division, city, liberty, borough, town, or place, within that part of Great Britain called England, be lawfully convicted of any felony of any robbery, or other felony, for which he or she shall by law be liable to suffer death without benefit of clergy, and his Majesty shall be graciously pleased to extend the royal mercy to any such offender, upon condition of being kept to hard labour at the place of confinement to be appointed for that purpose in manner herein after mentioned, and such intention of mercy shall be notified in writing, by one of his majesty's principal secretaries of state, to the judge or justice of oyer and terminer or general gaol delivery, in any county, city, or place, before whom such offender shall be convicted or condemned; it shall and may be lawful for every such judge or justice of oyer and terminer, or general gaol delivery, to make an order for allowing forthwith to every such offender the benefit of a conditional pardon, in the same manner as if there was a conditional pardon under the great seal, and may and shall adjudge that every such offender shall be kept to hard labour for the time specified in the notification from such secretary of state.

[When any offender shall be ordered to hard labour, the clerk of assize, &c. shall give a certificate to the sheriff or gaoler,]

XII. And be it further enacted, That when any offender shall be ordered to be kept to hard labour in manner aforesaid, the clerk of assize, clerk of the peace, or other clerk of the court by which such order shall be made, shall give to the sheriff or gaoler, having the custody of such offender, a certificate in writing under his hand, containing an account of the christian name, surname, and age of such offender, of his or her offence, of the court before whom he or she was convicted, and of the term for which he or she shall be ordered to hard labour;

[who shall deliver such prisoner, &c. to the keeper of the proper house of correction;]

and the sheriff or gaoler shall, with all convenient speed after the making of any such order, and receiving of such certificate, convey such offender, or cause him or her to be conveyed, to the proper house of correction and deliver such offender, or cause him or her to be delivered, together with the said certificate, into the custody of the master or keeper of such house of correction;

[who shall give a receipt for the same.]

and the person or persons to whom such offender shall be so delivered, shall give a proper receipt in writing, under his or their hand or hands, which shall be a sufficient discharge to the sheriff, gaoler, or other person, so delivering any such offender;

[Expenses of conveyance to be paid by the county, &c.]

and all expenses incurred by any sheriff or gaoler, in the conveyance of any such offender to the house of correction in manner aforesaid, shall be paid by the county, riding, division, city, liberty, borough, town, or place, for which the court ordering such punishment by hard labour shall be held, in the same manner as is herein before directed in respect to offenders ordered to hard labour in removing sand, soil, and gravel from, and cleansing the river Thames.

[Justices for every county, &c. in England to prepare their houses of correction for reception of offenders;]

XIII. And be it further enacted, That the justices of the peace for every county, riding, division, city, liberty, borough, town, and place, within that part of Great Britain called England, shall, at the first quarter or other general session of the peace, which shall be held next after the passing of this act, take into consideration the state of their respective houses of correction, in order that proper places within the same, or elsewhere, within each respective county, riding, division, city, liberty, borough, town, and place, may be prepared for the reception of such offenders as shall be ordered to hard labour therein, by force of this act, and for the purposes aforesaid;

[and to give directions for their government, and keeping them to hard labour.]

and for keeping such offenders to hard labour, and for their employment, regulation, and government, shall give such directions, and make such orders, as such justices shall think most fit and proper, and they are authorised to give or make by the laws now in force in respect to houses of correction, or by any of them: and the keeper of the place of confinement so appointed and prepared shall, in case of any abuse of the custody, or other misbehaviour in discharge of his office, be liable to the same punishment as a gaoler.

[Penalty on persons rescuing offenders ordered to hard labour;]

    XIV. And be it further enacted, That if any person shall rescue any offender, who by force of this act shall be ordered to hard labour, in removing sand, soil, and gravel from, and cleansing the river Thames, or in any place of confinement appointed by virtue of this act, either in his or her conveyance to the place appointed for such hard labour, or whilst such offender under this act shall be in the custody of the person or persons appointed for that purpose; or if any person shall be aiding or assisting in any such rescue; every such person shall be liable to the like punishment that is inflicted for breach of prison in cases of felony:

[or assisting in an attempt to make an escape, &c.]

and if any person, not having the actual custody of any such offender, shall be aiding and assisting in any escape, or shall by supplying arms, or instruments of disguise or escape, or otherwise in any manner be aiding and assisting in the attempt to make any such escape, though no such escape shall be made, every such person shall forfeit the sum of twenty pounds; which said penalty of twenty pounds shall be recoverable in any of his majesty's courts of record, by any person or persons who shall sue for the same, by bill, plaint, action of debt, information, or otherwise, wherein no essoin, protection, or wager of law, shall be allowed.

[Penalty on persons ordered to hard labour who shall escape from confinement, &c.]

    XV. And be it further enacted, That if any person who shall be ordered to hard labour under this act, either in removing sand, soil, and gravel from, and cleansing the river Thames, or at any place of confinement appointed by virtue of this act, shall, at any time during the term for which he or she shall be so ordered to hard labour, break prison, or escape from the place of his or her confinement, or from the person or persons having the lawful custody of such offender, he or she so breaking prison or escaping, shall on conviction, for the first escape, be punished by doubling the term of the service and hard labour in which he or she was at the time of such escape; and on conviction for a second escape, be adjudged guilty of felony without benefit of clergy, and suffer death accordingly.

XVI. And, to the intent that such conviction or convictions may be had with as little trouble and expense as possible, be it further enacted,

[Method of trial and conviction of offenders for making escape.]

That every offender or offenders, escaping in manner aforesaid, may and shall be tried before the justices of assize, oyer and terminer, or gaol delivery, for the county, city, or liberty, where he, she, or they, shall be apprehended and taken; and that the clerk of the assize and clerk of the peace, where such orders of confinement or hard labour shall respectively be made, and their successors for the time being, shall, at the request of the prosecutor, or any other in his majesty's behalf, certify a transcript briefly and in few words, containing the effect of every indictment and conviction of such man or woman, and of the order made for his or her confinement, or being sent to hard labour respectively, to the justices of assize, oyer and terminer, and gaol delivery, where such man or woman shall be indicted for any such escape from his or her place of confinement or of hard labour respectively, (not taking, for the same, above the sum of two shillings and sixpence;) which certificate being produced in court, shall be a sufficient proof that such person of persons have before been convicted and ordered to such place of confinement or hard labour respectively.

[Clerk of assize, &c. to be paid by the treasurer of the county, &c.]

XVII. Provided always, and be it further enacted by the authority aforesaid, That such clerk of the assize, clerk of the peace, or other clerk of the court, and the sheriff or gaoler, shall paid by the treasurer of the county, riding, division, city, liberty, borough, town, or place, the like satisfaction as hath been usually paid for the order of transportation of any offender.

[Offenders confined by virtue of this act, to be kept separate, &c.]

XVIII. Provided always, That the offender or offenders which shall be sent to, and shall by virtue of this act, be directed to be confined in, such places to be appointed as aforesaid, shall be kept separate from, and shall not be permitted or suffered to intermix with, any person or persons confined for any offence under the degree of petit larceny, or other crime not making the person or persons having committed the same, by the laws of this realm, subject to a sentence of transportation.

[Overseers of the places of confinement appointed by this act to make returns, on oath, of the names of the persons, &c. committed to their custody.]

XIX. And be it further enacted by the authority aforesaid, That the overseers of the several places of confinement to be appointed by virtue of this act, shall, from time to time, make returns, specifying the names of all and every the person or persons who shall be committed to their custody, the offences of which they shall have been guilty, the court before which each person was convicted, the sentence of the court, the age, bodily state, and behaviour of every such convict while in custody; and also the names of all and every the person or persons who shall have died under such custody or shall have escaped from such place of confinement, or shall have been released from thence by order from one of his majesty's principal secretaries of state;

[When, and to whom, the returns to be made.]

such returns from the overseers of the convicts to be employed in laborious service for the benefit of the navigation of the Thames, to be made the first day of every term, to his Majesty's court of King's Bench at Westminster; and from the overseers of the other places of confinement to be appointed by virtue of this act, to the justices of assize at each assize, and to the Justices of the Peace at each quarter or other general sessions of the peace, for the county, city, riding, division, or place, within which such place of confinement shall be situate; and that every such return shall be verified on the oath of the person making the same; such oath to be made before the court into which such return shall be delivered.

[Penalties of this act, how to be recovered and applied.]

XX. And be it further enacted, That any pecuniary penalties created by this act, for the recovery of which no mode is herein-before prescribed, shall be recoverable before two or more justices of the peace, in the county, riding, division, city, liberty, borough, town, or place, in which the offence shall be committed, on proof of the offence, by the oath or oaths of one or more credible witness or witnesses, or on confession of the offender, and shall belong to the informer or informers prosecuting for the same; and in case of non-payment, shall be levied by distress and sale of the offender's goods and chattels, by warrant under the hands and seals of such justices; and the overplus of the money raised, after deducting the penalty, and the expenses of the distress and sale, shall be rendered to the owner; and for want of sufficient distress, the offender shall be sent by such justices to the prison of such county, riding, division, city, borough, town, or place, for such term, not exceeding six months, as such justices shall think most proper.

[Persons prosecuted under this act, may plead the general issue.]

XXI. And be it further enacted, That if any suit or action shall be prosecuted against any person or persons for anything done in pursuance of this act, such person or persons may plead the general issue, and give this act, or the special matter, in evidence at any trial to be had thereupon, and that the same was done by the authority of this act; and if a verdict shall pass for the defendant or defendants, or the plaintiff or plaintiffs shall become nonsuit, or discontinue his, her, or their action or actions after issue joined; or if on demurrer, or otherwise, judgement shall be given against the plaintiff or plaintiffs,

[Treble costs.]

the defendant or defendants shall recover treble costs, and have the like remedy for the same as any defendants have by law in other cases; and though a verdict shall be given to any plaintiff in any such action or suit as aforesaid, such plaintiff shall not have costs against the defendant, unless the judge, before whom the trial shall be, shall certify his approbation of the verdict.

[Limitation of actions.]

XXII. And be it further enacted, That all actions, suits, and prosecutions, to be commenced against the person or persons for anything done in pursuance of this act, shall be laid and tried in the county, or place, where the was committed, and shall be commenced within six months after the committed, and not otherwise.

[Continuance of this act.]

XXIII. And be it further enacted, That this act shall continue to be in force for two years, and also to the end of the then session; or if the said term of two years shall not determine during any session, then till the end of the then next ensuing session of parliament.

Appendix 3

List of British Prison Hulks from Wikipedia

Name	Service	Location	Comments
HMS *Antigua*	1804–1816		*Antigua* was the former French privateer *Egyptienne*, which *Hippomenes* captured in 1804.
HMS *Antelope*	1824–1845	Bermuda	*Antelope* was a 50-gun Fourth-rate launched in 1802. She was used as a troopship from 1818, was placed on harbour service from 1824 and was broken up in 1845.
HMS *Argenta*	1919–1925	Belfast Lough Northern Ireland	*Argenta* was a U.S. cargo ship purchased as a hulk to intern Irish Republicans as part of Britain's 1922 Special Powers Act internment strategy[1] following the events of Bloody Sunday (1920). HMS *Argenta* was scrapped in 1925.
HMS *Bellerophon*	1815–1824	Sheerness	*Bellerophon* was a 74-gun Third-rate launched in 1786. Having taken part in the Battle of Trafalgar, she became a prison hulk in 1815, was renamed *Captivity* in October 1824 and was sold out of service in January 1836.
HMS *Belliqueux*	1814-1816		*Belliqueux* was a 64-gun Third-rate launched in 1780 at Blackwall. She was used as a prison hulk from 1814 and broken up in 1816.

HMS *Briton*	1841–1856	Portsmouth	*Briton* was built in 1812, Chatham.
HMS *Canada*	1810–1834	Chatham	*Canada* was a 74-gun Third-rate launched in 1765. She became a prison hulk in 1810 and was broken up in 1834.
HMS *Captivity*	1796–1816	Gosport and Devonport	The first *Captivity* was a former 64-gun Third-rate launched in 1772 as HMS *Monmouth*. She became a prison hulk and was renamed *Captivity* in 1796. She was broken up in 1816.
HMS *Captivity*	1824–1836	Gosport and Devonport	The second *Captivity* was a former 74-gun Third-rate launched in 1786 as HMS *Bellerophon*. She became a prison hulk in 1815 and was renamed HMS *Captivity* in 1824. She was sold in 1836.
Censor	1776–?	Woolwich	*Censor* was a former French Navy frigate of 731-tons. With *Justitia I* and *Justitia II*, she was one of the first prison hulks, and supplied by ship owner and merchant Duncan Campbell.
HMS *Ceres*	1787–1797	Woolwich	*Ceres* was a 32-gun Fifth-rate launched in 1781 and broken up in 1830.
HMS *Chatham*	1793–1805	Plymouth	*Chatham* was a 50-gun Fourth-rate launched in 1758. She was used for harbour service from 1793 and was a powder hulk from 1805. She was renamed *Tilbury* in 1810 and was broken up in 1814.
HMS *Coromandel*	1827–1853	Bermuda	*Coromandel* was a 20-gun storeship, formerly an East Indiaman that the Admiralty purchased in 1804, commissioned as a 56-gun Fourth-rate, and named HMS *Malabar*. She was refitted as a storeship in 1805 and renamed *Coromandel* in 1815. She became a prison hulk in 1827 and was broken up in 1853.

Name	Service	Location	Comments
HMS *Crown*	1798–1802 1806–15	Portsmouth	*Crown* was a 64-gun third rate ship launched in 1782. She was converted to serve as a prison ship in 1798, used as a powder hulk from 1802 until 1806, and then restored to a prison ship until being put in ordinary in 1815. She was broken up in 1816.
HMS *Cumberland*	1830–1833	Chatham	*Cumberland* was a 74-gun Third-rate launched in 1807, Northfleet. She was converted to a prison hulk in 1830 and was renamed *Fortitude* in 1833. She was put on the sale list in 1870 and was subsequently sold.
HMS *Dasher*	1832–1838	Woolwich	*Dasher* was an 18-gun sloop launched in 1797. She became a prison hulk in 1832 and was broken up in 1838.
HMS *Defence*	1850–1857	Woolwich and Portsmouth	*Defence* was a 74-gun Third-rate ship of the line, built in 1815 and accidentally burnt in 1857. Wreck broken up in 1857.
HMS *Defiance*	1813–1817		*Defiance* was a 74-gun Third-rate launched in 1783 Rotherhithe. She was used as a prison hulk from 1813 and was broken up in 1817.
HMS *Discovery*	1818–1834	Woolwich and Deptford	*Discovery* was a 10-gun sloop launched and purchased in 1789. She was converted to a bomb vessel in 1799, a prison hulk in 1818 and was broken up in 1834 at Deptford.
HMS *Dolphin*	1824–1830	Chatham	*Dolphin* originally an East Indiaman *Admiral Rainier*, which the Navy bought and renamed HMS *Hindostan*. The Admiralty purchased her in 1804 as a 50-gun Fourth-rate. Renamed again in 1819 as *Dolphin*, and once more in 1831 as *Justitia*, when she became a prison hulk. She was finally sold in 1855.

HMS *Dromedary*	1825–1864	Woolwich and Bermuda	*Dromedary* was an East Indiaman that the Navy purchased in 1805. First named *Howe* and then renamed *Dromedary* in 1808. She was converted to a convict ship in 1819, became a prison hulk at Bermuda in 1825, and was broken up there in August 1864.
HMS *Dunkirk*	1782–1792	Plymouth	*Dunkirk* was a Fourth-rate, built in 1754 at Woolwich. Converted to guardship in 1782, at Plymouth. Sold in 1792.
HMS *Edgar*	1814–1835		*Edgar* was a 74-gun Third-rate launched in 1779. She was converted to a prison hulk in 1813, renamed *Retribution* in 1814, and broken up 1835.
HMS *Essex*	1824–1834	Cork	HMS *Essex* was originally the USS *Essex* of the US Navy, a sailing frigate that participated in the First Barbary War, and in the War of 1812. The British captured her in 1814 and she then served as HMS *Essex* until she was sold at public auction in 1837. Having taken part in the Battle of Trafalgar and briefly served as Admiral Collingwood's flagship.
HMS *Euryalus*	1825–1847	Chatham and Gibraltar	*Euryalus* was decommissioned in 1825 and converted into a prison hulk for boys at Chatham. In 1847 she was moved to Gibraltar and was sold for breaking up in 1860.
HMS *Fortitude*	1833–1844	Chatham	HMS *Cumberland* was a 74-gun Third-rate launched in 1807. She was converted to a prison hulk in 1830 and was renamed *Fortitude* in 1833. She was put on the sale list in 1870 and was subsequently sold.

Name	Service	Location	Comments
HMS *Fortitude*	1795–1820	Chatham	*Fortitude* was a 74-gun Third-rate ship of the line launched in 1780. She served as a prison hulk from 1795 and was broken up in 1820.
HMS *Ganymede*	1819–1838	Chatham and Woolwich	*Ganymede* was the French frigate *Hébé* captured in 1809. She was converted to a prison hulk in 1819 and broken up in 1838.
HMS *Gelykheid*	1807–1814	Gillingham	Equally *Gelijkeidt*, *Gelykheidt*, or *Gelikheid*. On 8 May 1800 a court martial was held at Sheerness, on board HMS *Savage* on Lieutenant Wheatly and his Clerk, of the *Gelykheid* prison ship, at Gillingham, for drunkenness and neglect of duty, ungentlemanlike conduct, embezzlement of stores, tyranny, and oppression, but the charges being malicious and ill founded, they were acquitted. In 1803 was stationed in the Humber as Guardship and in 1807 she was fitted out as sheer hulk at Falmouth. She was disposed of in 1814.
HMS *Glory*	1809–1814		*Glory* was a 90-gun Second-rate launched in 1788. She was converted to a prison hulk in 1809, a powder hulk in 1814, was and broken up in 1825.
HMS *Goree*	1814–1817	Bermuda	*Goree* was the 16-gun sloop of war HMS *Favourite* launched in 1794. The French captured her in 1806 and renamed her *Favorite*; the British recaptured her in 1807 and renamed her HMS *Goree*. She became a prison hulk in Bermuda in 1814 and was broken up in 1817.

HMS *Hardy*	1824–1833		*Hardy* was a 14-gun gun-brig launched in 1804. She was used as a storeship from 1818 and a hospital ship from 1821, before being sold in 1835.
HMS *Hebe*	1839–1852	Woolwich	*Hebe* was a 46-gun Fifth-rate launched in 1826, made a receiving ship in 1840, hulked in 1861, and broken up in 1873.
HMS *Hector*	1808–1816		*Hector* was a 74-gun Third-rate launched at Deptford in 1774 and converted to a prison hulk in 1808, and broken up in 1816.
HMS *Justitia*	1812–1830	Sheerness	Vice Ad. Richard Onslow seized the *Zeeland* from the Dutch at Plymouth on 4 March 1796. She was renamed *Justitia* in 1812 and broken up in 1830, when her name was transferred to *Dolphin*.
HMS *Justitia*	1830–1855	Woolwich	*Justitia* originally an East Indiaman *Admiral Rainier*. The Admiralty purchased her in 1804 to use as a 50-gun Fourth-rate and named her HMS *Hindostan*. She was converted into a 20-gun storeship in 1811. She was renamed again in 1819 as *Dolphin*, and once more in 1830 as *Justitia*, when she became a prison hulk. sold in 1855.
HMS *Jersey*	1776–1783	New York	*Jersey* was a 60-gun Fourth-rate, built in 1736 as Plymouth. She was used as a prison hulk In New York during the American Revolutionary War, and subsequently burned by the British before they abandoned New York in 1783.
HMS *Laurel*	1798–1821	Portsmouth	*Laurel* was the Dutch sloop *Sireene* captured at the capitulation of Saldanha Bay in 1796. She was initially named HMS *Daphne*, but in 1798 was converted to a convict ship under the name of HMS *Laurel*. She was sold in 1821.

Name	Service	Location	Comments
HMS *Leven*	1827–1848	Woolwich and Deptford	*Leven* was launched in 1813 at Ipswich. She became a hospital ship in 1827 and then a prison hulk at Chatham. She became a receiving ship at Limehouse in 1842 and was broken up in 1848.
HMS *Leviathan*	1816–1848	Portsmouth	*Leviathan* was a 74-gun Third-rate ship of the line launched in 1790 at Chatham. She fought at the Battle of Trafalgar, was used as a prison hulk from 1816. In October 1846 she was used as a naval target and was sold out of service in 1848.
HMS *Lion*	1816–1837	Gosport	*Lion* was a 64-gun Third-rate launched in 1777. She was used as a sheer hulk from 1816 and was sold for breaking up in 1837.
HMS *Medway*	1850–1862	Bermuda	*Medway* was a 74-gun Third-rate launched in 1812. She was used as a prison hulk after 1847 and was sold in 1865.
HMS *Menelaus*	1832–1897		*Menelaus* was a Royal Navy 38-gun Fifth-rate frigate, launched in 1810 at Plymouth. In 1820 she moved to Chatham and in 1832 became a quarantine hulk. On 19 December 1848 she accepted sick from the convict ship *Hasemey*, which called in at Portsmouth enroute from the River Thames to New South Wales with a number of cases of cholera and diarrhoea. She remained with the Quarantine Service until 1890 and was sold in 1897.
HMS *Narcissus*	1823–1837		*Narcissus* was a 32-gun Fifth-rate launched in 1801 at Deptford. She became a prison hulk after 1823 and was sold in 1837.

Ship	Years	Location	Description
HMS *Oiseau*	1810–1816		*Oiseau* was a 36-gun Fifth-rate, originally a French ship called *Cleopatre* but captured in 1793. She was converted to a prison hulk in 1810, later lent to the Transport Board and sold in 1816.
HMS *Owen Glendower*	1842–1862	Gibraltar	*Owen Glendower* was launched in 1808 at Humber. She became a prison hulk in Gibraltar 1842, a receiving ship in 1876, and was sold in 1884.
HMS *Pegase*	1794–1810	Portsmouth	*Pégase* was a 74-gun ship of the line of the French Navy, captured in 1782. She served as a prison ship from 1794, a prison hospital ship from 1801, returned to being a prison ship in 1803 and was lent to the Transport Board in 1810. In 1811, she was still a Prison Hospital Ship (death on board of POW Pascal FURIC, a French sailor, "phthisis pulmonalis", on 6 May 1811) ref.: TNA ADM 103/357.
Phoenix	1824–1837	Sydney	*Phoenix* was a merchant sailing vessel damaged upon the Sow and Pigs Reef within Sydney Harbour and converted to a prison hulk.
HMS *Portland*	1802–1817	Langstone Harbour	*Portland* was a 50-gun Fourth-rate launched in 1770 at Sheerness. She was converted to a 10-gun storeship in 1800 and a prison hulk in 1802. She was sold in 1817.
HMS *Prothee*	1795–1815	Portsmouth	*Protée* was a 64-gun ship of the French Navy, captured in 1780. She served as a prison ship from 1795 until being broken up in 1815.
HMS *Prudent*	1779–1814	Woolwich	*Prudent* was launched in 1768 at Woolwich Dockyard. She was on put on harbour service in 1779 and sold in 1814.
HMS *Racoon*	1819–1838	Portsmouth	*Racoon* was an 18-gun sloop launched in 1808 at Yarmouth. She was used as a hospital ship for convicts from 1819 and was sold in 1838.

Name	Service	Location	Comments
HMS *Resolute*	1844–1852		*Resolute* was a 12-gun gun-brig launched in 1805 in Dover. She was used as a tender from 1814, a diving bell vessel from 1816 and a prison hulk from 1844. She was broken up in 1852.
HMS *Retribution*	1814–1835	Woolwich and Sheerness	*Retribution* was a prison hulk launched in 1779 as the 74-gun Third-rate HMS *Edgar*. *Edgar* was converted into a prison hulk in 1813, renamed *Retribution* in 1814 and broken up in 1835.
HMS *Royalist*	1856		*Royalist* was originally HMS *Mary Gordon* of six guns, purchased in China in 1841. Became a hulk in 1856.
HMS *Savage*	1804–1815	Woolwich	*Savage* was a 14-gun sloop launched in 1778. She became a hulk in 1804 and was sold in 1815.
HMS *Stirling Castle*	1839–1855	Portsmouth	*Stirling Castle* was a 74-gun Third-rate ship of the line launched in 1811 at Rochester. She became a hulk in 1839.
HMS *Success*	1814–1820	Hobart	*Success* was a 32-gun Fifth-rate launched in 1781 at Liverpool. She became a prison hulk in 1814 and was broken up in 1820.
HMS *Sulphur*	1843–1857	Woolwich	*Sulphur* was a 10-gun bomb vessel launched in 1826. She was used as a survey ship from 1835, and for harbour service from 1843. She was broken up in 1857.
HMS *Surprise*	1822–1837	Cork	*Surprise* was a 38-gun frigate, previously named HMS *Jacobs* and launched in 1812. She became a prison hulk in 1822 and was sold in 1837.

Ship	Years	Location	Notes
HMS *Temeraire*	1812–1815	River Tamar	*Temeraire* was a 98-gun Second-rate launched in 1798 at Chatham. She served as a prison hulk between 1812 and 1815, then as a receiving ship until 1836, and was broken up in 1838.
HMS *Tenedos*	1843–1875	Bermuda	*Tenedos* was a 38-gun Fifth-rate launched in 1812. She was used as a prison hulk from 1843 and was broken up in 1875.
HMS *Thames*	1841–1863	Bermuda and Deptford	*Thames* was a 46 gun Fifth-rate launched in 1823. She was converted to a prison hulk in 1841 and sank at her moorings in 1863.
HMS *Unite*	1832–1858	Woolwich	*Unite* was a 40-gun Fifth-rate captured from the French in 1793. She was taken into service as HMS *Imperieuse* and was renamed *Unite* in 1803. She was on harbour service from 1832 and was broken up in 1858.
HMS *Vengeance*	1808–1816	Portsmouth	*Vengeance* was a 74-gun third rate launched in 1774. She became a prison ship in 1808 and was broken up in 1816.
HMS *Warrior*	1840–1857	Woolwich	*Warrior* was a 74-gun Third-rate ship of the line launched in 1781. She became a receiving ship after 1818, a prison hulk after 1840, and was broken up in 1857.
HMS *Weymouth*	1828–1865	Bermuda	*Weymouth* was a 36-gun Fifth-rate, previously the East Indiaman *Wellesley*. She was purchased in 1804, and by 1811 had been converted into a 16-gun storeship. She was used as a prison hulk from 1828 and was sold in 1865.
HMS *York*	1820–1852	Gosport	*York* was a 74-gun Third-rate launched in 1807 at Rotherhithe. She was converted to a prison hulk in 1819 and served at Gosport and London from 1820 until 1848 when a serious rebellion broke out. Typically, she confined about 500 convicts. She was taken out of service and broken up in 1854.

Glossary

Assize Courts Since the twelfth century England and Wales had been divided into six judicial circuits, geographical areas covered by visiting judges. Hearings were held in the main county towns and presided over by visiting judges from the higher courts based in London. They were replaced by the Crown Courts in 1972.

Benefit of Clergy Of ecclesiastical origin, as the name would imply, and dating back to Roman times. Originally designed so that the church could look after its own with defendants being tried by the more lenient church courts, avoiding the secular courts. In 1351 this was made a more general defence with a lesser punishment given to those who could read, on the grounds that if educated they were more likely to be capable of reform. To prevent repeated claims the offender was branded on the thumb after their first appearance. This strange law was finally abolished by the Criminal Law Act of 1827.

Bloody Code A name given to the system of draconian laws and punishments from the late seventeenth to the early nineteenth centuries, so called because of the huge numbers of crimes for which the death penalty could be imposed and the vicious nature of lesser punishments.

Bridewell A 'house of correction', in which the inmates are made to work at various tasks for mainly minor offences or for just being on the streets. It took its name from the first one at St Brides in London.

Burgoo A thick oatmeal gruel or porridge served to convicts on certain days.

Capital Offence A criminal offence punishable by the death penalty. Suspended in the UK in 1965 and finally abolished in 1969.

Cony-catching Theft through trickery. It comes from the word 'coney', meaning a rabbit raised for the table and thus tame.

Cordage (nautical) A set of ropes and cords, especially those used for a ship's rigging.

Court Martial A military court empowered to determine the guilt of members of the armed forces subject to military law, and, if the defendant is found guilty, to decide upon punishment. Most navies have a standard court-martial that convenes whenever a ship is lost; this does not presume that the captain is suspected of wrongdoing, but merely that the circumstances surrounding the loss of the ship be made part of the official record. Usually, a court-martial takes the form of a trial with a presiding judge, a prosecutor and a defence attorney (all trained lawyers as well as officers).

Fencing or a Fence A person who receives stolen goods from a thief and sells them on for a profit. From a statute of 1691.

Felony A serious crime such as robbery that could incur the death penalty. Abolished by the Criminal Law Act of 1967.

Grand Jury A Grand Jury's role was to consider if an indictment, drawn up by a clerk, was a 'true bill' that could be sent for trial or 'ignoramus', which meant that there was no case to be brought. Their decisions were influenced by many factors including the type of charge, who the accused was, the apparent state of crime and the need at that moment for examples to be made to deter potential offenders. Abolished in 1948.

Habeas Corpus From Medieval Latin, literally 'that you have the body', is a recourse in law through which a person can report the unlawful detention or imprisonment to a court and request that the court order that the prisoner be brought to court, to determine whether their detention is lawful. If the custodian is acting beyond their authority, then the prisoner must be released. Any prisoner, or another person acting on their behalf, may petition the court, or a judge, for a writ of *habeas corpus*. One reason for the writ to be sought by a person other than the prisoner is that the detainee might be held incommunicado.

Hard Labour A form of compulsory work imposed as part of a prison sentence. Stone breaking, working the treadmill and picking oakum were common forms of hard labour.

House of Correction Since 1601 places where those who were 'unwilling to work', including vagrants and beggars, were set to hard labour typically beating hemp. Also known as a 'Bridewell', as above.

Hulk A dismasted sailing ship moored near the shore and used for the housing of convicts.

Ignoramus (literally 'we do not know') meaning that there was not enough evidence to pursue a case and that it was therefore dismissed.

Indenture A legal document or agreement between two or more parties.

Indentured Servitude A form of labour in which a person is contracted to work without salary for a specific number of years. The contract, called an 'indenture', may be entered voluntarily for eventual compensation or debt repayment, or it may be imposed as a judicial punishment.

Justice of the Peace (JP) Justices of the Peace were persons of some local social standing who were empowered to try minor offences. More serious crimes would be bound over for trial by judge and jury originally taking place in an informal setting such as a local inn.

Larceny Petty larceny was a charge brought for theft under the value of one shilling and normally tried by a magistrate, but the offender could still be tried as a felon and liable to transportation depending on the context of the offence. Punishments could include whipping, transportation or confiscation of goods. **Grand larceny** was a felony charge for amounts over the value of a shilling, which could mean transportation for a longer period or execution.

After 1827 the two categories were replaced by **Simple larceny**, removing the shilling barrier and resulting in all theft without aggravating circumstances constituting one offence, triable in the lower courts and no longer subject to transportation.

Lay on the Table A motion to set aside a pending question in Parliament when something else of immediate urgency has arisen. In such a case, there is no set time for taking up the matter again, but it can be resumed at the will of the majority and in preference to any new question.

Lighter A large, usually flat-bottomed barge, used especially in unloading or loading ships. In this context it would have been used to transport the convicts from ship to shore to carry out their labours and back again.

Mendicants A mendicant is a person who relies chiefly or exclusively on alms to survive, thus practising mendicancy.

Misdemeanour A crime less serious than a felony.

Mumping Begging as an impostor such as an old soldier, distressed gentleman, etc.

Mutiny A revolt among a group of people, typically a crew, to oppose, change or overthrow an organisation to which they were previously loyal. The term is commonly used for a rebellion among members of the military against an internal force. Mutiny does not necessarily need to refer to a military force and can describe a political, economic or power structure in which there is a change of power.

Night Watchmen Organised groups of men, formed to deter criminal activity and ensure that the dark streets were safe at night, variously engaged in fire watching, crime prevention, crime detection and recovery of stolen goods. Traditionally portrayed as bumbling oafs and replaced by an organised police force in 1829.

Of a Lesser Offence A jury could find the defendant guilty of a lesser offence to the one with which they were charged. Cases of burglary, housebreaking, shoplifting and robbery, all of which carried a death sentence, were occasionally recorded as a simple theft, leaving the judge free to waive execution in favour of a lesser punishment.

Ordinary of Newgate The chaplain of Newgate prison. It was his duty to provide spiritual care to prisoners who were condemned to death.

Order in Council A piece of legislation issued by the sovereign on the advice of the Privy Council.

Orlop The lowest deck in a ship where the cables are stowed, usually below the water line.

Quarter Sessions A court held four times a year by a Justice of the Peace to hear criminal charges as well as civil and criminal appeals. The term also applied to a court held before a recorder, or judge, in a borough having a quarter sessions separate from that of the county in which the borough was situated. Under the Courts Act of 1971, all the quarter sessions courts were abolished and their work was assumed by a system of courts called the Crown Court. They became situated between magistrates' courts below and assize courts above.

Oakum (Picking) Separating strands of worn-out, tarred rope taken from ships. Once separated the rope was hammered between the planks of a ship to help with waterproofing.

Panoptican A type of institutional building and a system of control designed by the philosopher and social theorist Jeremy Bentham in the eighteenth century. The idea was to allow all prisoners to be observed by a single security guard, without the inmates being able to tell whether they were being watched. As it was physically impossible for a single guard to observe all the inmates' cells at once, the fact that the inmates could not know exactly *when* they were being watched meant that they were motivated to act as though they were being watched all the time and in theory compelled to regulate their own behaviour. The architecture was to consist of a rotunda with the inspection house at its centre from which the manager or staff could watch the inmates. Despite repeated attempts at acceptance, Bentham's plans were finally rejected in 1813.

Partial verdicts A partial verdict occurs when a judge permits a jury to return verdicts on fewer than all the counts it has to decide, though it has not yet determined the remainder. The verdicts the jury has reached may or may not be announced immediately. The term may also be used in criminal or civil procedures.

Petty Sessions Local courts consisting of magistrates, usually based on the ancient county divisions known as Hundreds.

Petty Treason The murder of a master by a servant or husband by a wife, i.e. a social superior.

Pillory A wooden framework with openings for the head and hands, where prisoners were fastened to be exposed to public scorn.

Pious Perjury The jury undervalued the goods that had been stolen to change the term of the criminal action from larceny or burglary to theft for first-time offenders or those criminals charged with stealing slightly more than the definition of theft in entailed.

Poor Law A system of poor relief in England and Wales that can be traced back as far as 1536, when legislation was passed to deal with the idle poor and developed out of the codification of late-medieval between 1587 and 1598. Its history can be divided between two statutes: the Old Poor Law passed during the reign of Elizabeth I, and the New Poor Law, passed in 1834, which significantly modified the system, which continued until the modern welfare state emerged after 1945.

Scrofula Otherwise, mycobacterial cervical lymphadenitis, known historically as the King's Evil, as it was believed that the touch of a member of the royal family could cure it. The disease is associated with tuberculosis, usually as a result of an infection in the lymph nodes. The most obvious symptom is the appearance of a chronic, painless mass in the neck, which is persistent and usually grows with time.

Silent System Under this regime prison inmates were forced to do boring, repetitive tasks such as picking oakum, walking the treadmill, or turning crank handles thousands of times. The idea was that the silence and boredom would allow prisoners to reflect on their crimes. They slept on hard beds and ate basic food like bread and drank water. By the end of the nineteenth century it was realised that neither the separate or silent systems were working and they were dispensed with.

Skreen A sieve used for grading ballast in use at Woolwich.

Slave One who is the property of, and entirely subject to, another person, whether by capture, purchase or birth; a servant completely divested of freedom and personal rights.

Ticket of Leave (Australia) First introduced in 1801, tickets were given as a reward for good behaviour, permitting the holders to seek employment within a specified district, but not to leave it without the permission of a resident magistrate. Each change of employer or area was recorded on the ticket, which was originally issued without any relation to the period of sentence served. Some 'gentlemen convicts' were issued with tickets upon their arrival in the colony. From 1811 the need to have served some time in servitude was established, and in 1821 the following terms applied: four years for a seven-year sentence, six to eight years for a fourteen-year sentence, and ten to twelve years for those with a life sentence. Those issued were permitted to marry, bring their families from Britain and acquire property. Convicts who observed the conditions until the completion of one half of their sentence were entitled to a conditional pardon, which removed all restrictions except a ban on leaving the colony. Those in default could be arrested and would forfeit any property. The ticket had to be renewed annually. Once the full original sentence had been served, a 'certificate of freedom' could be issued.

Trinity House Established by Royal charter in 1514.

Vagabond Person who is homeless and goes around the country looking for money, often stealing from others to live. Both 'vagrant' and 'vagabond' ultimately derive from the Latin word *vagari*, meaning 'to wander'. The term vagabond is derived from Latin *vagab*.

Vagrant Vagrancy was a condition of homelessness without regular employment or income. Vagrants lived in poverty and supported themselves by begging, scavenging, petty theft and temporary work. They were associated historically with petty crime and lawlessness, and punished with forced labour, military service, imprisonment, or confinement in one of the houses of correction.

Bibliography

Alexander, C. *The Bounty*. Harper Collins, 2003

Barrington, G. *The Memoirs of George Barrington*. Google Books, 1790

Barrington, G. *A Voyage to Botany Bay*. Google Books, 1795

Barrington, G. *A Voyage to New South Wales*. Google Books, 1801

Beattie. J. *Crime and the Courts in England 1660-1800*. Princeton, 1985

Black, J. *An Authentic Narrative of the Mutiny on the Lady Shore*. John Bush, 1798

Branch-Johnson, W. *The English Prison Hulks*. Christopher Johnson, 1957

Brown, M. *Australia Bound! West Country Connections*. Ex Libris, 1988

Byrnes, D. *The Blackheath Connection*. A website, truly remarkable in its scope and erudition, essential for anybody with a serious interest in the Duncan Campbell era.

Campbell, C. *The Intolerable Hulks, 1776-1857*. Heritage, 1993

Campbell, D. *The Letterbooks of Duncan Campbell*. State Library of New South Wales, 2005

Carew, B. *The Life & Adventures of Bampfylde Moore Carew*. Google Books, 1835

Christopher, E. *A Merciless Place*. Oxford, 2011

Coldham, P. *Emigrants in Chains*. Alan Sutton, 1992

Cordingley, D. *Billy Ruffian*. Bloomsbury, 2003

Colquhoun, P. *A Treatise on the Police of the Metropolis*. Google Books, 1800

Crone, R. *Guide to the Criminal Prisons of 19c England*. Online, 2018

Currey, J. (ed) *Report of the Select Committee on Convicts*. (Bunbury Report) 1779

Davis, M. *Murders & Misdemeanours in Bath*. Amberley, 2022

Davis/Lassman. *Foul Deeds & Suspicious Deaths in and Around Frome*. Pen & Sword, 2018

Davis Family Archive. The Bishopsgate Institute, London. Deposited, 2021

Dixon, H. *The London Prisons*. Google Books, 1850

Duckworth, J. *Fagin's Children*. Hambledon & London, 2002

Dugan, J. *The Great Mutiny*. NEL, 1967

Ekrich, R. *Bound for America*. OUP, 1990
Frost, A. *Botany Bay Mirages*. Melbourne University Press, 1994
Garneray, L. *The Floating Prison*. Conway, 2003
Greetham, M. *Court Martial of Capt. Anthony Molley*. Google Books, 1795
Gulvin, K. *The Medway Hulks* Estuary Books, 2010
Hardie, E. *The Passage of the Damned*. Australian Publishing, 2019
Hawkins, D. *Criminal Ancestors*. History Press, 2009
Higgs, M. *Prison Life in Victorian England*. Tempus, 2007
Howard, J. *The State of The Prisons in England & Wales*. Google Books, 1797
Hughes, R. *The Fatal Shore*. Collins, 1987
Keneally, T. *The Commonwealth of Thieves*. Random House, 2006
Knap & Baldwin. *The Malefactors Register or Newgate Calendar*. Google Books, 1824
Lambert, R. *The Prince of Pickpockets*. Faber & Faber, 1930
Meyhew & Binny, *The Criminal Prisons of London*. Google Books, 1862
Mitchel, J. *Jail Journal*. Sphere, 1983
Moore, L. *The Thieves' Opera*. Viking, 1997
Morris/Rothman. (Eds) *The Oxford History of the Prison*. Oxford, 1998
O'Brian, P. *Joseph Banks. A Life*. Collins, 1988
O' Danachair, D. (ed) *The Newgate Calendar Volume 1*. Online, 1780
Old Bailey Archives. Online
Partridge, S. *Prisoner's Progress*. Hutchinson, 1935
Pelham, C. *The Chronicles of Crime Vol 1*. Online, 1891
Poulter, J. *The Discoveries of John Poulter*. Google Books, 1769
Scott, R. *The West Country's Australian Links*. Scott, 1988
TUC *The Martyrs of Tolpuddle 1834-1935*. Peter Gill, 1999
Vaver, A. *Bound with an Iron Chain*. Pickpocket Publishing, 2011
Williams, L. *Convicts in the Colonies*. Pen & Sword, 2018
Wikipedia entry used in Appendix 3: *List of British Prison Hulks*

Index